The Language of Per in Politics

This accessible introductory textbook looks at the modern relationship between politicians, the press and the public through the language they employ, with extensive coverage of key topics including:

- 'spin', 'spin control' and 'image' politics
- models of persuasion: authority, contrast, association
- pseudo-logical and 'post-truth' arguments
- political interviewing: difficult questions, difficult answers
- metaphors and metonymy
- rhetorical figures
- humour, irony and satire

Extracts from speeches, soundbites, newspapers and blogs, interviews, press conferences, election slogans, social media and satires are used to provide the reader with the tools to discover the beliefs, character and hidden strategies of the would-be persuader, as well as the counter-strategies of their targets. This book demonstrates how the study of language use can help us appreciate, exploit and protect ourselves from the art of persuasion.

With a wide variety of practical examples on recent issues relating to the US, UK and Europe, every topic is complemented with guiding tasks and queries with keys and commentaries at the end of each Unit. This is the ideal textbook for all introductory courses on language and politics, media language, rhetoric and persuasion, discourse studies and related areas.

Alan Partington is Professor of Political Linguistics at Bologna University, Italy and Editor-in-Chief of the *International Journal of Corpora and Discourse Studies*. He is the author of *Patterns and Meanings in Discourse* (with Alison Duguid and Charlotte Taylor, 2013), *The Linguistics of Laughter: A Corpus-Assisted Study of Laughter-talk at the White House* (Routledge, 2007), *Persuasion in Politics* (with Charlotte Taylor, 2010) and *The Linguistics of Political Argument* (Routledge, 2003).

Charlotte Taylor is Senior Lecturer in English Language and Linguistics at the University of Sussex (UK) and is editor of *CADAAD Journal*. Her publications include *Mock Politeness in English and Italian* (2016), *Patterns and Meanings in Discourse* (with Alison Duguid and Alan Partington, 2013) and *Persuasion in Politics* (with Alan Partington, 2010).

The Language of Persuasion in Politics

An Introduction

Alan Partington and
Charlotte Taylor

Routledge
Taylor & Francis Group

LONDON AND NEW YORK

First edition published 2018
by Routledge
2 Park Square, Milton Park, Abingdon, Oxon OX14 4RN

and by Routledge
711 Third Avenue, New York, NY 10017

Routledge is an imprint of the Taylor & Francis Group, an informa business

© 2018 Alan Partington and Charlotte Taylor

British Library Cataloguing-in-Publication Data
A catalogue record for this book is available from the British Library

Library of Congress Cataloging-in-Publication Data
A catalog record for this book has been requested

ISBN: 978-1-138-03847-9 (hbk)
ISBN: 978-1-138-03848-6 (pbk)
ISBN: 978-1-315-17734-2 (ebk)

Typeset in Sabon
by Sunrise Setting Ltd, Brixham, UK

Printed in the United Kingdom
by Henry Ling Limited

Contents

Figures and tables

Figures

Tables

Preface

An introduction to studies on language, power and persuasion

The relationship between *language* and *power* has been examined under a variety of guises in a variety of disciplines. These include: (i) the politics of language; (ii) critical discourse studies; and (iii) language *as* power, specifically, the power to persuade.

(i) The politics of language

In the field of the politics of language, much ink has been spilt on 'powerful languages'; that is, languages which for various military, economic and/or cultural reasons came to prominence. In Europe and the Middle East, traditional influential languages were Greek, for military and cultural reasons, Latin after the Roman conquests and Hebrew as the original language of the Bible. In the Middle East, these languages were eventually supplanted by Arabic, which eventually became the most powerful language after the Arab military conquests. In China, the situation is highly complex but forms of Mandarin dialect, originating in the powerful cities of northern China, have remained the language of power and prestige since at least the 14th Century. English, of course, became a powerful language only in relatively recent times.

One interesting case is the politics of the adoption of what eventually became 'standard Italian'. In many ways it is a great national achievement, but it was also mainly a political imposition and not the people's choice. In 1861, when the Kingdom of Italy was born, only one Italian in forty (2.5%) spoke the **dialect** of Italian (an antiquated form of Tuscan), which was to eventually become the basis of today's standard Italian, and only one in ten could read it. For 80% of the population, this dialect was seen as a foreign language and sometimes fiercely resented. The King himself spoke Piedmontese (when not speaking French); the great hero of Italian Unification, Camillo Cavour, thought that Sicilians spoke dialects of Arabic. The imposition of standard Italian, prioritised as national policy to 'create Italy', was eventually achieved through the education system, through economic discrimination against dialect speakers and by the state television service, the RAI (Radiotelevisione italiana S.p.A), whose explicit remit was to make Italians understand and speak the new 'standard Italian' (Gilmour 2011).

Today the language with greatest global influence, for a complex historical interplay of economic, military, cultural and scientific motives, is 'standard English'. But this term is something of a misnomer, since even 'standard English' exists in various different subforms, including standard American, standard Australian and standard British, all of which are spoken with very different accents even by first-language speakers. These all, however, derive from the same dialect – that of south-east England. English is also spoken worldwide in an almost infinite variety of dialects and accents as either a first language or a second or acquired language. The role of English can differ considerably in different countries; for instance:

> an average educated Nigerian commands two or three languages – the English language, his/her local language and Nigerian Pidgin. These are separate languages not varieties of the same language. For example, Nigerian English and Nigerian Pidgin are not the same language although they both serve the function of linqua franca within the multi-ethnic/linguistic community.
>
> (Mustapha 2011: 1337)

Another aspect of the relationship between language and power is that fluency in the powerful language of one's region can be an important factor in an individual gaining access to influential positions in society. As the economist Nandan Nilekani said of English in his native India:

> [A] big thing that has changed India is our attitude towards the English language. The English language was seen as a language of the imperialists. But today, with globalization, with outsourcing, English has become a language of aspiration. This has made it something that everybody wants to learn. And the fact that we have English is now becoming a huge strategic asset.
>
> (Nilekani 2009)

This cycle is not unique to English of course. Other languages too – Latin, Spanish, Arabic – may originally have become 'powerful' through an imposition which included military force, but they self-perpetuate through sheer commercial and political utility. Often, of course, the power recedes over time; Greek or Persian, for example, are no longer generally held to be languages of international power, as they once were.

One vexed question is the degree to which languages of power overshadow and eventually suppress (or 'kill off') other languages, and there are many examples from history. The Middle East has already been mentioned and many of the traditional languages of the region and of northern Africa disappeared under pressure from Arabic. Welsh Gaelic almost disappeared under pressure from the use of English and of misguided central government language policies, but is currently undergoing a revival. However, in many other situations, multilingualism is and was the norm: 'I speak Spanish to God, Italian to women, French to men, and German to my horse' said the Holy Roman Emperor, Charles V. A humble trader in Syria at the turn of the millennium might well have spoken Greek, Arabic, Persian and several dialects of Aramaic including Hebrew and Syriac. While it is very difficult to accurately assess levels of multilingualism, mono-lingual speakers are a minority in the world today too.

(ii) Language and power: differentials but development

Some fields of political linguistics such as critical discourse studies concern themselves with *language* and *power*, specialising in examining the power differentials of groups within societies, via their manifestations in language. There are various 'empowered' and 'disempowered' groups within societies, and 'empowered' groups have greater access to language resources and channels of communication, which is one of the principal means of maintaining and exercising power. Thus, 'empowered' groups have a greater ability to get their voices heard than 'disempowered' groups. During this course we will be examining some of these privileged voices, mainly politicians, the media and others whom we call 'professional persuaders'.

While this is no doubt true, we must be careful not to oversimplify and overgeneralise. First, not all 'powerful' voices are malicious: they might be powerful by possessing useful knowledge and skills, for example, healthcare workers, teachers and even many dedicated politicians. In the words of Abba Eban, the Israeli diplomat, 'it is our experience that political leaders do not always mean the opposite of what they say'.

Second, in reality, power relations can be much more complex than they first appear, and context is paramount. There are fundamental dangers to classifying by simple group identity, mainly because there are often far greater differences among members of groups than among the groups themselves (hence the use of the term 'intersectionality' in discourse studies). For example, a sweeping statement like 'white western males are an economically privileged group', can certainly be supported by economic data, but still needs to be treated with great caution. There are huge differences in economic well-being among the members of the group 'white western males'. So a more accurate language formulation would be: 'a disproportionately high number of those people with power in the West are white males'. But throughout history the majority of white, western men – and women – as individuals have had precious little power at all. Even today, many poorly educated and low-skilled white men in, say, the north of England and Scotland or the southern states of the US often enjoy few life chances; indeed, their life expectancy is lower than the average of many so-called 'developing countries' (that is low-to-middle-income countries).[1]

Nor is 'empowerment' and 'disempowerment' a binary distinction; there are degrees of (dis)empowerment and also different types. For example, it is unhelpful to think of, say, middle-class women or working-class men as equally disempowered or disempowered in a similar way. And both are far more advantaged than undocumented economic migrants of either gender. Most (but not all) ethnic minority groups are demonstrably on average economically disadvantaged in western societies, but not all to the same extent, with some groups faring much better than others and with large differences *within* groups.[2] A further complication is that women and girls, if they live in a highly conservative patriarchal community, can sometimes form 'a minority within a minority', being denied life opportunities and facing particularly extreme economic disadvantage relative to the rest of society. A 2016 UK government report listed 'poor English language skills' as both cause and result of the enforced social isolation of some groups of women.[3]

One phenomenon that early political linguists failed to predict was today's levels of human movement. Today of course, studies on migration, including its linguistic repercussions, abound. In their research on what are often termed 'underclasses', Johnson and Partington (forthcoming) found that (im)migrant groups were seen as particularly vulnerable to social deprivation in every national context they studied, which included the US, UK, India, Hong Kong and China. Government policy in all these places needs to focus on enabling the children of (im)migrants to gain access to education in order to prevent a single-generation underclass from developing into a permanent underclass. The question of access is also a linguistic one. In many countries the children of migrants can be severely disadvantaged if they do not speak the language used in school, and special provisions should be made to teach it.

Many of the topics in this book touch upon human socio-economic development from various perspectives, and we include the good news as well as bad. Another phenomenon that some early schools of political thought failed to predict was that the *producers* of wealth – the workers – would, in the second generation of an industrial revolution, also become *consumers* of the market for goods and services, thus acquiring a double value and considerable power; a phenomenon first seen in England, then in Europe and north America, then in parts of south-east Asia and now occurring throughout the so-called developing world (better described as middle-income countries). Industrialisation coincided with the spread of literacy and of education for ordinary people (first mainly for boys and then eventually also girls), since these new forms of work required educated labour. Thus, ordinary people also became consumers of information, a market for persuasion and even persuaders themselves. Historically the rise of political organisations such as trade unions and political parties went hand-in-hand with industrialisation and generalised education, and for the first time the people obtained a participatory voice and a degree of empowerment in the public sphere, a process which eventually led to universal voting rights and democracy as we know it now. The hope is that governments of once tightly controlled societies (whose control was maintained by monitoring language and eliminating dissenting voices) which are currently developing their own industrial revolutions will also be forced to empower the voices of their well-educated worker-consumers.

As a result, despite the increase in some kinds of inequality as global corporations expand, the good news is that the standard of life enjoyed by the majority of the human population, as measured by almost every metric such as life expectancy, nutrition and health, and access to education is higher today than in any previous stage in history.[4] The challenge is to ensure both that this trend continues and that the very poorest (the so-called 'Bottom Billion', Unit 3.3) also gain access to this unprecedented human development and are able to make their voices heard.

(iii) Language *as* power: the power of *persuasion*

In this book, of course, we will be mainly concerned with *language* as a principal means of achieving and exercising *power* in modern pluralistic democratic societies, with a focus on the English-speaking world. In a functional democracy, the principal use of language in politics is for persuasion in debate in both the political sphere, that is, among politicians, but also the public sphere, in the media, both mainstream and social media.

As Schäffner points out, language is vital to the process of transforming political will into social action, 'in fact, any political action is prepared, accompanied, controlled and influenced by language' (1997: 1). Fairclough goes further still. Politics, he says, is not just conducted through language, but much of politics is language: 'politics partly consists in the disputes which occur in language and over language' (1989: 23). Indeed, it is difficult to think of any political action which does *not* involve using language: political speeches, newspaper editorials, press conferences, cabinet meetings, Acts of Parliament, and so on (Unit 1).

For the purposes of the current work in political linguistics, we will adopt the definition that democratic politics is 'the art of persuasion', persuasion of the masses is generally via the mass media, and persuasion is achieved by the skilful use of language. At best, political language can be inspirational and galvanising:

> We hold these truths to be self-evident, that all men are created equal, that they are endowed by their Creator with certain unalienable Rights, that among these are Life, Liberty and the pursuit of Happiness.
>
> (The Declaration of Independence 1776)

But at its worst, as George Orwell reminds us:

> Political language . . . is [often] designed to make lies sound truthful and murder respectable, and to give an appearance of solidity to pure wind.
>
> (Orwell 1946)

Just as worryingly, the careless *misuse* of language can be downright dangerous, as in the cases of George W. Bush's promise of a 'crusade' against terrorists or of Obama's 'red line' **metaphor** which almost brought the US to war in Syria (see Unit 7 on metaphor).

But even if persuasion is an essential component in a functional democracy, even in a pluralistic society, that is, one where several competing voices can be heard in the public sphere, there are still many issues of concern. The power of persuasion of the media is considerable, and some worry that the concentration of ownership of media outlets is in the hands of too few organisations, such as news agencies like the Associated Press and Reuters or multi-media organisations like News Corp and Comcast. Another issue is how well or poorly informed the mainstream media are, as well as its inbuilt privileging of drama, crisis and alarmism – bad news sells – which results in a highly negative representation of the world. Recently we have also witnessed the rise of social media and blogging which allow individuals a voice in political debate but where questions of reliability of information are at least as pressing. Indeed, we are currently witnessing an epidemic of accusations of 'fake news' made by individuals and organisations of all political affiliations to attack their opponents' credibility. Conversely, the ownership of media sources by governments brings its own obvious dangers of censorship of dissident voices. And the technologisation of the media has also seen the ability of non-pluralistic states to give their voices global reach (for example, Russia Today, Press TV (Iran), Al-Jazeera (Qatar)).

The study of the art of persuasion in politics has never been so complex, but also never so fascinating, as today.

Further activity

Finally, if you enjoy a challenge, to discover how up-to-date your knowledge of the world is, you might like to take the 'ignorance test': www.gapminder. org/ignorance/

Notes

1 The average male life expectancy in Glasgow (UK) is 71.6 (https://en.wikipedia. org/wiki/Glasgow_effect). In Mississippi (US) it is 71.9 (www.worldlife expectancy.com/usa/life-expectancy-male). In China, it is 74.6 (World Health Organization, https://en.wikipedia.org/wiki/List_of_countries_ by_life_expectancy). As Professor Hans Rosling argues, the division of the world into two groups, namely developed and developing countries, no longer describes the modern world: 'Two groups are not enough. The World Bank did a promising attempt by creating four country groups by using cut-offs in Gross National Income per capita at $1,000, $4,000 and $12,000. The cut-offs defined low-income, lower middle income, upper middle income and high income countries' (www.edition.cnn.com/2013/12/10/opinion/ gapminder-hans-rosling/).
2 For data on differences in earnings by ethnic origin in the US see government census data (www.census.gov/prod/2013pubs/p60-245.pdf. A simplified version can be found here: https://en.wikipedia.org/wiki/List_ of_ethnic_groups_in_the_United_States_by_household_income). For data in the UK, see the Joseph Rowntree Foundation report (www.jrf.org.uk/ sites/default/files/jrf/migrated/files/inequality-ethnicity-poverty-full.pdf).
3 The Casey Review Report (www.gov.uk/government/uploads/system/ uploads/attachment_data/file/575973/The_Casey_Review_Report.pdf).
4 For an enlightening survey of progress in human development, see Gapminder (www.gapminder.org/).

References

Fairclough, N. (1989) *Language and Power*, London: Longman.
Gilmour, D. (2011) *The Pursuit of Italy*, London and New York: Penguin.
Johnson, J. and Partington, A. (forthcoming) 'Corpus-assisted discourse study of representations of the "underclass" in the English language press', in E. Friginal (ed.) *Studies in Corpus-based Sociolinguistics*. London: Routledge, 295–320.
Mustapha, A.S. (2011) 'Compliment response patterns among speakers of Nigerian English', *Journal of Pragmatics* 43(5): 1335–1348.
Nilekani, N. (2009) 'Ideas for India's future', TED talk . Available at: www.jrf. org.uk/sites/default/files/jrf/migrated/files/inequality-ethnicity-poverty-full.pdf
Orwell, G. (1946) *Politics and the English Language*, London: Horizon.
Schäffner, C. (1997) 'Editorial: Political speeches and discourse analysis', in C. Schäffner (ed.) *Analysing Political Speeches*, Clevedon: Multilingual Matters, 1–4.

Acknowledgements

Some of the material in this book appeared in an earlier publication by the same authors, *Persuasion in Politics* (2010, LED).

Animal Farm by George Orwell (Copyright © George Orwell, 1945) Reprinted by permission of Bill Hamilton as the Literary Executor of the Estate of the Late Sonia Brownell Orwell.

Every effort has been made to contact copyright holders. Please advise the publisher of any errors or omissions, and these will be corrected in subsequent editions.

1 Politics and the language of persuasion

The limits of my language are the limits of my world.

(Wittgenstein)

Words are the only things that last forever.

(Churchill)

1.1 Politics is conducted through language

Language is vital to the process of transforming political will into social action, 'in fact, any political action is prepared, accompanied, controlled and influenced by language' (Schäffner 1997: 1). Or as Corlett puts it:

> Communication is the currency of politics. Politicians trade in discourse and argument, public statements, speeches, pamphlets and manifestos. How they express themselves determines who they are and whether they will succeed in their profession. Keeping quiet for a politician is as useful as a shopkeeper who never opens his store.[1]

To paraphrase the Wittgenstein aphorism above, the limits of a politician's language set the limits of their careers. In this series of lessons we will look, first of all, at the many ways in which politicians use language, the tool of their trade, but also at what we can learn about politics and politicians themselves from how they use language. The topics we look at include: common models for structuring an argument, how to tell logic from pseudo-logic, rhetorical figures for effective speech-making, metaphor and metonymy (attractions and dangers), the tricks of political interviewing, humour, irony and satire, and how election campaigns are run.

It is possible to define politics narrowly as the working of institutions of governance or, more broadly, as the interrelations of social groups, some with more power than others, within a given society. It is similarly possible to define the *language* of politics narrowly as the language used by institutions of governance to conduct their business, to communicate with other institutions and with the rest of society, or, more broadly, as all the discourses produced by groups within a society which relate to issues of the management of power and of social governance. Both of these definitions are relevant to the kind of studies of political language found in this book.

However, most ordinary people rarely have experience of politics directly. In many countries it is possible to meet with elected politicians at appointed times, or attend local events, such as town hall meetings. But most of the time our experience of politics is 'mediated', that is, we experience it via the media, the TV and radio, the paper press and increasingly through websites. As Wilson (2001: 411) similarly concludes:

> defining political discourse is not a straightforward matter. Some analysts define the political so broadly that almost any discourse may be considered political. At the same time, a formal constraint on any definition such that we only deal with politicians and core political events excludes the everyday discourse of politics which is part of people's lives.

And so we will also scrutinise some of the ways in which the media employ language, also the tool of *their* trade and the ways in which political issues are discussed by non-politicians.

TASK 1: *Language in politics*

It is difficult to think of any political action which does not involve using language: political speeches, newspaper editorials, press conferences, cabinet meetings, Acts of Parliament, and so on.

1) How many more political actions or events involving the use of language can you think of?
   Which involve spoken language, which involve written language and which involve both?
2) Can you think of any political actions or events which do NOT involve using language at some stage?
3) From which sources (news websites, TV news, newspapers, social media, conversations with friends, etc.) do you obtain your information about politics?

In this book, the types of political language we will look at include newspaper articles, blogs, interviews, speeches, expert talks, debates, press briefings, election campaign language, slogans, aphorisms, tweets, political humour, satire and even insults.

TASK 2: *Politics is . . .*

1) Can you match the following six definitions with the six speakers listed below them?

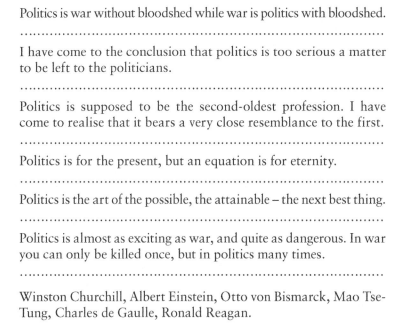

Politics is war without bloodshed while war is politics with bloodshed.

I have come to the conclusion that politics is too serious a matter to be left to the politicians.

Politics is supposed to be the second-oldest profession. I have come to realise that it bears a very close resemblance to the first.

Politics is for the present, but an equation is for eternity.

Politics is the art of the possible, the attainable – the next best thing.

Politics is almost as exciting as war, and quite as dangerous. In war you can only be killed once, but in politics many times.

Winston Churchill, Albert Einstein, Otto von Bismarck, Mao Tse-Tung, Charles de Gaulle, Ronald Reagan.

2)　Which of the definitions do you empathise with most? (Free response)

For the purposes of the current work in political linguistics, we will adopt the definition that democratic politics is 'the art of persuasion' – also known more formally as *rhetoric* (terms which are in bold and italics are explained in the Glossary). Persuasion is achieved principally by the skilful use of language. And persuasion is of itself neither good nor bad, neither beneficial nor harmful, but in practice it can be both or neither. Rhetoric is language at work, and language at play:

> It is what persuades and cajoles, inspires and bamboozles, thrills and misdirects. It causes criminals to be convicted and then frees those criminals on appeal. It causes governments to rise and fall [. . .] and perfectly sensible adults to march with steady purpose towards machine guns.
>
> (Leith 2012: 6)

1.2 Persuasion and rhetoric in a democratic society

In an absolutist or totalitarian regime (from the Roman Empire to Nazi Germany or the Soviet Union), those in power rule by using the twin weapons of coercion and the manipulation of information (for a current example of the latter, browse the North Korean regime's official Twitter feed @uriminzok_engl).

In a pluralistic democracy, instead, the principal use of language in politics is for persuasion in debate. In fact, the art of political persuasion in this sense was born with the first democracy in ancient Greece. The Greeks developed what they termed the art of rhetoric, which is none other than the skill of persuasion. More formal rhetoric was generally felt to have three main fields of application: for politics (*agora*, that is 'public space'), for law (*forensic*) and for speeches of public praise or blame (*epideictic*). As Charteris-Black (2013: 3) points out, the most frequent adjective which modifies *rhetoric* in the British National Corpus is *political*, followed by *public*. Thus, rhetoric is still seen as central to both senses of political discourse. Aristotle also identified three basic *appeals* of rhetoric. The first, *ethos*, is the attempt to establish the credentials to justify why you should be listened to, perhaps because you are interesting and witty or, if a politician, strong, honest and experienced. An adversary may well attempt to *delegitimise* your ethos, by questioning your character or discrediting your credentials to make certain claims or hold certain powers (we will meet several types of attempted delegitimisation in this book). The second basic appeal is *logos*, the attempt to present a plausible argument in a logical or at least apparently logical way. And the third is *pathos*, the attempt to appeal to the audience's emotions. We shall come across these appeals in different disguises during the rest of this book, including in more informal acts of persuasion (Aristotle 2012).

But rhetoric right from the beginning had a mixed reputation, and still today the word can have a number of meanings. It can be defined simply, following Aristotle, as we said above, as the 'arts of persuasive discourse' (Cockcroft and Cockcroft 1992: 3), that is, the use of words by human agents to form attitudes or to induce actions in other human agents. Aristotle argues that we employ the art of persuasion every day in our normal and natural relations with other people; indeed, his theory of rhetoric is also essentially a theory of human interaction. In other words, people use language all the time 'to attempt to influence the beliefs and the behaviour of other people' (Partington, Duguid and Taylor 2013: 5). In terms of one important approach to language study, namely speech act theory, studying rhetoric means studying the perlocutionary intent of utterances, that is, the effect speakers wish them to have on their audience.

In real life, of course, attempts to influence and convince others are often met with suspicion and resistance; the more blatant the attempts, the deeper the suspicion. Such resistance to rhetoric is anything but new: 'The success of rhetoric rapidly drew upon itself a counter-attack, recorded in Plato's Gorgias, where Socrates deplores the skill taught by sophists (teachers of rhetoric) as a mere "knack" to disguise falsehood or ignorance as plausible truth' (Cockcroft and Cockcroft 1992: 5).

For Plato himself the rhetorician is a 'speech-rigger' (*logodaidalos*) (Cockcroft and Cockcroft 1992: 20). Rhetoric, in this view, is manipulative and there is somehow a deficit between complex-sounding rhetorical argument and 'the truth' which, in his view, could only be discovered and explained by – who else? – the philosopher. Plato was scandalised by the thought that the plausible orator might be more convincing than a virtuous philosopher like himself. The irony is of course that, according to the definitions given above, Socrates' own methods of persuasion, famously through asking questions, were just as 'rhetorical'.

Rhetoric of course has yet another sense, equivalent to 'grandiloquence' or the use of high-sounding but 'empty' language. This meaning derives from the obscurantist associations that rhetoric acquired after the codification of its persuasive techniques and language tropes (or figures) that took place in the Middle Ages by the Scholastic (or pseudo-Scholastic) orators. Geoffrey Chaucer satirises this misuse of rhetoric in *The Canterbury Tales* (the Host is addressing the Oxford Clerk, a student of Rhetoric):

Tell us a cheerful tale [. . .]
But don't preach, as friars do in Lent,
To make us all for our old sins weep,
And don't tell a tale to send us to sleep.
Tell us some merry adventurous things,
And your fancy terms, your rhetorical figures and rhymes,
Keep them to yourself for some other times,
No 'High style', like when you'd write to kings.
Speak nice and plain this time, I you pray,
So we can all understand what you say.
(Chaucer, The Clerk's Prologue 2000)[2]

'Rhetoric', in this sense, is an 'over-the-fence' or 'outsider' word (see Unit 2.3); that is to say, it is used to describe what others do, is only applied to other people or an outsider group and is often roughly equivalent to 'bluster':

COLONEL CROWLEY: [. . .] What we've heard today from Iraq is a great deal of rhetoric. We've heard this bluster before. We've seen this petulance before.
(White House press briefing;
Partington 2003: vi–vii)

This view can be recognised today in the contempt frequently expressed for 'mere rhetoric', which somehow substitutes 'real substance'. In recent times, Barack Obama's rhetorical fluency aroused much suspicion in some quarters. The Republican politician Rick Santorum called him 'just another élitist who worked with words' and Hillary Clinton (his opponent for the Democrat candidacy in 2007) tried to dismiss him as a man who just 'gives speeches' (Leith 2012: 14).

TASK 3: *Definitions of rhetoric*

1) We have seen that rhetoric is used with three distinct meanings. Briefly, these are:

   i)
   ii)
   iii)

2) Which of these did Aristotle subscribe to?

   And which did Plato subscribe to?

3) Which definition of 'rhetoric' do you think is being used in the following statements about various political speech-makers?

   1. Obama: Oratory and originality. Barack Obama's rhetorical skill, his ability to captivate and inspire audiences with his powerful speeches, has led some writers to describe him as the greatest orator of his generation.

      (*BBC News* 19 November 2008).

   2. Salman Rushdie has attacked the 'hate-filled religious rhetoric' that 'persuades hundreds, perhaps thousands of British Muslims to join the decapitating barbarians of Isis', describing it as 'the most dangerous new weapon in the world today'.

      (*Guardian* 10 October 2014).

   3. Donald Trump's campaign dismissed a night-long offensive from top Democrats at the party's national convention as 'empty rhetoric'. At the Democratic National Convention, speaker after speaker took to the stage to denounce Trump, whose senior policy adviser, fired back saying the DNC had obsessed over Trump and 'offered no solutions'.

      (*The Hill* 2016).

4) Another way of viewing the different senses of *rhetoric* is through examining which words behave in similar ways, that is to say which words share the same kind of lexical company. If we examine *rhetoric* using the Thesaurus tool available on the Sketch Engine suite of language analysis programs, we can see the words which are used in the most similar ways in newspaper discourse. The results are shown in Figure 1.1 (see www.sketchengine.co.uk for information on this tool):

Figure 1.1 Rhetoric in the Sketch Engine Thesaurus

Q1

In your opinion, how do the terms shown in Figure 1.1. relate to the different senses of rhetoric? (Free responses)

1.3 Professional persuaders and the art of the 'spin-doctor'

In modern times, for many political commentators, then, the word 'rhetoric' enjoys a bad reputation. Knowledge of how to employ the techniques of persuasion is seen as one of the principal ways in which the 'powerful' both express and reinforce their power over the 'powerless', for example, in situations such as the courtroom, the workplace and also in the mass media.

Although this may frequently be the case, it is not necessarily always the case. The relationship between rhetoric and power has not always been a cosy one. In many periods of history, rhetoric has been subversive of authority – Giordano Bruno, Thomas Paine and the pamphleteers of the 17th and 18th Centuries spring to mind – and authority has always been most wary and intolerant of rhetoric and orators it could not control. Moreover, the very need for the organs of state to avail themselves of persuasion, of the arts of rhetoric, has tended to coincide historically with periods of relative freedom (for some sections of society at least). It is, therefore, as we said, no coincidence that it first enters the arena of history with Greek democracy because absolute, despotic, coercive power has little need of rhetoric for persuasion.

If persuasion is such a powerful tool in those societies where speech is relatively free, for obtaining, wielding and contesting power, then it is no surprise that such societies host a wealth of different kinds of what we might term 'professional persuaders'. These include both the more obvious categories such as politicians, spokespersons, media opinion-makers, lawyers, publicity and public relations experts, but also types which may be slightly less in the public eye like speech-writers, newspaper editors and lobbyists.

Recently, much attention is being paid to the phenomenon of what has been termed *spin*, that is, the tailoring of news and information on its release to the public to cast a favourable light on the institutions of authority. The term itself is a ***metaphor*** (see Unit 7) deriving from the sport of baseball, 'spin' being the twist effect put on the ball by the pitcher (thrower) in order to make the ball curve through the air in order to evade the batter. Thus, the politician or his/her agent hopes to spin their political message so that it will reach the public without the intervention of a critical press. From the politicians' point of view, the process is necessary because the modern press, in the UK and often in the US at least, is obsessed with conflict and scandal and is forever 'distorting' their (the politicians') messages. At the time of writing there is even an epidemic of accusations by politicians or their agents that the media is spreading 'fake news' to damage their image:

> President Donald Trump kicked off his campaign rally in Florida by attacking the media as purveyors of **fake news** and part of the corrupt system [he] accused the 'dishonest media' of publishing one false story after another as his administration gets under way.
>
> (*Irish Examiner* 2017)

> Jeremy Corbyn has accused the BBC of peddling '**fake news**' after being challenged on persistent rumours he was preparing to quit as Labour leader.
>
> (*Independent* 2017)

as well as media accusations against other media:

> Xinhua, the Chinese government's official news agency [. . .] accuses western media of **fake news** about human rights.
>
> (*Guardian* 2017)

As Richard (Dick) Cheney, who became Vice-President of the Bush administration, once put it: 'You don't let the press set the agenda. They like to decide what's important and what isn't important. But if you let them do that, they're going to trash your presidency' (in Maltese 1992: 2).

In democratic countries, then, all the major political parties have press officers, responsible for maintaining relations with and communicating the party's message to the media. These officers frequently become very unpopular with the journalists they are dealing with, who accuse them of manipulating or hiding 'the truth' (whatever that might be). They are informally labelled *spin-doctors*. The verb *to doctor* has the slang meaning of to 'tamper' or to 'interfere' with something.

Another modern development is the employment by major companies of public relations personnel whose job it is to present the best possible image of their employer to the world; for example, to present an oil company as more 'eco-friendly' than it actually is.

Yet again, pressure groups, lobbies, charities and non-governmental organisations (NGOs) are also commercial operations who employ spin-doctors, in the form of both spokespersons and political lobbyists, not only to raise awareness of their cause but also to raise as much money as they can.

We also live in the age of the press release. Politicians, police, large companies and NGOs employ agents to write documents for the media giving a favourable account of their actions and policies. These same agents make it their business to be on friendly terms with relevant journalists, politicians with political correspondents, technology companies with science correspondents, Green NGOs with environmental correspondents, and so on.

But are these terms – spin and spin-doctor – simply new names for an old game? Persuading people to accept your version of events, of 'the truth' – in competition with other versions – is at the very dialogic heart of rhetoric. Kings and Emperors have often kept official biographers and religious leaders have often maintained a monopoly on literacy to promote their particular traditions. Similarly, writers and portrait painters were often involved in presenting political leaders in a favourable or unfavourable light (depending on who commissioned the work). To take just one well-known example, many now argue that Shakespeare's portrayal of an evil King Richard III was partly political spin, designed to discredit the old King. And just as Socrates was alert to the efforts of the doctors of sophistry, we need to build and maintain our modern defences against the doctors of spin.

TASK 4: *Metaphors of spin*

Briefings is the name given to press conferences which are held on a regular basis. The White House has its own press secretary whose job it is to meet the press and respond to their questions more-or-less every day. The press audience includes representatives of various types of news agencies. Pride of place is given to the representatives of press agencies (also known colloquially as the 'wire services'), such as Associated Press and Reuters. Press agencies collect as many news stories as they can, which they then sell on to other news outlets around the world including newspapers and TV news networks, both national and local. The major US broadcast news services, including ABC, CNN and Fox send representatives as do the wealthier US newspapers such as the *Washington Post* and *New York Times*, and the financial press, including the *Wall Street Journal*, *Bloomberg* and the *Financial Times*. This book contains numerous extracts from White House briefings because they can give us useful insights into the relationship between the political world and the press.

Read the text below entitled 'The spin-doctor and the wolf-pack' (from Partington 2003). What do you notice in general about the metaphors used to describe the White House press briefings and their participants, that is, the spokesperson, also known as the podium (the press secretary) and the journalists? The metaphors can be grouped into certain categories, for example, 'sporting', 'military'. Try to sort as many of the metaphors as you can into such categories.

The spin-doctor and the wolf-pack

1) A quite remarkable variety of metaphors have been employed by commentators, many of whom are unsympathetic towards the participants, in describing the briefings held daily at the Office of the White House Press Secretary. They are 'a political chess game' (Reaves White), in which 'both sides view everything the other side does as a mere tactic' (Kamiya). Alternatively, they are 'rhetorical combat' (Kurtz), a 'war zone' in which 'combatants with a multitude of agendas [. . .] prepared for battle' (Reaves White). They are 'a wrestling match' and a duel or 'face-off' (Reaves White) but also 'a weird formulaic dance' (Kamiya).*

2) The spokesperson (or podium) is a soldier under 'hostile media fire [. . .] on the front lines for Clinton on nearly every major battle' (Baker and Kurtz) but also a sailor who must 'navigate the treacherous waters of the daily briefings' (*CNN Allpolitics*) and is frequently found 'desperately scrambling and bailing to keep a torrent of scandals from sinking the battered ship of state' (Jurkowitz). He is both a pugilist who has 'bobbed and weaved and jabbed [. . .] his way through all manner of Clinton scandals' but also a street thug who 'beats up on reporters' (Kurtz). He has even tried to be 'an ambassador between a president who disdained the press and reporters who didn't much trust the president' (Kurtz). Less nobly, he is 'a propagandist and a smear artist' (Irvine and Kincaid), 'a master at keeping the press in its place by doling out exclusives to reporters who will play ball with him and actually sandbagging those who will not' (Zweifel). Above all he is a 'spinmeister extraordinaire' (Kurtz) eternally spinning the truth, whatever that might be.

3)   There are slightly fewer metaphors to describe the journalists, probably because most of the commentators are themselves press people. Nevertheless, they are wild animals, the 'wolf-pack' of my title, which 'fights over morsels' (Warren). They too can be boxers out to 'pummel' the spokesperson, who has 'to stand at the podium and take whatever abuse the fourth estate wanted to dish out' (Kurtz). They are 'cynical chroniclers' (Kurtz), 'petty and manipulative [who] simply cannot put aside their "gotcha" mentality' (Zweifel). 'They like to destroy people. That's how they get their rocks off' (Dunham, supposedly quoting President Clinton). At the same time, however, they are 'a lot of dupes' (Irvine and Kincaid) and 'the White House reporter is not much more than a well-compensated stenographer' (Warren). On a more exalted note, their 'job is to transcend The Spin to find The Truth' (Dunham).

*References to Kurtz are from Kurtz (1998). All other references in these three paragraphs are from various websites. Baker, P. and H. Kurtz for *The Washington Post*; Dunham, R. for *BusinessWeek*; Irvine, R. and C. Kincaid for *Media Monitor*; Jurkowitz, M. for *The Boston Globe*; Kamiya, G. in *Salon*, Internet magazine; Reaves White, S. for the Amazon Website; Warren, J. for the *Chicago Tribune*; Zweifel, D. in *The Capital Times*.

Transcripts of the press briefings are available at:

www.whitehouse.gov/briefing-room/press-briefings

The White House has its own *YouTube* site:

www.youtube.com/whitehouse

which, naturally, provides a platform for the President's rhetoric of persuasion.

Q2

The more-or-less daily briefings held at the White House and presided over by the White House press secretary are generally held in a special room, the briefings room. It is not especially large and seats just forty-nine journalists. The seating assignments are organised by the White House Correspondents' Association, not by the White House press staff. The front row is assigned to the representatives of what are thought to be the most important and influential media, the second row for the slightly less important media, and so on until the back row. Which media organisations do *you* imagine are thought to be the most important, and are therefore awarded seats in the front row? See Figure 1.3 in the Keys below for the answers.

1.4 Epilogue: when persuasion is superfluous to requirements, even in some 'democracies'

There are, unfortunately, a number of situations where processes of persuasion of the population of the kinds described in this book are not necessarily relevant or are regularly abused.

The first of these situations is that of extreme poverty. In societies where people's basic needs are barely met, it is not rare to find politicians paying money for or bartering goods in return for people's votes. In pre-modern Britain, before the 19th Century, it was quite common, particularly in parliamentary constituencies with very small populations, for the richest local family to buy the votes of the constituents to elect one of the family members to Parliament. Such constituencies came to be called 'Rotten Boroughs' (that is 'corrupt areas'). There have been many allegations of contemporary vote-buying in several democracies around the world, not to mention strong rumours of buying of members' votes at the United Nations, the International Olympic Committee and the International Football Association (FIFA).

Another factor to consider is that the poorest societies also tend to be ones with high levels of illiteracy. Since democracy depends upon the availability of information about the choices available, can a largely illiterate society make such choices well and to what degree can information sources which do not necessarily require the ability to read (for example, TV, radio, online videos) fill the gap?

The second situation in which persuasion can be irrelevant is that which is sometimes called 'identity politics', that is, situations where people vote because of who or what they are, not for what they might think or believe. Put more precisely, in societies where people vote according to the group (race, religion, tribe) they belong to, not for any political ideals. One European example has been that of Northern Ireland, where voters traditionally voted along religiously sectarian lines, Protestants for 'Protestant' political parties, that is, organisations which promoted the interests of the Protestant community, and Roman Catholics for 'Catholic' political parties. Since it was clearly in people's self-interest to vote for parties promoting their own group, there was little attempt by politicians on either side to persuade voters to vote across the sectarian divide. An analogous situation has arisen in current post-invasion Iraq, where post-dictatorship political parties in the Arab parts of the country have coalesced according to sectarian identities, with Shia-Islam-aligned parties and Sunni-Islam-aligned parties.

Situations in which people vote according to racial or religious identity very often lead to the third hindrance to balanced and functional democracy, namely, the 'winner takes all' mentality. In both Northern Ireland in the past and Iraq, one sectarian group has a larger share of the population and, therefore, a larger number of voters than the other;

in the first case, the Protestants are a larger population than the Roman Catholics, and in the second, the Shia Muslims outnumber the Sunni Muslims. This means that the set of parties representing one of the sectarian groups has an inbuilt permanent majority of seats in Parliament and, therefore, is likely to always control the government; they can become effectively 'elected dictatorships'. Unless there are political checks and balances to protect the rights of the minority groups, the latter come to feel permanently disenfranchised and excluded from power:

> Democracy is not freedom. Democracy is two wolves and a lamb voting on what to eat for lunch. Freedom comes from the recognition of certain rights which may not be taken, not even by a 99% vote.
>
> (Simkin, *Los Angeles Times* 1992)

In both Northern Ireland and Iraq, the sense of being alienated from power has resulted in some members of the minority group resorting to violence against the State and against the members of the dominant sect. Furthermore, the individual members of a party which does not fear being removed by elections are often tempted to use their permanent power to their personal financial advantage (being the 'winners', they 'take all'): with no effective political rivals, no one will hold them

Figure 1.2 When you educate a girl

Source: Courtesy of Unicef and photographer Manpreet Romana.

to account, and they may well use their powers to close down the free press. With no accountability, one-party states are generally extremely corrupt, even where the party is *voted* into power. In 2014, Transparency International, an NGO dedicated to monitoring corruption, calculated Iraq to be 170 out of the 175 countries examined for levels of corruption, with the lowest possible score – zero – for governmental budget openness.

One final form of flawed democracy is the kind where the educational opportunities of girls and young women are limited or even forbidden. In such societies, even if nominally democracies, women will tend to vote as instructed by their fathers or husbands. In other words, natural democratic persuasion through language does not reach half the population, the female half. Investment in the education of girls is particularly worthwhile, because she will go on to educate her own children in turn. In the words of a Unicef campaign: 'Educate a girl and you educate a nation'.

Q3

Discussion. Checks and balances.

A democratic government that respects no limits on its power is a ticking time bomb, waiting to destroy the rights it was created to protect' (J. Bovard).

What are the checks and balances necessary to protect the interests of minorities in societies where people vote according to racial or religious *identity*? How is it possible to guard against the 'winner takes all' mentality that often arises in such societies?

Further reading

Cockcroft, R. and Cockcroft, S. (2013) *Persuading People: An Introduction to Rhetoric*, Basingstoke: Palgrave Macmillan.

Charteris-Black, J. (2013) *Analysing Political Speeches: Rhetoric, Discourse and Metaphor*, Basingstoke: Palgrave Macmillan (Part 1).

Keys and commentaries

TASK 1: *Language in politics*

The list is a long one. We might include:

- Spoken language: political interview, TV debate, cabinet meeting, trade negotiations, etc.
- Written language: party manifesto, election poster, newspaper or blog articles, peace treaty, tweets, etc.

- Mixed: parliamentary business is a mixture of debates, transcriptions of debates, writing and rewriting of drafts, discussion of improvements, until a final document is voted upon and becomes a written Law.

Political acts not involving language are few and far between. We might include a terrorist attack or initiation of hostilities without a declaration of war (e.g. Pearl Harbor), where language has been deliberately suppressed to exploit the element of surprise. Even these thankfully infrequent activities are prepared using language and are often followed by a claim of responsibility on the part of the perpetrators.

TASK 2: *Politics is . . .*

- Politics is war without bloodshed while war is politics with bloodshed. *Mao Tse-Tung.*
- I have come to the conclusion that politics is too serious a matter to be left to the politicians. *Charles de Gaulle.*
- Politics is supposed to be the second-oldest profession. I have come to realize that it bears a very close resemblance to the first. *Ronald Reagan.*
- Politics is for the present, but an equation is for eternity. *Albert Einstein.*
- Politics is the art of the possible, the attainable – the next best thing. *Otto von Bismarck.*
- Politics is almost as exciting as war, and quite as dangerous. In war you can only be killed once, but in politics many times. *Winston Churchill.*

TASK 3: *Definitions of rhetoric*

1) The art of persuasion in the attempt to influence the behaviour of others. A natural and everyday human activity.
2) The manipulation of an audience for personal ends. The use of complex-sounding language to hide the truth or the speaker's ignorance.
3) 'Grandiloquence' or the use of high-sounding but 'empty' language.

Aristotle argued the first of these, Plato the second.

1) Obama: Oratory and originality: rhetoric as the art of persuasion.
2) Salman Rushdie: hate-filled rhetoric of 'jihadi cool' is persuading British Muslims to join Isis: rhetoric as manipulation and persuading people to do things against their own interests.
3) Trump campaign dismisses Democratic attacks as 'night of empty rhetoric': rhetoric as grand-sounding talk with no substance.

TASK 4: *Metaphors of spin*

The metaphors of war and sport both suggest combat and competition between the two sides:

War: *war zone, combatants, hostile media fire*, etc.
Sport: *wrestling match, a pugilist* (that is boxer), and perhaps *chess game.*

Other metaphors emphasise the skill required to do the job: *a sailor navigating dangerous waters, an ambassador* and *a master.* The metaphor of *dance* suggests both skill and also coordination with rather than competition against the press. The metaphors used for the journalists suggest hyper-aggression: *wolf-pack*, fighters who *pummel* and who want to *destroy* people.

Q2

In the very front row we find the two biggest US press news agencies, Associated Press and Reuters. News agencies are organisations which collect news stories from around the world and sell them to other news broadcasters who have an account with them (which include the vast majority of mainstream newspapers of any repute). The other font row seats are reserved for TV channels. Only by the second row do we find the renowned US newspapers represented. The lesson is that today, TV broadcasting is more influential than the paper press.

PODIUM						
NBC	Fox News	CBS News	Associated Press	ABC News	Reuters	CNN
Wall Street Journal	CBS Radio	Bloomberg	NPR	Washington Post	New York Times	Associated Press Radio
AFP	USA Today	McClatchy	American Urban Radio Networks	POLITICO	Tribune	ABC Radio
Foreign Pool	MSNBC	Washington Times	The Hill	Fox News Radio	Voice of America	National Journal
Bloomberg BNA	TIME	New York Daily News	Hearst, S.F. Chronicle, Baltimore Sun	New York Post	Real Clear Politics	Chicago Sun-Times, Al Jazeera
Washington Examiner	Yahoo! News	Salem Radio Network	Media News Group, The Daily Beast	Christian Science Monitor	Sirius XM	Dow Jones
Talk Radio News Service	Dallas Morning News	Roll Call	CBN News	BBC, The Boston Globe	Scripps, BuzzFeed	Financial Times, The Guardian

Figure 1.3 The White House press room seating chart (2015)

Q3

Checks and balances. In circumstances where there is an inbuilt majority and minority, some form of power sharing needs to be guaranteed by the constitution; for instance, certain political posts have to be assigned to minority leaders.

Checks and balances include: the ability of Parliament to control the government; judges, even if appointed by the government, cannot be removed by it; if the government dissolves Parliament, new elections need to take place quickly; the press must be free to criticise the government, the Parliament and the judiciary – yet another confirmation that politics is conducted through language, and that democracy is not possible without freedom of expression.

Notes

1 www.communication-director.com/issues/power-persuasion/language-and-politics#.WLwMajvyvIU
2 Translated into modern English by the authors: *weep* = 'cry'; *pray* = 'ask'.

2 Evaluation

What's good and what's bad

Do not wait for the last judgment. It comes every day.
(Albert Camus)

The sad souls of those who lived without praise or blame.
(Dante Alighieri)

2.1 Evaluative language

Language which expresses the opinion, attitude and point of view of a speaker or a writer is called evaluative language. *Evaluation* is intended, in simple terms, as 'the indication of whether the speaker thinks that something is good or bad' (Thompson 1996: 65; Hunston 2004: 157). Not necessarily good or bad in a strictly moral sense, but also as favourable or unfavourable in an almost infinite number of wider senses: good can be intended as 'profitable', 'enjoyable', 'healthy', 'sensible', and so on; bad as the opposite of all these, 'wasteful', 'painful', 'unhealthy', 'idiotic', and so on.

Evaluation (or 'judgement' in Camus's words) is clearly the very basis of persuasion, in politics as in life. The persuader uses evaluative language to try to convince his or her audience that their own opinions are good, alternative ones are not good, that their proposals are worthy and logical (that is, good), those of their opponents illogical or dangerous (that is, bad), that they themselves are honest and trustworthy (good) and maybe that others who disagree with them are not (bad). Put another way, the persuader attempts to have the audience adopt his or her *preferred evaluations* of the topics in hand.

As Charles Darwin himself observed, humans are inherently *evaluating animals*. Probably all animals are; the ability to differentiate between a good thing and a bad thing is fundamental to survival. In politics, as in the rest of life, we constantly evaluate our own and other's behaviour and when we evaluate some behaviour as good we praise it, and when we evaluate it as bad we blame it and the people who commit it. As Charles Darwin argued, all social life revolves around people's pursuit of praise and fear of blame:

We may therefore conclude that primeval man was influenced by the praise and blame of his fellows [. . .] the members of the same tribe would approve of conduct which appeared to them to be for the general good, and would reprobate that which appeared evil [. . .]

It is, therefore, hardly possible to exaggerate the importance during rude times of the love of praise and the dread of blame.

(Darwin 1874: 89)

Evaluation can be expressed overtly or covertly. The second of these, covert or implicit evaluation, is so called because the speaker or writer provides no obvious linguistic clues, but exploits the audience's ability to recognise a good – or bad – thing when they see it. Thompson and Hunston (2000) argue, for instance, that what is good or bad is frequently construed in terms of goal achievement, and so all the actions in a narrative are meant to be evaluated in reference to an explicit or implicit goal (such as, say, 'survival' or 'getting the girl/boy one desires'). Implicit evaluation also depends upon expecting one's audience to share with you similar moral and socio-political values such as, say, the importance of democracy, of gender equality, of wage growth and – one of the most commonly evoked in political speeches – patriotic pride. And so, a statement such as:

Large parts of the Middle East have little experience of democracy
(Hamid 2011)

would be taken implicitly as an unfortunate state of affairs while:

More women are finding top posts in US politics and business
(Pew Research Centre 2015)

should, one hopes, be understood implicitly as a good thing, as, very commonly, are political slogans such as:

Make our country great again.

Overt or explicit evaluation, on the other hand, can be achieved through grammatical, textual or lexical means, as shown below.

2.1.1 Grammatical evaluation

Comparatives (better/worse than, richer/poorer than, etc.) are an obvious indication of evaluation.

The system of **transitivity** (also sometimes called **agency**) is the grammatical structuring which tells us 'who does what to whom (and how)': In simple terms, it tells us who is the 'Doer' of an action and who is the 'Done-to' of an action or event, it enables (and in fact forces) the language user to place the participants and events in a particular order and allows him or her to express evaluations of responsibility. If the action the 'Doer' is said to have done is a positive one then transitivity is a means of assigning praise, and if the action is negative, it is a way of apportioning blame. In some cases it can also be a way of hiding blame: compare 'A shot B', 'B was shot by A', 'there was a shooting' (Mooney et al. 2011: 70).

Consider the differences between:

John argued with Sue;
Sue argued with John;
John and Sue argued.

In the first John seems to be responsible, in the second Sue and in the third they are co-doers and so co-responsible. Consider too the differences among:

William and Mary got a divorce;
William divorced his wife, Mary;
Mary was divorced by William;
William got a divorce (where no other participant is mentioned except William).

Or between the following two headlines which describe the 'same' event which took place in Rhodesia (now Zimbabwe):[1]

Police shoot 11 dead in Salisbury riot (*Guardian*)
Rioting blacks shot dead by police (*Times*)

Q1

In how many different ways could you formulate a headline to describe the conflict which broke out between the Russian Federation and Ukraine in 2014?

Participants involved: Russia (Putin); Ukraine
Action involved: attack, invade, fight, war

See the Extension task at the end of this Unit for a case study in how the examination of grammatical evaluation can reveal non-obvious meanings in a text.

2.1.2 Textual evaluation

Evaluation can also be expressed by the particular positioning or ordering of 'blocks' of language in certain places in a text.

The final paragraphs of newspaper editorials tend to indicate favoured solutions to problems proposed in the previous parts of the text (Morley 2004).

Similarly, if a speaker, a politician perhaps, presents two alternative policies to her audience, one of which she agrees with and wishes to persuade the audience to adopt, and one of which she does not, she will generally talk of the one she does not approve of first and the one she wants to promote second. (This is called the 'straw man' technique, from medieval battle training where the aim was to knock down a straw dummy using a stick or a sword.) See also the problem–solution model of argument discussed in Unit 3.

Speakers often open their speech with a strong and clear evaluative statement to attract the audience's attention and also often try to end their speech with a 'rhetorical flourish' or finale, consisting of a particularly emphatic and sometimes quite poetic summation of their evaluative argument. This means the opening and closing sections of speeches are frequently especially interesting from a discourse analyst's point of view.

2.1.3 Lexical evaluation

Probably the most obvious signs of evaluation are contained in the lexis, that is, the words and phrases a speaker or writer uses. If we divide all the words in the language into two types:

> grammar words, which include determiners (e.g. *the, a, one, some*), linkers (e.g. *and, because, since*) and prepositions (e.g. *in, at, from, by, across*);

and

> content words, which include nouns, verbs, adjectives and adverbs;

we find that an enormous variety of the latter type, content words, have evaluation as part, often most, of their meaning. Consider, for instance, the adjectives *splendid, miserable, untrue*; the adverbs *happily, unfortunately*; the nouns *success, failure*; and the verbs *win* and *lose*.

One way we can see how central evaluation is to us is to look at language change because evaluative adjectives are one of the most innovative categories. Try it out – can you think of five adjectives to describe something as good/bad which people older than you would not use?

TASK 1: *Evaluation in action*

Read the following extract from the US presidential election debates held in late 2004. The two candidates were the incumbent President George W. Bush and the challenger Senator John Kerry.

Underline the language you think is evaluative in function, both favourable and unfavourable. You will see how not only individual words express evaluation but entire phrases too. (Mr Lehrer, of the Public Broadcasting Service, was the so-called 'moderator' who put the questions.)

Can you spot any instances of implicit evaluation?

Mr Lehrer: New question, Mr President. Two minutes. Do you believe the election of Senator Kerry on Nov. 2 would increase the chances of the US being hit by another 9/11-type terrorist attack?

1) Mr Bush: I don't believe it's going to happen. I believe I'm going to win because the American people know I know how to lead. I've shown the American people I know how to lead. I have – I understand everybody in this country doesn't agree with the decisions that I've made. And I've made some tough decisions. But people know where I stand. People out there listening know what I believe. And that's how best it is to keep the peace.

2) This nation of ours has got a solemn duty to defeat this ideology of hate. And that's what they are, this is a group of killers who will not only kill here but kill children in Russia. That will attack unmercifully in Iraq hoping to shake our will. We have a duty to defeat this enemy. We have a duty to protect our children and grandchildren.

3) The best way to defeat them is to never waver, to be strong, to use every asset at our disposal. It's to constantly stay on the offensive. And at the same time spread liberty. And that's what people are seeing now is happening in Afghanistan. Ten million citizens have registered to vote. It's a phenomenal statistic. That if given a chance to be free they will show up at the polls. Forty-one percent of those 10 million are women.

4) In Iraq, no doubt about it, it's tough. It's hard work. It's incredibly hard. You know why? Because an enemy realizes the stakes. The enemy understands a free Iraq will be a major defeat in their ideology of hatred. That's why they're fighting so vociferously.

5) They showed up in Afghanistan when they were there because they tried to beat us and they didn't. And they're showing up in Iraq for the same reason. They're trying to defeat us and if we lose our will we lose. But if we remain strong and resolute we will defeat this enemy.

Can you spot any instances of implicit evaluation?

Note the particular rhythmical rhetorical flourish he employs to conclude his turn (see Unit 5.3 on the three-part list and 5.4 on contrasting pairs), as mentioned above as a mechanism of *textual* evaluation.

Q2

Televised debates

Such highly organised televised debates are, of course, acts of attempted persuasion. The questions are asked by the moderator and the responses are formally addressed to him. But who do you think are the real targets of the act of persuasion? The question was about Senator Kerry, but Bush does not mention him in the answer. What does he talk about instead? What 'shared values' does Bush appeal to in this response? Do you think Bush's response is a successful one in terms of an act of persuasion?

2.2 Evaluation by language choice

2.2.1 Denotation and connotation

There are, of course, many ways of saying the 'same' thing and speakers and writers can, indeed *must* in practice, choose one among these many potential ways. The choice of vocabulary that a speaker/writer makes can tell us a great deal about how they evaluate the topic in question, and so a great deal about their opinions and/or intentions.

Compare, for instance, the following set of descriptions, applied to old items for sale:

used, second-hand, pre-loved, vintage, antique

or these applied to a politician:

obstinate, stubborn, firm, decisive, resolute, pig-headed.

In both cases, the basic meaning of the words, that is, their ***denotational*** meaning, is roughly the same, but they differ radically in the evaluation or the ***connotational*** meaning they express. A seller is unlikely to label their items as *used* or even *second-hand*, but *vintage* and *antique* are often used in shop names and advertising because these are definitely more favourable and complimentary. The denotation of an item is the definition we might find in a dictionary; the connotations of an item are the associations it has for us, especially the evaluative ones.

Speakers and writers, then, very frequently can make a choice of which word or expressions to describe a person, an event, an entity, etc. The political and civil unrest which broke out in North Africa and the Middle East has been given various names, including:

The Arab revolts
The Arab uprisings

> The Arab Spring
> The Arab Awakening

We have listed the terms in order of evaluative connotation, from the least positive – *revolts* – to the most positive –*Awakening*.

Some words acquire a good or bad sense over time; for example, as Beard (2000) points out, *politics* and *politician*, especially in the UK, have acquired a negative sense. The denotation would be something like:

> Politician: One versed in the theory or science of government and the art of governing; one skilled in politics; one practically engaged in conducting the business of the state; a statesman;

while the connotation, for most people at least, is likely to be:

> Politician: a shrewd schemer; a crafty plotter or intriguer.

And perhaps this bad connotation is not as recent as is sometimes imagined:

> You can't use tact with a Congressman! A Congressman is a hog! You must take a stick and hit him on the snout!
>
> (Cabinet member 1906)

TASK 2: *Forms of government*

Using a dictionary and other Internet resources, try to find the general evaluative connotations of the following items used to describe forms of government and fill in Table 2.1 below.

regime, junta, democracy, dictatorship, one-man rule, administration

In 'Notes', add any other observations you might have, e.g. the associations of the item, where in the world it is applied, and so on.

Table 2.1 Forms of government

Word	Evaluation	Notes
Regime	Bad	Military

Using corpora to check language

Corpora are collections of text which you can use to check how words are actually used. For this study, you could also make use of the free corpora available at http://corpus.byu.edu/

- Choose the *Corpus of Contemporary American English*. This corpus gives you a snapshot of current language in the US.
- Choose the option 'compare'.
- Type in two of words you want to compare, e.g. *regime* and *junta*.
- You will then get a list of words which more typically co-occur with one of the words, compared to the other. This can help you to understand the *connotations* for each term.

At the beginning of 2011, political protest spread across the Arab world. In Libya, a section of the population rose in violent conflict against the government, headed by Colonel Gadaffi (sometimes written Qadaffi, along with twenty-six other variants according to the London newspaper the *Evening Standard*). The graph below shows how, within a very short space of time, from January to March 2011, the White House spokesperson stopped using the normal, default, diplomatic designation *Libyan government* and began to use *Libyan regime* and finally *Qadaffi regime*.

This change of language shows how quickly the US both distanced itself from the Syrian administration and personalised the conflict. As so often in a conflict, it is rhetorically convenient to '**metonymise**' (Unit 7) one's opponent, that is, to identify one's antagonist in the figure of a single person.

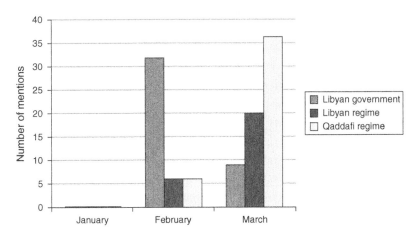

Figure 2.1 How the Libyan administration is referred to by the podium in the first three months of White House press briefings in 2011

2.3 'Insider' words (good), 'outsider' words (bad)

Closely related to the question of good or bad evaluative connotation is the question of the difference between the labels a group chooses to describe itself and those used by those outside the group to describe it (as we saw with the term *rhetoric* in the previous Unit). A very large number of governments, of both western capitalist or eastern communist form, although they have very little else in common, have called themselves *democratic*, such is the favourable connotation of the label. Few have chosen to call themselves *dictatorships*, though their opponents may well call them that. A group which employs violence to obtain political ends may call itself a *resistance movement*, which is thus an 'in' or 'insider' word, while those outside it or unsympathetic to it may call it an *extremist organisation*, which is thus an 'out' or 'outsider' word.

All this leads us to one of the most important observations to be kept in mind throughout these lessons. The use of a word or expression or a certain type of language tells us as much about the person speaking/writing as about the topic of the discourse itself.

TASK 3: *Opponents of those in power*

Using a dictionary, a corpus such as those available at http://corpus. byu.edu/ and/or other resources on the Internet, try to find the general evaluative connotations of the following items used to describe opponents of those in power:

> *revolutionary, fundamentalist, dissident, separatist, militant, protester, freedom-fighter, terrorist*

If you find a word is sometimes good, sometimes bad and sometimes neutral, you may decide that its evaluation depends on the context it is used in.

The term *terrorist/s*, *terrorism* and *terror* merit special attention. Many journalists and media critics argue that they should not be used

Table 2.2 Opponents of those in power

Word	Evaluation	Notes

at all, since they convey a negative evaluation in contexts where a more neutral term might be appropriate. They repeat the old cliché that: 'one man's terrorist is another man's freedom fighter'. A large variety of alternative terms are often found in the media after an incidence of violence, including *shooters, assailants, attackers, militants, gunmen, bombers, lone wolf.*

Others argue instead that *terrorism* indicates a *method* rather than a political stance. It indicates the more or less indiscriminate use of violence to attempt to force another group of people to do what the perpetrators wish them to do. They argue that the term, being descriptive, is entirely appropriate and does not make a value judgement. It is, in fact, possible to be a freedom-fighter *and* a terrorist, if one chooses to terrorise as a method of achieving one's goals.

Anecdotally, the current authors have noticed that even the first group, those who recommend avoiding the terms *terrorism* and *terrorist*, are more likely to disregard their own advice if an incident occurs geographically or culturally close to home than if it occurs far away. The BBC's guidelines advise their journalists to avoid the term:

> The word 'terrorist' itself can be a barrier rather than an aid to understanding [. . .] Terrorism is a difficult and emotive subject with significant political overtones and care is required in the use of language that carries value judgements. We try to avoid the use of the term 'terrorist'
>
> (BBC Editorial Guidelines[2])

But several BBC reporters and commenters showed no hesitation in referring to terrorism to characterise the violent events which took place in Paris in January and November 2015, for example:

Paris attacks: a new terrorism and fear stalks a city

> It's just 10 months since Paris was the scene of multiple **terrorist** attacks, first the massacre of staff at the satirical magazine Charlie Hebdo and then a hostage-taking at a Jewish supermarket.
>
> (*BBC News* 2015)

And when *British* people are victims of an attack, there is no reticence at using the word *terrorist*:

> Thirty UK citizens were among 38 people killed in a terrorist attack in Tunisia on 26 June.
>
> (*BBC News* 2015)

Finally, when one of the BBC's own journalists was killed and another maimed for life, the latter had no reserves about using the word:

> Frank Gardner: I will never forgive the terrorists who did this to me.
> (*Daily Telegraph* 2014)

TASK 4: *Political positions*

Using a dictionary and other resources on the Internet, try to find the general evaluative connotations of the following items used to describe various political positions:

> *activist, hawk, extremist, radical, moderate, liberal, reactionary, populist*

Occasionally words may change their insider or outsider status, for example, in the process of 'reclaiming' of the terms *queer* (gay) and *nigger* (black person), and, from the political sphere, *suffragette*, which was coined as a dismissive term for women trying to obtain equal access to politics through voting reforms. While these words were/are very highly derogatory when used by outsiders, they have now been reclaimed and may be used by speakers who belong to the group in question to describe themselves or others from their inside group. This is also illustrated in the following headline from the *Guardian* newspaper (*Paki* is a derogatory term for a person of Pakistani origin):

> 'I'm a Paki and proud'
>
> Businessman Abdul Rahim says he wants to reclaim the P-word from racists – and he's using his 'PAK1' clothes label to do it.
> (*Guardian* 2004)

Table 2.3 Political positions

Word	Evaluation	Notes

2.4 Hooray words and boo words

The New Zealand philosopher Jamie Whyte coined the term 'hooray' word for a term which has a socially positive connotation and almost automatically arouses a sense of approval in an audience, and the term 'boo' word for one which, instead, has a negative connotation and automatically arouses a sense of disapproval in the hearer. As Whyte points out, such items are frequently exploited by professional persuaders. They often have little core meaning when subjected to close scrutiny; in fact, their meaning or function lies almost entirely in their positivity or negativity.

Two of the most common 'hooray' words found in advertising are *natural* and *authentic*. It is hard to argue that something is *not* authentic – everything is authentically itself – but the term itself seems to suggest *reliability*. Nor is there a legal definition of what is *natural*. Very little of the food we eat today existed in the form we know it 1000 years ago. Most of it undergoes some form of processing and uses products developed by agriculturalists or scientific crop-breeders; there is no, say, *pasta* plant in nature. It is made by milling, baking then drying a special human-domesticated variety of wheat. But few would object to pasta being called a *natural* food. One especially curious example is the 'contains 100% natural tobacco' claim by certain cigarette manufacturers; no unhealthy additives, then, to the carcinogens already contained in the natural tobacco plant.

'Hooray' words in modern English-language politics are too many to list but include items like *modernisation, justice, equality, diversity, initiative, fairness, sustainable, freedom, choice, respect, efficiency, hope* and *democracy*. It is hard to imagine any politician and party declaring themselves to be *against* any of the above. When a politician is against one of these, s/he will choose a different term to describe it. For instance, if a politician is critical of, say, the ethnic or religious *diversity* brought about by immigration, they might talk positively instead about national *traditions*.

When 'hooray' words are used, everyone in an audience can be expected to be in favour, at least until further investigation into what the politician might actually mean. The US claims to be a democratic nation, but so does China and so did the notoriously oppressive DDR, East Germany, the self-proclaimed *Democratic* Republic of Germany. No party will declare themselves to be against *social justice*. But left-leaning and right-leaning parties define it very differently. For the former, social justice would imply reducing inequality and involve high levels of redistribution of wealth, in the form of taxation, from the haves to the have-nots. For the second, high taxes are a form of theft and they discourage hard work and wealth creation. For the right, social justice implies allowing people to hold on to the rewards of their ambition, talents and industriousness.

Sometimes the notions, when they exist, behind hooray words, may even be in conflict. Some forms of *modernisation* may not necessarily be *sustainable*. A group which feels its *freedom* is under threat may not opt for *peace*. What a government calls *savings*, an opposition will call *cuts*. *Equality* and *diversity* may also be perceived to clash in multicultural societies which strive for an ideal of equality of rights and opportunities between men and women. However, some communities within such societies may not see equality of the sexes as desirable and may practise serious discrimination against the girls and women in those communities. The question then arises: is it possible to support *equality* and respect cultural *diversity* at the same time?

Many boo words are the simple antonyms of hooray words, derived from them by a prefix; for example, *inequality, unfairness, unsustainable, injustice*. *Natural* has two antonym boo words, *unnatural* and *artificial*. Yet again there is no agreement over what counts as *unnatural*; consider the controversies over what is and is not *un/natural* sexual behaviour. Given that hospitals, most medicines, houses, trains and even bicycles are not natural products, however, another antonym of *natural* is *science* and *technology* – hardly boo words for most people.

While most hooray words have general appeal, many boo words, in contrast, are highly 'sectarian', that is, they are boo words for one group but not for others. The term *capitalist* is a boo word for many on the left, just as *socialist* is a boo word for their opponents on the right. At the time of writing there are a number of metonymic (see Unit 7.3) place-name boo words in UK and US political rhetoric. For opponents of the UK's membership of the European Union, *Brussels*, a metonym for the EU as a whole, is a boo word (see the exercise in Unit 7.3). Similarly, for Scots who want to leave the UK, *Westminster*, the part of London where the UK Parliament is situated, is a boo word. In the US, the term *Washington* is a boo word for many Republicans, as is *Wall Street* for many Democrats, both seen by the respective groups as acting against or at least ignoring the interests of 'ordinary Americans' (Unit 10.1). What this shows us is that the connotations of many words and phrases can vary for different groups of people.

TASK 5: *Hooray words and boo words 1*

The box below contains a number of politically relevant hooray words and boo words; that is, words which have either a strong positive or negative connotation for large numbers of people. Which are which?

unsustainable	genuine	the people
bureaucracy	our children	artificial
environmentally friendly	cuts	traditional
green	moderate	politicians
discrimination	diversity	community
cost-effective	big government	

Hooray: ....

....

Boo: ....

....

TASK 6: *Hooray words and boo words 2*

In section 2.1 above we examined President Bush's response to a question posed during a presidential debate. It contains a number of hooray and boo words and phrases. Can you find them?

2.5 Evaluation by *selection of information*: what to leave in and what to leave out

Textbooks on journalism often teach that a news story has to answer the readers' six 'wh' questions, four of which can be relatively simple:

What happened?
When did it happen?
Where did it happen?
Who was involved, that is who were the main actors, sometimes expressed as 'who did what to whom?' (see Grammatical evaluation in 2.1 above).

and two which are frequently much more complex:

How did it happen?
Why did it happen?

In books of grammar, *what*, *when*, *where* and *who* are often known as the 'closed' wh-questions since their answers can be quite short, while *how* and *why* are known as open questions, since they often not only require long answers but are frequently answered in very different ways according to people's background knowledge and experiences, points of view and political standpoint.

The following is the recounting on the *BBC News* website of a tragic event which took place in a suburb of London (the full article can be found at: https://tinyurl.com/PiP-2-5):

A four-year-old girl has been found dead at an address on an east London housing estate at 1530 GMT on Thursday after reports of a knife incident.

A woman, 36, believed to be the girl's mother, has been sectioned under the Mental Health Act after being arrested on suspicion of her murder.

TASK 7: *Information in the BBC report*

How much information can be extracted on the journalistic wh-questions from the BBC article:

What happened?..

When?..

Where?..

Who was involved? ....

How? ....

Why?..

An article relating to the same event was published by the British tabloid newspaper the *Daily Mail* with a headline suggesting that the death was somehow part of a 'religious ritual'. The body of the article goes on to elucidate:

> The 35-year-old woman was allegedly chanting verses of the Koran as her daughter's disembowelled corpse lay next to her in the home in Clapton, East London. The woman, believed to be from Somalia, had her MP3 on full blast as she listened to the Muslim holy book.

The full article is available at: https://tinyurl.com/PiP-Task7. The names, all of non-European origin, of the child, her mother and father are given. The latter, we are also informed, is 'believed' (though we are not told by whom it is believed) to be a convert to Islam.

TASK 8: *Information in the Daily Mail report*

How much information can be extracted on the journalistic wh-questions from the extracts from the *Daily Mail* article:

What happened?..

When?..

Where?..

Who was involved? ....

How? ....

Why?..

It could be argued that the BBC article is 'information-poor' in that it gives minimalistic detail of what occurred and leaves the reader in the dark about how the death occurred. The *Daily Mail* story is much more 'information-rich' but the reader might question the relevance of some of the information, why religion is mentioned so often and why the non-British origins of the actors are stressed. The BBC article is as non-evaluative an account as it is possible to construct. But does the *Daily Mail*'s inclusion and repetition of certain information invite readers to perform too much negative evaluation?

2.6 Evaluation and modality

2.6.1 Modality as your degree of commitment to a belief

In standard grammars, modality refers to the grammatical systems which speakers can use to express their degree of commitment to their belief that:

> something did or did not happen (degree of past certainty); will or will not happen (degree of future possibility/probability); or should or should not happen (degree of necessity),

or to their belief that:

> someone did or did not do something (certainty); is able or unable to do something (ability); is wanting/willing or unwilling to do something (willingness or 'volition'); should or should not do something (necessity or moral responsibility).

As Thompson (1996: 57) says, a 'simple starting definition of modality is that it is the space between "yes" and "no"'. The following is an illustration of the degrees of *past certainty* between 'yes, someone certainly did it' and 'no, someone certainly didn't do it':

> the politician took the bribe; the politician probably took the bribe; the politician might have taken the bribe; the politician probably didn't take the bribe; the politician didn't take the bribe.

It is also possible to 'hyper-commit' to a belief. For example:

> the politician *definitely* took the bribe; I'm *absolutely convinced* the politician didn't take the bribe.

Expressions of modality might also include: the politician shouldn't have taken the bribe; the politician shouldn't have been allowed to take the bribe (moral responsibility); there's no way the politician could have taken the bribe (ability); the politician is probably going to take the bribe; it wouldn't surprise me if the politician took the bribe

(future possibility and maybe willingness); the politician had no need
to take the bribe (necessity and moral responsibility).

Note how all expressions of other types of modality also presuppose a commitment on the certainty–uncertainty belief scale.

It is not difficult to see from these examples how expression of
modality is intertwined with the expression of evaluation. Of course,
the modal expressions of moral responsibility are the most overtly
evaluative, but since taking a bribe is generally thought of as a bad
thing, even the degree of commitment to the belief in the certainty or
ability or willingness or necessity that she or he did it or not can be an
evaluation of them.

2.6.2 Modality and evaluation in political comment

The modality in newspaper reports such as the BBC piece on the death
of the child in London can be relatively straightforward, a simple
statement of what is believed to be known. In contrast, the modality
in newspaper opinion pieces can be concentrated and highly complex.
The following extracts are all from political editorial opinion pieces
from the *Sun* newspaper. The most frequent modality is that of necessity and moral obligation, that something *needs* to be done and someone *should be* doing it:

> THE new Government **needs to** get serious about defence spending.

> The starting point for any review of Whitehall budgets **should be**
> that two per cent of our GDP will be spent on Our Boys to keep the
> nation safe.

> We wish it wasn't as **vital** as it is. But the world is more dangerous
> now than for 70 years. **This is not the time** to refuse to commit to
> Nato's target.
>
> (*Sun* 2015)

Vital and *This is not the time* are also modal expressions of necessity.
On other occasions, necessity and obligation are followed by an
explanation in terms of future prediction:

> BRITAIN **needs** its nuclear deterrent. In an increasingly dangerous
> world, that **should be** beyond dispute.

> **Chances are we'll never use it.** But **consider the threat** from Russia,
> North Korea, a destabilised Pakistan, or Iran **if it gets the bomb**.
>
> (*Sun* 2015)

Needs denotes necessity, *should be* an obligation to know these facts.
The second paragraph contains two obvious future predictions, one

probable *chances are* the other possible *if it gets the bomb.* In addition, *consider the threat* weds explicit evaluation (*threat*) to modal possibility, that the four countries named *may* some day constitute a menace to the UK.

In the next passage, necessity, moral obligation, possibility and volition are all intertwined:

> The PM [David Cameron] said the EU **must** face the fact that voters **want** their own individual countries to be sovereign.
>
> He added: 'We **need** more for nation states. It **should be** nation states **wherever possible** and Europe **only where necessary**. We **need** people running these organisations that really understand that – and **can** build a Europe that is about openness, competitiveness and flexibility. Not about the past'.
>
> (*Sun* 2014)

The modality bears the weight of various evaluations; a positive evaluation of the nation state (*wherever possible*), a less negative evaluation of the EU or 'Europe' (*only where necessary*) and a negative evaluation of EU managers (we *need* 'people' who understand better what the voters *want* [volition], which implies that we do not as yet have them).

TASK 9: *Forms of modality and their contribution to evaluation*

A high proportion of opinion pieces look to the future, first outlining negative situations in the present, predicting possible future events and suggesting, even exhorting, a particular course of action, obviously positively evaluated. Read the following extract from an editorial. Find the expressions of modality, specify which sort they are and think about how they contribute to guiding the readers' evaluation of the topics.

Why should [the conflicts in Syria] concern us? First, there is the humanitarian crisis, with hundreds of thousands of refugees streaming into makeshift camps [. . .]

Second, other countries in the region risk being drawn into the conflict, especially Iran, which could spark a full-blown sectarian war.

Requests for help will be difficult to resist. Third, there is the threat of the export of further hardline Islamist terror to countries including Britain.

We cannot afford to have Islamist extremists coming home with British passports, having waged successful jihad across the Middle East.

> That is why it is absolutely imperative that Isis is defeated [. . .]
> Many will be tempted to say it is not our problem, that it is something happening far away. That would be the wrong conclusion to draw.
> If Isis wins in Iraq, then it could easily become an ungoverned space that encourages and trains terrorists even more than Afghanistan before 9/11 – and we all know the cost we had to bear as a consequence.
> It is absolutely essential that we do not allow that to happen.
>
> (*Sun* 2014)

2.7 Extension task. What examining grammatical evaluation can reveal: a case study of the *US Declaration of Independence*

The language of the *Declaration of Independence of the United States* has been studied many times, and we return to it in Unit 5.6. It is available for download at www.constitution.org/us_doi.pdf, while the image of the actual signed parchment can be viewed here: www.archives.gov/founding-docs/downloads

It is, above everything else, an attempt at *persuasion*. The authors, principally Thomas Jefferson, flood the document with messages favourable to a particular worldview, namely, the secessionist agenda of the revolutionaries. But, to recoin a phrase, one man's revolutionary is another man's traitor and, indeed, many American colonists remained loyal to the British Crown (as witnessed by the large-scale exodus to Canada at the end of the Revolutionary War), and the conflict was as much a civil war, with Americans fighting Americans, as a struggle for independence. Those Americans who fought against secession and with the British called themselves 'Loyalists', those who fought for independence/secession called themselves 'Patriots', both good examples of 'insider words' (see section 2.3 above).

The *Declaration*, therefore, constitutes two attempts at persuasion; first, an appeal for unity to an internal audience, the colonists, and an appeal for legitimacy and understanding of motivation to an external audience, both in Britain and elsewhere. To understand how Jefferson makes his persuasive argument, we can study the patterns of agency he weaves in the choices made in the grammatical system of transitivity.

If the language being studied is English, one useful way of studying transitivity and agency is to look at the use of pronouns. Pronouns constitute the only remaining relict of the case system in English, they change according to whether a participant is active *Do-er*, so *I, he, she, we*, etc., or passive *Done-to*, so me, him, her, us, etc., or possessor, so *mine, his, hers, ours*, etc. One can then look at the verbs associated with the Do-er and Done-to pronouns and the semantic categories these verbs belong to, and the sorts of nouns following the possessive pronouns.

Jefferson carefully avoids the *Us* vs *Them* rhetoric of so many political documents, presenting the reader instead with an *Us* versus *Him*, or rather *He*, evaluative dichotomy or opposition. The item *He* occurs nineteen times in the document, always referring to the King of Great Britain, George III, and always in sentence- or clause-initial position. In all but one occasion *He* is followed by *has* + verb participle. The item *him*, in contrast, is never used in the document; in other words, the King is always cast in active 'Do-er' role and never in passive 'Done-to' role.

Q3

The complaints against the King

The verbs following *He has* ... fall into two semantic categories. What overall sense do the verbs in each category convey?
Category 1:

- He has abdicated Government here.
- He has dissolved Representative Houses repeatedly.
- He has forbidden his Governors to pass Laws of immediate and pressing importance.
- He has obstructed the Administration of Justice, by refusing his Assent to Laws for establishing Judiciary powers.
- He has refused for a long time, after such dissolutions, to cause others to be elected.
- He has refused his Assent to Laws, the most wholesome and necessary for the public good.
- He has refused to pass other Laws for the accommodation of large districts of people.
- [. . .] he has utterly neglected to attend to them.

Category 2:

- He has destroyed the lives of our people.
- He has excited domestic insurrections amongst us.
- He has plundered our seas, ravaged our Coasts, burnt our towns.

In contrast, the primings constructed around the *We* group are more complex. They are active Do-er (*we*) and passive Done-to (*us*) on an equal number of occasions, eleven.

Q4

Here is a selection of the use of *we*. What is the semantic category of verbs associated with *we*?

- **we** have Petitioned for Redress in the most humble terms.
- **we** have warned them from time to time of attempts.

- **we** have reminded them of the circumstances of our emigration and settlement here.
- **we** have appealed to their native justice and magnanimity.

When Done-to (that is *us*) it is always 'Done-to' by the King:

- imposing Taxes on **us** without our Consent:
- depriving **us** in many cases, of the benefits of Trial by Jury.
- transporting **us** beyond Seas to be tried for pretended offences.

The agency priming is that of apportioning blame to the single figure of George III; the rebels even claim to have *not* been 'wanting in attentions to our British brethren (brothers)' and talk of 'the ties of our common kindred' in order to reinforce this message that the King alone is to blame (another example of the useful metonymisation of the enemy into a single person, mentioned in section 2.2 above).

However, and perhaps more surprisingly, by far the most common pronoun in the document is the possessive *our*, which occurs twenty-six times. If we compare the frequency of occurrence of these three items – *we/us/our* – in the *Declaration* with that in the one-million-word Frown corpus of mixed (or 'heterogeneric') American English texts,[3] we discover a considerable difference. In the *Declaration*, the three pronouns occur once every twenty-three words, in the Frown corpus once in every 256 words:

	Declaration	Frown corpus of US English
we/us/our	1:23	1:256

The 'we' group is clearly an extremely important notion in Jefferson's priming of the reader. But we also note that the proportions among the three items are strikingly different, as illustrated in Figures 2.2 and 2.3.

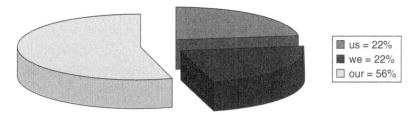

us = 22%
we = 22%
our = 56%

Figure 2.2 The proportions of *we*, *us* and *our* in the *Declaration of Independence*

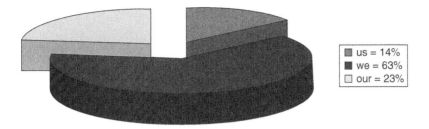

us = 14%
we = 63%
our = 23%

Figure 2.3 The proportions of *we*, *us* and *our* in the Frown corpus

The possessive *our* is thus proportionally far more frequent in the *Declaration* than in the Frown corpus which represents American English more generally.

A study of the grammar of the *Declaration*, especially the way pronouns are used, reveals how Jefferson attempts to flood the discourse with messages beyond the more obvious ones of 'liberty' and 'tyranny'. These include: the agency of the King as Do-er and guilty party; the agency of the rebels as responsibly minded, judicious but long-suffering Done-to victims and also the message of *unity* by continually talking of *we*, *us* and *our* in reference to the colonists, which was far from the actual case (note also how the title itself talks of a *'unanimous' Declaration*). But the relative frequency of *our* is evidence of how the *Declaration* is as much a declaration of *ownership* as of *freedom*, both naturally evaluated positively. This should come as no surprise in hindsight; the dependency of liberty upon property rights seemed natural to the 18th-Century political mind.

Further reading

Bednarek, M. (2006) *Evaluation in Media Discourse: Analysis of a Newspaper Corpus*, New York and London: Continuum.

Partington, A., Duguid, A. and Taylor, C. (2013) *Patterns and Meanings in Discourse*, Amsterdam: John Benjamins. Chapter 2: 'Evaluation in discourse communication'.

Thompson, G. and Hunston, S. (2000) 'Evaluation: An introduction', in S. Hunston and G. Thompson (eds.) *Evaluation in Text*, Oxford: Oxford University Press, 1–27.

Case studies

Cabrejas-Peñuelas, A.B. and Díez-Prados, M. (2014) 'Positive self-evaluation versus negative other-evaluation in the political genre of pre-election debates', *Discourse & Society* 25(2): 159–185.

Ghachem, I. (2015) 'A sociocognitive approach to agency framing in David Cameron's 2010 pre-election discourse', *Critical Approaches to Discourse Analysis Across Disciplines* 7(2): 263–282.

Keys and commentaries

Q1

In how many different ways could you formulate a headline to describe the conflict which broke out between the Russian Federation and Ukraine in 2014?

Suggestions:

Russian forces invade Ukraine.
Ukraine invaded by Russian forces.
The Russian invasion of Ukraine.
Russia and Ukraine are at war.
Ukraine is invaded.
War breaks out in Ukraine.

TASK 1: *Evaluation in action*

In the first paragraph of Mr Bush's reply, the evaluation is positive, as we might expect since he chooses to speak about himself and his past record; for example, 'I believe I'm going to win', 'the American people know I know how to lead', and so on. In the second paragraph, when he speaks of us, 'this nation of ours', the evaluation remains good while when he speaks of 'them', the killers, the evaluation is, in contrast, highly unfavourable; for example, 'kill children', 'attack unmercifully'. Notice how odd the last expression is: it would be more normal to say 'attack mercilessly'.

We need to be careful, however. It should be noted that in the sections of good evaluation we often find items which, by themselves, might seem to carry an unfavourable evaluation, such as [tough decisions] or [ideology of hate]. But if we look at the surrounding context the speaker reverses the polarity: it is a good thing to be (able to take [tough decisions]) and to (defeat this [ideology of hate]). The round brackets indicate positive evaluation and square brackets negative. The outside brackets are those which dictate the overall evaluation.

A probable candidate for implicit evaluation is provided in the final sentence of the third paragraph: 'Forty-one percent of those 10 million are women'. Mr Bush relies on his audience judging the high degree of participation of women in elections in a country where women have traditionally been excluded from politics as a very good thing.

Q2

Televised debates

The real target of the act of persuasion is, of course, the TV audience. Instead of talking about Senator Kerry, Bush talks about himself, his qualities of leadership in the struggle of 'us' against 'them'.

Not talking about the challenger is a common strategy for the incumbent candidate (see Unit 3.2).

The shared values include: strong leadership, patriotism, belief in democracy, a role for women in politics.

Do you think Bush's response is a successful one in terms of an act of persuasion? (Open response).

TASK 2: *Forms of government*

Table 2.1 Key: forms of government

Word	Evaluation	Notes
Regime	Bad	Military
Junta	Bad	South American military regime
Democracy	Good	All other forms of government are negative by comparison
Dictatorship	Bad	
One-man-rule	Bad	Somehow not as bad as 'dictatorship'
Administration	Neutral	Often deliberately used not to pass a critical evaluation

TASK 3: *Opponents of those in power*

Table 2.2 Key: opponents of those in power

Word	Evaluation	Notes
Revolutionary	Depends on the context	
Fundamentalist	Bad	Intolerant religious movement
Dissident	Good	Always applied to groups in foreign countries, the opponents of a regime
Separatist	Bad	An outsider term. The insider term would be 'independence-seeker'
Resistance	Good	Overtones of resistance to Nazism
Militants	Neutral	Often deliberately chosen not to pass an evaluation
Freedom-fighters	Good	

TASK 4: *Political positions*

Table 2.3 Key: political positions

Word	Evaluation	Notes
Activist	Neutral to good	Political campaigners might self-identify as activists
Hawks (also hawkish)	Bad	In favour of military action, in distinction to 'doves'
Extremist	Bad	
Radical	Depends on the context	But 'radicalisation' has come to mean conversion to religious extremism
Moderate	Good	Sometimes found as an insider term for 'conservative'
Liberal	Good	But sometimes used as criticism in the USA to mean 'too leftwing'
Reactionary	Bad	Likely to be used by leftwing person to describe rightwing person, instead of using 'conservative'

TASK 5: *Hooray words and boo words 1*

Hooray: *genuine, the people, our children, environmentally friendly, traditional, green, moderate, diversity, community, cost-effective.*

Boo: *unsustainable, bureaucracy, artificial, cuts, politicians, discrimination, big government.*

TASK 6: *Hooray words and boo words 2*

Hooray: *the American people, lead, peace, this nation of ours, duty, liberty, free, women.* You may wish to add some more.

Boo: *enemy, killers.*

TASK 7: *Information in the BBC report*

How much information can be extracted on the journalistic wh-questions from the BBC article:

What happened? A four-year old girl has been found dead.

When? At around 15:00 on Thursday.

Where? In East London

Who was involved? All we are told is that the mother has been arrested on suspicion.

How? All we are told is that there was a 'knife incident'.

Why? We are not told, but the mother has been sectioned (confined) under the Mental Health Act. We might infer that she had mental health problems.

TASK 8: *Information in the Daily Mail report*

How much information can be extracted on the journalistic wh-questions from the *Daily Mail* article:

What happened? A four-year old girl, [name given] has been found dead, disembowelled, etc.

When? On Thursday.

Where? Clapton, East London.

Who was involved? The mother [name given] who is from Somalia, the neighbours as witnesses, the father [name given] who discovered the scene. The woman has two other children.

How? The journalist implies that the girl was stabbed and dismembered by the mother using a kitchen knife. We are spared no details of the 'gruesome scene'.

Why? The headline focuses on 'religious ritual'. The journalist claims that the mother was 'chanting verses of the Koran' though no evidence is given. The claim is then repeated that she was listening to the 'Muslim Holy book'. Only in paragraph four do we learn that the mother has been sectioned under the Mental Health Act, and that mental illness rather than religion, might be the reason for the killing of the child.

TASK 9: *Forms of modality and their contribution to evaluation*

Why **should** [the conflicts in Syria] concern us? First, there is the humanitarian crisis, with hundreds of thousands of refugees streaming into makeshift camps [. . .]

Second, other countries in the region **risk** being drawn into the conflict, especially Iran, which **could** spark a full-blown sectarian war.

Requests for help **will be difficult** to resist. Third, there is **the threat of** the export of further hardline Islamist terror to countries including Britain.

We **cannot afford to** have Islamist extremists coming home with British passports, having waged successful jihad across the Middle East.

That is why it is **absolutely imperative** that Isis is defeated [. . .]

Many will be tempted to say it is not our problem, that it is something happening far away. That would be the wrong conclusion to draw.

If Isis wins in Iraq, then it **could easily become** an ungoverned space that encourages and trains terrorists even more than Afghanistan before 9/11 – and we all know the cost we **had to bear** as a consequence.

It is **absolutely essential** that we **do not allow** that to happen.

(*Sun* 2014)

Q3

The complaints against the King

The first category of verbs all convey 'obstruction' and 'refusal' to do something which ought to be done. The second category of verbs convey 'violence'.

Q4

The verbs associated with *we* convey responsible requesting. Jefferson wishes to say *we* are reasonable people but our patience is at an end.

Notes

1 These examples are from a classic study by Trew (1979).
2 www.bbc.co.uk/editorialguidelines/guidance/terrorism-language/ guidance-full
3 This may be accessed through Sketch Engine at www.sketchengine.co.uk. For more information on the contents, compilation and availability of the Frown corpus, see: www.helsinki.fi/varieng/CoRD/corpora/FROWN/

3 Ways of persuading

Persuasive speech, and more persuasive sighs;
Silence that spoke, and eloquence of eyes.

(Alexander Pope)

Authors on rhetoric have categorised the many and varied methods of persuasion in different ways. One frequently cited general level of division is between 'persuasion by appeal to reason' and 'persuasion by appeal to the emotions': 'rationalize rhetoric and she speaks to your mind: personify her and she speaks to your soul' (American Rhetoric website). The distinction is similar to that made by Aristotle between the appeals he calls *logos* and *pathos* (Unit 1). One practical illustration of this was provided by Frank Luntz, a 'communication professional' (yet another form of spin-doctor) to the Republicans in 1997, who found that, in his focus groups, 'women consistently respond to the phrase "for the children" regardless of the context in which it was used. From balancing the budget to welfare reform, "for the children" scores highest of all arguments offered'. He also went on to emphasise that 'politics remains an emotional arena' and the importance of using the words 'hope' and 'dream' in speeches and so on (reported in Tannen 2003). Before his election in 2008, Barack Obama produced two books, one entitled (our italics) '*Dreams* from My Father' (2004) and the other 'The Audacity of *Hope*?' (2006).

A fundamental concept in sociolinguistics and communication theory is that of *face* and *facework* (Goffman 1967; Brown and Levinson 1987). 'Face' is defined as the image we all project of ourselves to the outside world and 'facework' is the behaviour we employ to project that image. The concept of face and its projection has much in common with Aristotle's notion of *ethos* (see Unit 1). Partington has shown that politicians (and many other professional persuaders) have two separate kinds of face, namely *competence* face and *affective* face (Partington 2006: 97–98 et passim). Competence face is one's image as well informed, an expert, in control and authoritative. Affective face is one's image as likeable, good humoured, normal, 'one of us'.

However, one problem that politicians have is that the two kinds of face are not fully compatible; it is not always possible to project an image of authority and expertise at the same time as one of a normal, easy-going person. It is a political skill to know when to prioritise one over the other in front of an audience.

Another distinction similar to that between persuasion by appeal to reason and by appeal to emotion is between **ideational** or conceptual persuasion, in which a speaker projects primarily their competence face and **interpersonal** persuasion in which the speaker projects primarily their affective face. In the first, an author attempts primarily to persuade an audience of the veracity, logic or usefulness of his or her ideas and, if a politician is speaking, the effectiveness of their actions, as in the following:

> A new tower rises above the New York skyline, al Qaeda is on the path to defeat, and Osama bin Laden is dead.
>
> (President Obama 2012)

In the second case, an author attempts to convince others that he or she is honest, interesting and worthy of attention, respect, friendship or some other desired interpersonal service or product; or, alternatively or concomitantly, tries to persuade them that they, the audience, are lacking some quality, product or service – for example, wealth, power, safety, health – which the speaker/writer is able to provide, a sort of persuasion by inducing desire or anxiety (see the campaign advert at the beginning of Unit 5), as crystallised in:

> Everyday Americans need a champion and I want to be that champion.
>
> (Hillary Clinton 2015)

A quick Google trawl revealed that in 2015–2016 pre-election Americans also 'needed' Bernie Sanders, Donald Trump, Ted Cruz and other candidates (not mention 'to work more hours', 'fuel choice' and, controversially, 'more guns').

The projection of affective face also often takes the form of expressing positively evaluated shared values such as compassion, patriotism and faith:

> Yes, our path is harder – but it leads to a better place. Yes our road is longer – but we travel it together. We leave no one behind, knowing that Providence is with us, and that we are surely blessed to be citizens of the greatest nation on Earth.
>
> (Obama 2012)

Another strategy of interpersonal persuasion is to flatter one's audience:

> The election four years ago wasn't about me. It was about you. My fellow citizens – you were the change.
>
> (Obama 2012)

Affective persuasion is less concerned with influencing the audience's political opinions and more with 'rallying the troops'; that is, encouraging one's own party faithful to keep up the good fight and, of course, to support you (see Unit 7.2, 'Making the right noises').

In practice, most real-life attempts at persuading a particular audience are likely to combine elements of both ideational and interpersonal persuasion.

Five models

Expanding on this simple two-part distinction between ideational and interpersonal persuasion, in the rest of this Unit we will examine the structure and use of five major models of persuasion, namely:

1) the appeal to authority
2) comparison and contrast
3) problem – solution
4) hypothesis – evidence – explanation
5) association

3.1 Authority

In persuasion by authority, the 'persuader', that is, the person responsible for the persuasive message (who, it is vital to remember, may not be the actual speaker: think of spokespersons or actors in TV commercials), appeals to some sort of higher authority to convey and strengthen their message. One obvious example of this kind of appeal is in religion. Religious services tend to use appeals to religious writing, known as sacred scripture (note how the word scripture – meaning literally 'writings' – itself underlines the importance of the concept of language) as a high authority. Scripture appeals to the highest authority of all (God or Gods) to persuade us that it expresses certain truths.

Academic and scientific writing is also largely based on appeals to authority. Even in this book you will occasionally come across references to what previous authors – the more illustrious the better – have said. In academic communication writers continually back up their arguments with claims of the sort: 'I am not the only person to think this. Other important people have said the same'. Even Plato himself in the Dialogues puts his arguments in the mouth of Socrates, his dead mentor. The following example is from the political philosopher Hobsbawm (1994), who appeals to three previous authors (Albers, Goldschmidt and Oelkepp):

> Nobody with even minimal experience of the limitations of real life, i.e. no genuine adult, could have drafted the confident but patently absurd slogans of the Parisian May days of 1968 or the Italian 'hot autumn' of 1969: *tutto e subito*, we want everything and we want it now.
>
> (Hobsbawm 1994: 324)

TASK 1: *Appeals to authority*

1) Since we live in a world permeated by advertising, we all come into contact with both blatant and sophisticated attempts at persuasion every day. Can you think of any advertisements (TV/radio commercials, posters, newspaper/magazine ads, social media campaigns, etc.) which try to employ persuasion by appeal to authority? What kinds of 'authoritative people' do advertisements employ?

2) What sort of appeals to authority do we find in political discourse? The authority chosen will also depend on the context; for example, in 2003 the UK Prime Minister Tony Blair included this in a political speech:

> The spread of freedom is the best security for the free. It is our last line of defence and our first line of attack.
> And just as the terrorist seeks to divide humanity in hate, so we have to unify it around an idea. And that idea is liberty.
> We must find the strength to fight for this idea and the compassion to make it universal.
> Abraham Lincoln said: 'those that deny freedom to others, deserve it not for themselves'.

The choice of the appeal to Abraham Lincoln as a persuasive authority to support (and therefore positively evaluate) his argument was no doubt influenced by the fact that he was speaking to the US Congress.

If we look at the debates in the UK Parliament (using the free Hansard corpus from corpus.byu.edu), we can discover which sources are quoted most frequently and are considered to carry more authority in the context of British politics.

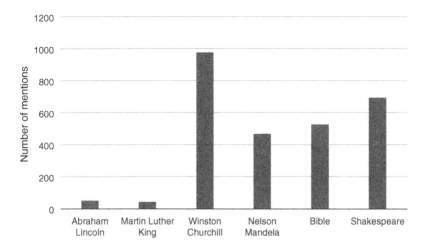

Figure 3.1 Frequency of mentions of 'authorities' in the British Parliament 1990–2005

And a study of the works of US Supreme Court judges found that the most quoted fictional authors were Shakespeare, perhaps to be expected, and Lewis Carroll, author of the *Alice* stories (Dodson and Dodson 2015), while another study has found that the US Supreme Court is far more likely to rely on dictionaries as an authority than the UK Supreme Court.[1]

3) Who might you expect to find used as an authority in political speeches in your country?

4) What is the appeal to authority made by the interviewer in the next example?

Interviewer: GMTV this week commissioned a poll and in fact 71% of the British public said they would be against British involvement in any attack on Iraq. Would you be prepared to send British troops into the region without full public support?

Appeal to ....

5) What are some potential problems with the authority model of persuasion?

At the present time, there is a very interesting case study in the use of authority in argument in the discussion about the origin of the universe as the creationist movement increasingly uses the language of science, appealing to science (some would say 'pseudo-science') rather than to religion as their authority.

For example, there is now a large 'Institute for Creation Research' (www.icr.org) which claims to 'explore the evidence of creationism', providing proof by 'leading scientists' for Biblical stories such as the Flood and that 'the first human beings were specially created in fully human form from the start'. At the same time, the scientific topic of evolution is discussed in terms of whether people 'believe' in it or not (see below), partly due to the mismatch between lay and scientific uses of the word 'theory'. In science, 'theory' denotes (or should denote) a model of how a system behaves which has been subjected to rigorous examination. In popular parlance, however, it can mean almost the opposite: just one idea among many possible ideas, e.g. 'well, it's a theory I suppose'.

Climate change is also sometimes discussed using quasi-religious language. For instance, with references to 'climate change believers' and 'climate change deniers':

> The world is warming up. And it's still our fault. But not as quickly as we thought. So says the Intergovernmental Panel on Climate Change. Believers always say it's worse than we imagine, deniers that we're led astray by faulty climate modelling.
>
> (*Daily Mail* 2013)

The latter, 'deniers' is an outsider term (Unit 2.3), with echoes of 'Holocaust deniers'. The insider term would probably be climate change 'sceptics'.

We should not perhaps be too surprised that expressions such as 'I don't believe in climate change' or 'I believe in evolution' are commonly heard. We simply do not have the time to study all complex scientific theories about the world, we are all of us – even the most intelligent among us – non-experts in most fields of study. And so we normally believe what we are told by experts who have studied that particular field. However, where there is a scientific controversy, we may well choose to believe those who tell us what is most congenial to our own personality and mindset.

Finally, it is no exaggeration to say that, philosophically speaking, the majority of things we claim to 'know' we do not in reality 'know' at all, at least not through personal experience. Instead, we *believe* them to be the case because we have been told they are by what we consider reliable *authority*. To take a mundane example, we firmly believe in the existence of places we have never personally visited and people we have never met. And most people also 'believe' in evolution, plate tectonics and black holes, despite never having had personal experience of them. It is no exaggeration to say that persuasion by belief in authority is the most common form of persuasion of all.

3.2 Comparison and contrast

3.2.1 'Us' against 'them'

In this model of persuasion, the persuader invites us to compare and contrast an argument, policy, product, etc., with one or more others. Evaluation plays a role when this model is used since there is usually the assumption or implication that one is *better* than the others. The following were slogans used in the 2016 election campaign in the US:

A. When they go low, we go high (Michelle Obama/Hillary Clinton).
B. I'm With Her (Hillary Clinton's campaign).
C. I'm With You, the American People (Donald Trump's campaign reply).

TASK 2: *Slogans*

What is each one of these slogans implying about other political parties?

A. Are you better off than you were four years ago? US Republicans, 1980.
B. You can only be sure with the Conservatives, UK Conservatives, 1997.
C. Keep the Bastards Honest, Australian Democrats, 1990s.

At election time, the incumbent party (that is, the party in power at the time of the election) – of whatever political leaning, left, right or centre – tends to produce slogans warning electors of the *dangers* of change, that things could get worse. In contrast, opposition parties, or challengers, tend to produce slogans holding out the *hope* of a future that will be better than the present.

Q1

Of the three slogans in Task 2 above, which do you think was produced by the incumbent party and which by challengers?

It is common among political analysts to make a distinction between two types of election campaigning, namely positive and negative campaigning. In the first, a party declares and promotes its own virtues whereas, in the second, one party reveals and attacks the presumed failings of its adversary. The second, negative campaigning, is natural in majority or 'first-past-the-post'-style electoral systems, such as that of the UK or the US, where two main parties are in opposition to each other.

Positive slogans are often criticised as being too bland and general ('Yes, America Can!', Bush 2004), although Obama's (2008) 'Yes we can!' was both popular and successful. Negative slogans are sometimes criticised as being unfair or frivolous, as when the UK Conservative Party attempted to 'demonise' Tony Blair by depicting him in an election poster as having 'demon eyes', and he went on to win the election (the poster can be seen by typing 'New Labour, New Danger' into your search engine). Or it can be very effective. The Conservative poster, produced in 1979 when they were in opposition to the Labour government, depicting a long queue of unemployed people, headed with the slogan 'Labour Isn't Working' is considered by some to be one of the most successful campaign posters of all time, and indeed the Labour Party lost the following election.

Q2

What is the play on words in the campaign slogan 'Labour Isn't Working'?

Very generally, incumbents tend to opt for positive campaigns to stress their virtues and minimise attention on the opposition. Opposition parties and their members do not usually get the daily media exposure that governing parties and their top members get, and incumbent parties naturally like to keep the opposition starved of media attention. Opposition parties, of course, will tend to indulge in negative campaigning to attack the record of the party in power.

In the two referendums we examine in Unit 10, the 2014 Scottish and 2016 Brexit Referendums, the two campaigns for 'Staying' (in the UK and in the European Union, respectively) found themselves as the proponents of the status quo, in a position very similar to that of an incumbent party, running largely on the message of fear of change, while the two campaigns for 'Leaving', that is, for change, were in a similar position to that of a challenging party, running largely on the message of hope of a better future.

In the somewhat unusual case of the Scottish National Party, we have an example of a party that has been both an incumbent party and an opposition party at the same time. In 2015, the SNP campaigned in the UK general election as an opposition party with the slogan 'Stronger for Scotland', triggering a comparison which unfavourably evaluated the other parties. While in 2016, they fought the elections for the *Scottish* Parliament as the governing party and the slogan on their manifesto was simply 're-elect'. The Scottish Conservative Party adapted the SNP's 2015 slogan and campaigned for the 2016 Scottish elections with 'A strong opposition – a stronger Scotland'.

TASK 3: *Positive and negative slogans*

Which of the following slogans are positive and which are negative?

1) *With you, for you, for Singapore,* People's Action Party (Singapore), 2015.
2) *Make America Great Again,* Donald Trump, US Republican, 2015.
3) *Are you thinking what I'm thinking?*
   'I mean how hard can it be to clean a hospital?', UK Conservatives, 2005.
4) *Labour isn't working* (with a picture of unemployed people), UK Conservatives, 1979.
5) *People, planet, peace,* UK Greens, 2005.
6) *Let's Get Our Country Back,* UK Independence Party (anti-EU), 2005.
7) *Proven leadership for a strong Canada,* Conservative Party (Canada), 2015.
8) *Everyday Americans need a champion. I want to be that champion.* Hillary Clinton, 2015.
9) *Create an Earthquake. UKIP, A Real Alternative,* UK Independence Party, 2014.
10) *Real Change,* Liberal Party (Canada), 2015.
11) *Honesty is Our Best Policy: The Real Alternative,* UK Liberals, 2005.
12) *There's no God now we Communists are in Power* (with a picture of gunmen), South African National Party, 1994.

Q3

Two of these were produced by an incumbent party. Which? How do you know?

To follow up, you might like to visit the following site which shows what the British newspaper, the *Guardian,* considers to be the top ten UK campaign posters in history. You might like to consider why these particular ten were chosen by this paper, perhaps bearing in mind its centre-left, pro-Labour Party political leanings: https://tinyurl.com/PiP-posters

In fact, in a two-party system, persuasion by comparison – in the form of 'we are better than them' – is endemic throughout political debate, a natural part of political thinking in an adversarial system. The following is a question and response from Prime Minister's Questions in the UK Parliament, which illustrates very clearly the 'us' versus 'them' dualism:

> Q: When will the P.M. live up to his promise of eliminating cor-
> ruption from local government? Is it not obvious, even to him,
> that Labour councils are rotten to the core?

> Mr Blair: Every time there have been allegations of corruption in
> Labour councils we have investigated them, in stark contrast to
> a Conservative party which allowed corruption and wrongdoing
> to carry on and for years did nothing – but that is the differ-
> ence between Conservative and Labour values.

(Quoted in Beard 2000: 106)

3.2.2 Beyond 'us' against 'them'

Highlighting the contrast between two entities, notions, states of affairs, sets of behaviours, and so on, is one of the most useful and frequent ways of furthering a political or sociological argument. Such contrasts can come in very many forms, including the following:

- Geographical: One place/area vs another
- Historical: One time/era vs another
- Conceptual One idea/philosophy vs another
- Political: One policy vs another

as well as:

- What people have done in the past vs What we should do now and in the future.
- What people generally believe vs How things really are.
- How things are now vs How things should be.
- What other thinkers have argued (another's hypothesis) vs What I argue (my hypothesis).

We should note, once again, that these sorts of contrast are often *evaluative*: a choice is proposed between something negative and something positive (or at least less negative).

TASK 4: *Contrasts (and evaluation)*

What contrasts are being created in the following introduction to a 'Technology, Entertainment, Design' (TED) talk?

China or India? Yasheng Huang (economist MIT)

My topic is economic growth in China and India. The question is whether democracy has helped or hindered growth. You may say I'm selecting two countries to make a case against democracy. Actually I'm going to use these two countries to make an economic argument for democracy, not against democracy. (edited)

www.ted.com/talks/yasheng_huang.html

....
....
....
....

Find and list all the contrasts in the following book review (Vinen 2000). Do any of them involve an evaluation?

A HISTORY IN FRAGMENTS. Europe in the twentieth century. By Richard Vinen. 724 pp. Little, Brown. £25.

1) It might seem perverse of Richard Vinen to proclaim in the title that his book is composed of 'fragments'. But he has his reasons. Previous histories of twentieth-century Europe, he claims, have been too neat, set out in tidy divisions: East versus West, capitalism versus socialism. They have tended, moreover, to devote most of their attention to the dramatic and violent period which ended in 1945, surveying the subsequent decades in a cursory overview and leaving detailed exploration of them to the social scientists.

2) This book is different. It constantly juxtaposes and compares the fates of all European nations, north and south, east and west. It focuses on the different varieties of capitalism and socialism, and shows how they evolved. It gives full weight to the post-war period – 384 pages as against 255 pages for pre-1945 – and weaves a full account of the 1990s into the general texture. It treats political, social, economic and cultural history with equal acumen, giving as much attention to the lives of ordinary people as to the gestures of statesmen. It is a thoughtful and challenging book, often brilliantly perceptive and innovative on subjects where one had thought debate was exhausted. (*Times Literary Supplement*)

....
....
....
....

What are the contrasts made in the following? What is the metaphor (Unit 7) which the writer uses to describe the relationship between China and America? Who are the 'East Chimericans' and who are the 'West Chimericans'?

> ### 'Chimerica', Neil Ferguson
>
> Welcome to the wonderful dual country of 'Chimerica' – China plus America. For a time Chimerica seemed like a marriage made in heaven. The East Chimericans did the saving. The West Chimericans did the spending. The Chinese did the exporting, the Americans the importing. The more China was willing to lend to the United States, the more Americans were willing to borrow. Chinese imports kept down US inflation. US wage costs were kept down by Chinese labour (Ferguson, *The Ascent of Money*, 2008: 335, edited).
>
> But how might it end?
>
> It's like one of those marriages between a compulsive saver and a chronic spender. Eventually the parsimonious one gets disillusioned with the spendthrift. It reminds me of one of those domestic tiffs in which the saver says to the spender: 'You overspent on the credit cards once too often, honey' (Ferguson, *Newsweek* 2009, edited).

....
....
....
....
....

3.2.3 Surprise tactics and the Garden Path diversion

Leslie Chang is a US journalist of Chinese origin. She spent a year living alongside young female workers who migrate from rural areas to work in China's big industrial cities as research for her book *Factory Girls: From Village to City in a Changing China*. This, she says, is how the migrant worker's life often begins:

1. The city does not offer them an easy living. The pay for hard labor is low often lower than the official minimum wage [. . .] and work hours frequently stretched beyond the legal limit of forty-nine hours per week. Get hurt, sick or pregnant, you are on your own. Local governments have little incentive to protect workers; their job is to keep the factory owners happy, which will bring in more investment and tax revenue.

2. But suffering in silence is not how migrant workers see themselves. To come out from home and work in a factory is the hardest thing they have ever done. It is also an adventure. What keeps them in the city is not fear but pride. To return home early is to admit defeat. To go out and stay out – *chuqu* – is to change your fate.

(Chang 2008: 11, edited)

In the first part she describes the objective harshness of their lives, with a series of negative evaluations. *But* then, in the second part, after the adversative *But* – which very frequently acts as a signal of evaluative switch – she takes the reader by surprise and presents the picture as seen through the eyes of the 'girls' themselves, no longer as seen by an objective observer, with far more positive evaluations: *an adventure, pride, to change your fate.*

Sometimes, a writer or speaker deliberately creates or presents a narrative which draws the reader in and positively invites them to agree with it, only to then argue that this narrative is completely mistaken. This is known as the 'Garden Path' technique, a metaphor describing how the reader is led along a false trail, from which they must then return in order to take the correct one.

TASK 5A: *The Garden Path technique 1*

Read or watch the first 2 minutes 18 seconds of Leslie Chang's TED talk entitled 'The Voices of China's Workers', available at: https://tinyurl.com/PiP-Chang

What contrasts does Chang create? ………………………………...…………

…………………………………………………………………………...…...……

…………………………………………………………………...……………

What is the false narrative ('Garden Path') that she leads her audience along? ………………………………………………………................………

…………………………………………………………………………...…………

……………………………………………………………………...……………

What is the correct narrative she then communicates to her audience?………………………………………………………......………...…..

………………………………………………………………………...…....……

……………………………………………………………………......……...

With what language does she inform her audience of the falsehood of the first narrative? ……………………………………………………...…………

……………………………………………………………………...….......…..

……………………………………………………………………......……...

How are Chinese factories and Chinese workers evaluated in the first narrative? ....
....
....

How does Chang evaluate Chinese industry and Chinese workers in the second narrative? ....
....
....

How does she evaluate her audience? ....
....
....

TASK 5B: *The Garden Path technique 2*

Finally, read or watch the first 1 minute 53 seconds of Pinker's TED talk entitled 'The Surprising Decline in Violence', available at: https://tinyurl.com/PiP-Pinker

What contrasts does Pinker create? ....
....
....

What is the (in his view) false narrative ('Garden Path') that he leads his audience along? ....
....
....

What is the correct narrative he then communicates to his audience?
....
....
....

With what language does he inform his audience of the falsehood of the first narrative? ....
....
....

How is modernity evaluated in the first narrative? ....
....
....

How does Pinker evaluate modernity in the second narrative? ....
....
....

How does he evaluate his audience? ....

....

....

3.3 Problem–solution

In the problem–solution method of persuasion, the persuader first proposes and outlines a supposed problem and suggests that he or she has the solution to the problem.

3.3.1 The simple problem–solution model

In its most synthetic form, as found in slogans, the problem is more or less implicit in the solution offered by the slogan sponsors:

> It's not racist to impose limits on immigration.
>
> (UK Conservatives 2005)

The slogan asserts that the problem is immigration; the Conservative's solution is to impose limits. The solution is evaluated positively 'it's not racist'.

In more extended cases, the problem is usually given first and then the author goes on to offer us his or her solution. This solution is usually accompanied by a positive evaluation.

> Why are some nations more prosperous than others?
>
> *Why Nations Fail* sets out to answer this question, with a compelling and elegantly argued new theory: that it is not down to climate, geography or culture, but because of institutions. Drawing on an extraordinary range of contemporary and historical examples, from ancient Rome through the Tudors to modern-day China, leading academics Daron Acemoglu and James A. Robinson show that to invest and prosper, people need to know that if they work hard, they can make money and actually keep it – and this means sound institutions that allow virtuous circles of innovation, expansion and peace.
>
> (Acemoglu and Robinson 2013)

The main problem presented in the extract is the relative poverty of some nations compared to others. Various reasons for this are mentioned – climate, geography, and so on – but are dismissed. The authors then supply what they feel is the correct solution, namely, 'sound institutions', which allow people to make money and keep it. This solution is evaluated positively with the expression *virtuous circles*.

TASK 6: *Problem–solution. The 'Bottom Billion'*

The following text is the publisher's presentation of the book *The Bottom Billion* by Paul Collier (2008), expert in international development. Identify the parts of the following discourse which present the problem, those which describe solutions and those which give evaluations.

The Bottom Billion

Global poverty is falling rapidly; but in fifty or so failing states the world's poorest people – the 'bottom billion' – face a tragedy that is growing inexorably worse. Why do these states defy all attempts to help them? Why does current aid seem unable to make a difference?

In his award-winning bestseller, Paul Collier pinpoints the issues of corruption, political instability, and resource management that lie at the root of the problem, and offers hard-nosed solutions and real hope for a way of solving one of the great crises facing the world today.

3.3.2 The complex problem–solution model

In a still more sophisticated version of problem–solution persuasion, the author outlines the problem then offers a preliminary solution (or pseudo-solution), which s/he goes on to reject, evaluating it as wrong or inadequate or unjust. The author then goes on to suggest an alternative solution, which s/he then evaluates as correct, satisfactory or fair. There might finally be some sort of concluding coda. We might illustrate this as:

- Problem
- Solution 1
- Evaluation (negative)
- Solution 2
- Evaluation 2 (positive)
- Conclusion or coda

Here is a real-life example:

Bus security

Your newspaper suggests that the reintroduction of bus-conductors would avert terrorist acts. But London bus staff are not security guards, able to prevent suicide-bomber attacks.

There are now over 1,000 police officers who travel on bus services in London, due to a mayoral initiative unique in the UK.

(Letter to the Guardian 2005, edited)

The problem is introduced in the letter's title: Bus security, or how to make travelling on buses in Britain safer, especially in the light of a terrorist bomb explosion on a London bus which had taken place two weeks earlier. The first solution is the one offered in a previous article which proposed 'that the reintroduction of bus conductors would avert terrorist acts' (a bus conductor is an official who travels on the bus to collect fares and issue tickets). This is evaluated as negative on the basis that such people would not be qualified to act as 'security guards' and could not have prevented the terrorist attacks. The rest of the letter, from the manager of the London Transport Authority, sets out, as the correct solution, the one already adopted by his agency, which is evaluated favourably: 'a mayoral initiative unique in the UK'.

TASK 7: *Identifying a complex problem–solution model*

Watch, listen or read the transcript of the first 2 minutes 35 seconds of the TED talk entitled 'New Rules for Rebuilding a Broken Nation', given by Paul Collier, available at: https://tinyurl.com/Collier-PiP

The topic of the talk is on how best societies which have just experienced a major conflict should manage themselves:

- What is the problem and how is it presented?
- What is the first solution and how is it evaluated negatively?
- What is the second, alternative solution and how is it evaluated positively?

As we shall see in Unit 8, politics is full of question–response discourse, for example, interviews, press conferences, MP's meetings with their constituents and Parliamentary Question Time. Questions generally outline problems, the interviewee's response attempts to outline solution(s) or 'pseudo-solution(s)'.

The following is a typical political 'pseudo' response giving no proper solution to the problem posed in the question:

Q: Can I ask what progress you are making in talks with the Americans about the British suspects in Guantanamo Bay?

PM Blair: Well, we are still in discussion, but there are the two alternatives that we have outlined and we are finding the talks with the Americans immensely co-operative.

This type of 'pseudo' response is frequently the target of satire (discussed in Unit 10), as, for example, in the classic BBC fictional political satire 'Yes, Minister' (Jim is the government minister, Bob is a TV interviewer):

Bob: Minister are you laying the foundations for a police state?
Jim: You know, I'm glad you asked that question.

Bob: Well Minister could we have the answer?

Jim: Well yes, of course, I was just about to give it to you, if I may. Yes as I said I'm glad you asked me that question because it's a question that a lot of people are asking, and quite so, because a lot of people want to know the answer to it. And let's be quite clear about this, the plain fact of the matter is that it is a very important question indeed and people have a right to know.

Bob: Minister, we haven't yet had the answer.

Jim: I'm sorry, what was the question?

(Lynn and Jay 1989, 'Big Brother')

3.4 The hypothesis–evidence–explanation model

In this model, the speaker or writer introduces, first of all, his or her principle argument in terms of a hypothesis. The following sections of the discourse then provide evidence to support or corroborate the hypothesis. This section is often followed by one or more explanations, which propose to clarify why the original argument or hypothesis should be the case. This model is clearly very rational or rational-seeming. However, listeners and readers need to be aware that speakers and writers attempting to corroborate or 'prove' their own hypothesis are not always likely to include any counter-examples or inconvenient evidence in their discussion. It is also a common model in legal argumentation where, just as in politics, it is not necessarily the responsibility of the arguer, in making their case, to provide any counter-evidence, that being the job of the opposing side.

TASK 8: *Hypothesis–evidence–explanation*

Read or watch the TED talk 'The Surprising Decline in Violence' by Steven Pinker at: https://tinyurl.com/PiP-Pinker

1) What is Pinker's main <u>hypothesis</u>?
2) In constructing this hypothesis he makes an argument by Contrast (Unit 4.2). What is the contrast?
3) What is the <u>evidence</u> he supplies for:

   a) Violence in the pre-historical distant past
   b) Violence in the historical past and Middle Ages
   c) The decline of violence in the recent past

4) What are the four potential <u>explanations</u> for the decline of violence over time that he outlines?

   i)
   ii)

iii)

iv)

4)   What is the coda or conclusion to Pinker's talk?

3.5 Association

Persuasion by association is largely conducted through resources other than language. Music, images, colours, clothes, logos, and so on, are all used in the hope of creating favourable associations in our mind about a person, party or policy. Critics claim that there has been a huge increase in the use of associative techniques in political propaganda. It is called, disparagingly, 'image politics', the implication being that image politicians favour form over substance of ideas (recall also Unit 1.3. on spin):

> we have a prime minister who has admitted to spending more than £1,800 on cosmetics over the past six years while Italian PM Silvio Berlusconi has spent a fortune on a facelift and hair transplant [. . .] the average British woman, by comparison, spends only £195 per annum on make-up and skincare.
>
> (*Daily Telegraph* 2005, edited)

Some politicians have themselves been known to judge their rivals by their looks rather than their words or ideas, and women have traditionally been especially targeted (Unit 10.1.3). The Italian politician Silvio Berlusconi, during a televised debate, referred to the female politician Rosy Bindi by saying with heavy irony, 'You are more beautiful than intelligent', implying that she was neither. Hillary Clinton was often accused of having a shrill voice (a term that is rarely applied to a man's voice), including the 'renaming' as 'Shrillary'. Journalists are no better. *The Guardian* newspaper in 2013 accused the German Chancellor Angela Merkel of looking like a 'prudent housewife' (her PhD is in quantum chemistry). The Labour MP, Liz Kendall, told a journalist to 'fuck off' after being asked how much she weighed. She later explained to the BBC:

> It's unbelievable that in the 21st Century women still get asked such very different questions from men.
>
> Can you imagine a newspaper asking the weight of a male politician?
>
> I cannot wait for a world when women are judged the same as men and not by those kinds of questions.
>
> Liz Kendall MP (BBC Radio 5 2015, edited)

This kind of image-centred evaluation, however, is not entirely exclusive to female politicians. Many male politicians are made fun of for their looks. Silvio Berlusconi, three times Italian Prime Minister, was often derided for his lack of height and general appearance (alleged hair transplant and face-lift) and given nicknames such as 'the eighth dwarf'. Donald Trump is constantly being mocked for his outlandish hairstyle, his mannerisms and 'orange skin'.

Nevertheless, in the past too, image was important and politicians have always understood the importance of attractive or impressive associations, indeed we might recall Aristotle's advice to project an inspiring *ethos* and to appeal to emotion (*pathos*) as well as to reason (*logos*) (Unit 1). Parties have always had a symbolic logo to represent them. In the UK the Labour Party has a red rose (a patriotic symbol). The Conservatives used to have a burning torch, symbolic of leadership and victory, but in 2006 changed it into a more environmentally friendly tree. More recently they changed it yet again to the British flag. The Liberal Democrats have chosen a dove (symbol of peace). Parties have their own colour (red for Labour, blue for the Conservatives, yellow for the Liberal Democrats) and often their own theme song. In the UK, for instance, the Labour Party used to be keen on The Internazionale until it was considered too left-wing by New Labour; the Conservatives were happier with the national anthem.

India is a country with a large population and also a large number of political parties. Among the political symbols chosen by the various parties we find: the elephant, the lotus, both national symbols, the hammer and sickle, international symbol of communism, the open hand, the bicycle and the clock.

In terms of dress, too, politicians were expected to dress formally, which carries its own connotations of gravity. At election time, shaking hands and kissing babies – hardly rational argumentation – have also always had a prominent place in 'persuading' electors.

TASK 9: *Association*

1) What logos and other symbols do political groups in your country employ? What are their associations?
2) Ever since the early 19th Century the US Democrats have chosen the donkey to represent their party, while the Republicans have chosen an elephant. What do you think the positive associations of these might be?
3) Using an Internet search engine, look at the logos used by the parties and candidates (Clinton, Sanders, Trump) in the 2015–2106 US primaries and presidential campaigns (see Unit 10). What differences in associations do you note?

4) Do the same for the logos used by the Leave and Remain sides during the Scottish Independence Referendum of 2014. What difference in associations do you note (Unit 10)?

TASK 10: *Rational and non-rational persuasion*

Which of these five forms of persuasion – by authority, by comparison, by problem–solution, by hypothesis–evidence–explanation and by association – are logical/rational and which are not? Put them in order from the least to the most rational:

Least rational

1)
2)
3)
4)
5)

Most rational

TASK 11: *Models of persuasion in TV commercials*

Four of the five models outlined here – authority, comparison, problem–solution and association – are also those regularly encountered in other spheres of persuasion; it is not difficult to encounter them, for instance, in the world of advertising.

Here are five TV commercials. Match each commercial to one of the models of persuasion.

1) A car is shown driving fast along a deserted road which winds itself around spectacular cliffs above a steep drop to an angry sea. Dramatic music builds to a climax which at the end of the commercial coincides with the slogan: 'Product name (car): the Drive of your Life'.

    Model ....

2) A handsome young man appears perplexed at being ignored by a beautiful young woman. A friend tells him he has dandruff! He first tries one shampoo, to no effect. He then washes his hair with Product name (shampoo) and the commercial ends with him happy, smiling and surrounded by adoring females.

    Model ....

3) A famous footballer is shown in a domestic setting. He drinks Product name (mineral water) and tells us how healthy and tasty it is, and advises us to try it.

    Model ....

4) The viewer is shown the different rates per minute for telephone calls offered by various phone companies. Those provided by Product name (telephone company) are strikingly lower. We are exhorted to change our telephone service provider.

Model ....

In the following, two or even perhaps three models are combined. Which?

5) A housewife is looking at her washing on the washing line, clearly dissatisfied. An older, very friendly looking woman appears and asks the first what the problem is. The first explains that, try as she might, she can't get her washing any whiter. The older woman explains that she has been using the wrong product and should try Product name (washing powder). The commercial ends with both looking happily at gleaming white sheets on the line.

Models ....

Keys and commentaries

TASK 1: *Authority*

1) Free response. The kinds of 'authoritative people' advertisements employ are usually celebrities and models but rarely, say, real scientists or doctors.
2) For example: in references to earlier politicians or statespersons, De Gaulle in France, J.F Kennedy in the US, De Gasperi in Italy, Churchill in the UK. In references to political or economic thinkers, e.g. Marx, Adam Smith. In appeals to abstract political ideals, e.g. socialism or the free-market economy.
3) Free response.
4) The authority invoked is 'the British public', as Whyte (2003: 22) notes 'in a democracy The People is the ultimate political authority'. The strength of the statement is also enhanced by the reference to a specific statistic '71%' which invokes a quasi-scientific authority.
5) For example, in the model of authority seen in 4, public opinion, we should remember that just because a majority believe in something does not mean that it has any basis in fact. It was once firmly believed that the sun went round the earth. And if one religion does indeed reveal the truth then all the others, with their millions of adherents, must in some aspects at least have got things wrong.

Another problem is that the authoritative source may indeed be an authority – but in another field. For instance, Einstein used to be invoked as an authority on absolutely any field. But are his views on morality or religion any more valid than another person's? Therefore, we need to look at why a source is given an authoritative status and whether it is logically justified. Especially pernicious is the way the modern media often use media celebrities as authorities. Are Madonna's views on adoption any more significant than your own?

TASK 2: *Slogans*

What is each one of these slogans implying about other political parties?

A. That the other (governing) party has failed to make us richer.
B. You can't be sure with anyone else and so changing government could be dangerous.
C. The other parties would be dishonest if we were not there to keep an eye on them.

Q1

The slogan B was produced by the incumbent party. Being in power, it evokes fear of change.

Q2

What is the play on words in the campaign slogan 'Labour Isn't Working'?
'Labour does not function' and 'Labour is creating a lack of work, jobs'.

TASK 3: *Positive and negative slogans*

1) *With you, for you, for Singapore,* People's Action Party, Singapore, 2015.
   Positive.

2) *Make America Great Again,* Donald Trump, US Republican, 2015.
   Negative: a criticism of those in power who have failed to keep America as it should be.

3) *Are you thinking what I'm thinking?*
   'I mean how hard can it be to clean a hospital?', UK Conservatives, 2005.

Negative: those in power cannot manage to keep a hospital clean and are, therefore, not to be trusted to manage the Health Service. Presumably they are supposed to be just as incompetent at everything else.

4) *Labour isn't working* (with a picture of unemployed people), UK Conservatives, 1979.
   Negative: the Labour Party has failed to combat unemployment.

5) *People, planet, peace*, UK Greens, 2005.
   Positive.

6) *Let's Get Our Country Back*, UK Independence Party (anti-EU), 2005.
   Negative: the other parties have given the country away.

7) *Proven leadership for a strong Canada*, Conservative Party (Canada), 2015.
   Positive.

8) *Everyday Americans need a champion. I want to be that champion*, Hillary Clinton, 2015.
   Negative and positive: Americans are in need (negative) and I will come to their aid (positive).

9) *Create an Earthquake. UKIP, A Real Alternative*, UKIP, 2014.
   Positive.

10) *Real Change*, Liberal Party (Canada), 2015.
    Positive, although the use of 'real' suggests some criticism of the 'change' offered by other parties.

11) *Honesty is Our Best Policy: The Real Alternative*, UK Liberals, 2005.
    Mainly positive, although there is the implication that the other parties are not honest.

12) *There's no God now we Communists are in Power* (with a picture of gunmen), South African National Party, 1994.
    Negative: the right-wing National Party want to imply that the 'Communists' will kill those who try to worship God.

Q3

Two of these were produced by an incumbent party. Which? How would you know?

Number (1) and (7). Positive campaigning is generally associated with the incumbent. In (7), as the party in power, the Canadian Conservatives try to stress their own virtue by focussing on the experience they have gained while in power. Most of the others, from opposition parties, attack the policy of those in power. The other positive ones are (5), (9) and (10). Number (8) is both negative – Clinton is not the actual incumbent President – and positive – but she does belong to the incumbent party at the time, the Democrats.

TASK 4: *Contrasts (and evaluation)*

China or India?: China vs India; democratic economics vs non-democratic economics; what you expect me to say vs what I'm actually going to say.

A History in Fragments: East vs West, socialism vs capitalism; the period before 1945 vs the period after 1945; the lives of ordinary people vs the gestures of statesmen; this book vs other books with a positive evaluation of the former.

Chimerica: China vs America; saving vs spending, exporting vs importing, lending vs borrowing; a serene vs a problematic relationship; the compulsive saver (the parsimonious one) vs the chronic spender (the spendthrift). The metaphor is the relationship as a marriage. The 'East Chimericans' are the Chinese, the 'West Chimericans' are the Americans.

The Surprising Decline in Violence (paragraphs 1–2): what people generally hear, read and believe (modernity is more violent than ever) vs the way the world's history really is (modern existence contains less violence than in the past).

TASK 5A: *The Garden Path technique 1*

What contrasts does Chang create?
The West vs China; the beneficiaries vs the victims of globalisation; western perceptions vs the way things are in China.

What is the (in her view) false narrative ('Garden Path') that she leads her audience along?
That westerners drive millions of Chinese workers to migrate to the cities and factories and are, therefore, guilty for the suffering of Chinese workers.

What is the correct narrative she then communicates to her audience?
That Chinese workers chose to migrate to the cities in search of a better life.

With what language does she inform her audience of the falsehood of the first narrative?
'But it's also inaccurate and disrespectful'.

How are Chinese factories and Chinese workers evaluated in the first narrative?
The factories are oppressive and the workers feel oppressed.

How does Chang evaluate Chinese industry and Chinese workers in the second narrative?
Chinese industry is efficient and the workers are largely self-motivated.

How does she evaluate her audience?
As not only misguided and self-obsessed but also disrespectful of Chinese workers. There is a hint of accusation of racism.

TASK 5B: *The Garden Path technique 2*

What contrasts does Pinker create?
Violence (of modernity) vs peacefulness (of natural past life); the 'common understanding' vs the way things really are.

What is the (in his view) false narrative ('Garden Path') that he leads his audience along?
That modern times are far more violent than past times.

What is the correct narrative he then communicates to his audience?
That instead we are living in the most peaceful times in our species' existence.

With what language does he inform the audience of the falsehood of the first narrative?
'Now, you're all familiar with this treacle … the original title of this session was, "Everything You Know Is Wrong"'

How is modernity evaluated in the first narrative?
Negatively, as more violent than ever.

How does Pinker evaluate modernity in the second narrative?
Positively, as less violent than previous times.

How does he evaluate his audience?
He is less openly challenging than Chang, but he does perhaps imply that they should be better informed.

TASK 6: *Problem–solution. The 'Bottom Billion'*

The problems: (i) a billion people have been stuck living in economies that have been stagnant for forty years, and hence diverging from the rest of mankind, and (ii) how can we give credible hope to that billion people?

The solutions: (i) Compassion for a human tragedy and (ii) enlightened self-interest, because if that economic divergence continues for another forty years, combined with social integration globally, it will build a nightmare for our children.

TASK 7: *Identifying a complex problem–solution model*

Problem: Why has the record on post-conflict resolution been so poor?

Solution 1: (the one generally practised in the past): Prioritise the political resolution.

Evaluation 1: 'That approach denies reality'. A quickly organised election produces a winner and a loser and the latter is 'unreconciled'.

Solution 2: Prioritise economic development of the area.

Evaluation 2: 'The politics become easier as the decade progresses if you're building on a foundation of security and economic development'.

TASK 8: *Hypothesis–evidence–explanation*

1) Professor Pinker's main hypothesis is that, contrary to many people's belief and contrary to the romanticisation of the past by the media, 'today we are probably living in the most peaceful time in our species' existence' (paragraph 2).

2) What is the evidence he supplies:

   a) Violence in the pre-historical distant past. The extremely high 'likelihood that a man will die at the hands of another man' in hunter-gatherer societies (paragraph 5).

   b) Violence in the historical past and Middle Ages. The genocidal nature of warfare in ancient times (paragraph 6). The prevalence of capital punishment and torture (paragraph 7). The high rates of murder or homicide (paragraph 8).

   c) The decline of violence in the recent past. Statistics show a steep decline since 1945 in wars among states ('interstate wars'), as well as 'fewer civil wars, fewer genocides' and a 'precipitous decline' in violent crime since the 1990s (paragraph 9).

3) What are the four potential explanations for the decline of violence over time that he outlines?

   1) Thomas Hobbes's 'Leviathan' theory. 'In a state of anarchy there is a constant temptation to invade' – and kill – 'your neighbors before they invade' – and kill – 'you' (paragraph 12).

The rise of powerful centralised states ('Leviathans'), with a system of justice that can keep order among its citizens, by punishing and therefore dissuading those who commit violence against others.

2) James Payne's increasing value of life theory. 'As technology and economic efficiency make life longer and more pleasant, one puts a higher value on life in general' (paragraph 14).

3) Robert Wright's non-zero-sum game theory and increasing cycles of reciprocity theory. Technology has allowed 'the trade of goods, services and ideas over longer distances and larger groups of people'. When different parties trade with each other, all parties gain (thus the 'non-zero-sum' outcome). The result is that other people are more economically and culturally valuable and useful alive than dead and 'violence declines for selfish reasons' (paragraph 15). Moreover, the market economy based on trade has made ordinary people doubly valuable; for the first time in history, they are valuable not only as producers (serfs and slaves) but also as consumers.

4) Peter Singer's 'expanding circle' theory, which argues that human empathy for others has expanded over history from a small group of intimates to a much wider set (paragraph 16), powered perhaps by the reasons given by Wright above in the previous cycles of economic and cultural reciprocity theory.

4) What is the coda or conclusion to Prof Pinker's talk?
The entire final paragraph and in particular '[the historical decline in violence] should force us to ask not just, why is there war? But also, why is there peace? Not just, what are we doing wrong? But also, what have we been doing right?'

TASK 9: *Association*

Free responses.

TASK 10: *Rational and non-rational persuasion*

Least rational

1) Association
2) Authority
3) Comparison
4) Problem–solution
5) Hypothesis–evidence–explanation

Most rational

TASK 11: *Models of persuasion in TV commercials*

1) Association
2) Problem–solution
3) Authority
4) Comparison
5) Problem–solution, comparison and the older woman may well be intended to be seen as an authority.

Note

1 https://tinyurl.com/PiP-Dictionary

4 Cave emptor![1]
Arguments good and bad, true and false, logical and non-logical

Truth is rarely pure and never simple.
In matters of grave importance, style, not sincerity, is the vital thing.
(both Oscar Wilde)

Each year the *Oxford English Dictionary* chooses its 'word of the year', a word which is felt to have played a prominent role in Anglophone discourse in that year. In 2016 the item chosen was 'post-truth', defined as 'relating to or denoting circumstances in which objective facts are less influential in shaping public opinion than appeals to emotion and personal belief'. While acknowledging it is not a new term, the dictionary nevertheless claims it has gone from being 'a peripheral term to being a mainstay in political commentary' and is often used in the expression 'post-truth politics'. And yet all this somehow suggests that there once was a past golden 'age of truth', when honesty reigned and deception was unknown. It also suggests that there is one absolute knowable truth, but it is widely recognised that political debate is nothing if not a clash of and competition among different conceptions, beliefs and narratives about what is supposedly 'true'.

In this Unit, then, we continue the overall focus on types of argumentation, but look at some methods of argument which might be described as non-rational, or non-logical, some perhaps even to the point of being misleading or even deceitful. We have already met one such technique in Unit 2, the 'straw-man argument' defined as 'caricaturing an opposing view so that it is easy to refute'. We will outline a few more of the tricks of the orator's trade, not all of which would always stand up to the scrutiny of the cold light of logic or complete moral propriety; which does not necessarily, in the right context, of course, render them any less effective as forms of persuasion. Otherwise they would not be so useful and so widely used. Unfortunately, in real life, the most logical and the most moral arguments do not always win the day. And perhaps, just as unfortunately, the most logical argument is not always the most moral and vice versa.

4.1 Euphemism and dysphemism

Political rhetoric is characterised by **euphemism** and **dysphemism**, both of which involve choosing lexical items which have a particular evaluative **connotation** (Unit 2) for persuasive purposes. We may describe euphemism as the deliberate renaming of negative, controversial or downright harmful actions in neutral terms in order to sanitise them. In history we can several find extreme examples, for instance mass murder described as *ethnic cleansing* or *cleansing the bush* (the Rwanda massacres in 1994) or as a *Cultural Revolution* (Mao's deliberate systematic destruction of China's middle classes) or the *Final Solution* (the Nazi's plan and execution of systematic genocide against European Jewry during World War II). Some more modern instances of euphemisms can be found in Unit 7.

The opposite of euphemism is **dysphemism**, the use of language to portray some entity, event or policy in an exaggeratedly negative light. In western societies with their aging populations, the state of the healthcare system is an enormously contentious political issue. While some political parties talk highly euphemistically of *modernisation* when they refer to privatisation and reduced access to health services, others may talk dysphemistically of *destruction* in response to proposed changes. Thus, we find accusations of attempting to *destroy, dismantle* or *wreck* the existing healthcare system (the NHS is the *National Health Service*, the Tories are the Conservatives, in government at the time):

Miliband (leader of the Labour opposition) claimed that the NHS greatest institution of our country 'has been wrecked' by the Tories.
(*Daily Mirror* 2013)

Similarly, the Democrats' attempts at healthcare reform in the US met with hyperbolic criticism from the Republican opposition:

[. . .] the White House sticks to its guns and refuses to be held hostage by Republican[s] . . . who keep contending that Obamacare is a train wreck.
(*New York Times* 2013)

In bipartisan politics, each side naturally tends to describe its own policies with euphemistic terms, the other's with dysphemisms. Whenever a government decides to spend less money in any area, it describes the reduction as 'savings for the taxpayer' (our emphasis):

New figures published today reveal that the government has **saved the taxpayer** 3 billion since 2010 and reduced the number of public bodies by over a third.
(www.gov.uk 2015)

while the opposition describes it as 'cuts' or even 'axing' and 'slashing':

22,000 cops facing axe in savage cuts

BRUTAL Tory **cuts** could result in the number of police officers being **slashed** by 22,000 to its lowest in nearly 40 years.

(*Daily Mirror* 2015)

Dysphemisms in politics are thus a form of what is called rhetorical *delegitimisation,* which we can define as the attempt to discredit the right or ability of an opponent to make a certain claim or argument or to hold a certain power. We will come across several types of delegitimisation in the course of this book.

On those rare occasions where the opposition cannot find anything wrong with government policy or even agrees with it, it will nevertheless refrain from praise, calling it perhaps 'insufficient' or 'not going far enough':

On the food Bill, Sen too said that the Bill **did not go far enough,** but said that given that there appeared to be public support for greater food security and an 'overwhelming case for passing it, Parliament needs to carry out what the public has been demanding'.

(*Times of India* 2013)

Euphemistic and dysphemistic descriptions are, of course, yet further expressions of spin (Unit 1) and evaluation (Unit 2) which run like a thread throughout political discourse. Euphemism is exaggerated or unmerited *positive* evaluation while dysphemism is exaggerated *negative* evaluation. Both euphemisms and dysphemisms are used to try and *persuade* the audience of course.

4.2 The *ad hominem* argument

The *ad hominem* (sometimes *ad personam*) is one of the most common of the classical non-rational arguments. We can define it as attacking a person rather than his or her arguments, and it is another form of attempted delegitimisation of an opponent. The person might be either the opponent in an argument or some authority called upon in support of an argument we oppose.

TASK 1: *ad hominem 1*

What *ad hominem* does Ms Shiva employ to attack her critics in the following:

'Bullshit Award for Sustaining Poverty' Awarded Today to Vandana Shiva

In front of a rapt crowd of farmers from Africa and Asia, the award –
a plaque mounted with cow manure, representing the traditional
agricultural technology that the winner favours – was bestowed on
Ms. Vandana Shiva.

(www.libertyindia.org/events/bullshit_
award_28august2002.htm)

The farmers are demanding the freedom to use modern technology
to improve food production, and to trade unhindered by bans on
GM produce.

Shiva hit back saying her critics are people whose minds have been
bought and that proponents of GM foods are third-rate scientists,
corrupt politicians, and pawns of multinationals.

(*The Times of India* 2002, edited)

Occasionally the attack is not so much on the person him/herself but
a group he or she belongs too; the person in question is thus negatively
evaluated by association, as in Task 2, below.

TASK 2: *ad hominem 2*

In the following extract on 'Charles's fantasy farming', with which
group is Prince Charles associated? How is this group brought into
ridicule? What is the real object of criticism and how does the *ad
hominem* argument attack it?

> In response to 19th-century industrialisation, the British aristocracy
> rediscovered medieval chivalry, jousts, castles and armour. Now, in
> response to modern agriculture, Prince Charles has rediscovered
> organic peasant farming. Again it has its comic side, but [. . .] organic
> peasant agriculture is a solution for the angst of affluence, but not
> hunger.

(*Guardian* 2008)

Responding to these kinds of attacks in verbal interactions can be
challenging for the target because they are 'derailments' of the debate,
that is, an *ad hominem* remark during a speech diverts attention from
the topic in hand. If the speaker, who has been targeted by the
ad hominem remark, attempts to counter the attack, they accept the
derailment, but if they ignore it, then they allow the attack to stand.
This problem has been recognised and even codified in European parliamentary rules which dictate when such responses are permitted.
The European Parliament rules of procedure (Article 145) state that:

1. A Member who asks to make a personal statement shall be heard
at the end of the discussion of the item of the agenda being dealt

with or when the minutes of the sitting to which the request for leave to speak refers are considered for approval.

The Member concerned may not speak on substantive matters but shall confine his observations to rebutting any remarks that have been made about his person in the course of the debate [. . .]

4.3 *Tu quoque* (also known as: 'you're just as bad' or 'two wrongs make it all right')

This is a subcategory of the *ad hominem* technique in which the person making an argument is accused of having spoken or acted in a way inconsistent with the argument. In one variant, someone proposing a course of action involving *not* doing something is accused themselves of having done it, or something similar. In another variant, if person A criticises the actions of person B, a *tu quoque* response is that A has acted in the same way.

Thomas Jefferson, principal author of the *Declaration of Independence* which contains the fine and famous words 'we hold these truths to be self-evident, that all men are created equal' (Unit 4.7), and who called slavery 'this great political and moral evil', in fact himself owned a large number of black slaves and even had a relationship with one of his slaves, with whom he had children.

Thomas Jefferson

Jefferson's champions [are] no longer able to evade or sweep aside the central, terrible contradiction at the core of his life: that the author of the noblest phrases ever penned in the English language about equality, and liberty, and self-governance, held other human beings in bondage. The apparent confirmation of long-standing rumors regarding his relationship with Sally Hemings has cast a harsh light; no longer can we think of Jefferson as merely a 'participant' in the 'institution' of slavery, in some abstract and disembodied sense; he was, we now see, and not to put too fine a point on it, engaged in sexual relations with a chattel slave, a woman – a girl, really – whom he *owned*.

D. Post: 'Words Fitly Spoken': Thomas Jefferson,
Slavery, and Sally Hemings
http://www.temple.edu/lawschool/dpost/slavery.PDF

Q1

Whether or not we consider Jefferson to have been a hypocrite, the question to be asked is: does his personal life detract from the truth, the integrity and the force of his actual arguments, namely, that all men are created equal, and that slavery is a great moral evil? (Free response)

Q2

The following extract poses explicitly the question of personal 'credibility'. If Mr Gore's lifestyle does not exactly fit his message, does this have any effect on the scientific reality – or otherwise – of anthropogenic (or *man-made* or *human-induced*) climate change? Does the fact that his behaviour does not seem to reflect the urgency of his message make his message less reliable? And if Mr Gore consumes energy as extravagantly as this newspaper claims, why shouldn't we? (Free response).

Al Gore insists the world must embrace a 'carbon-neutral lifestyle'. To do otherwise will result in a cataclysmic catastrophe but he does very little. He lives in a 10,000-square-foot, 20-room, eight-bathroom home in Nashville, and a 4,000-square-foot home in Arlington, Va. (He also has a third home in Carthage, Tenn.)

USA Today 2006, edited

TASK 3: *ad hominem 3*

Is the *ad hominem* technique ever justifiable; in other words, might there be circumstances in which it is fair to attack the character or characteristics of an opponent or an opponent's ally, supporter or group?

Consider the following:

a) How can [politician X] possibly be a socialist when he is so wealthy?
b) You are a woman, so you should vote for a female candidate like Angela Merkel.
c) Why follow what the Vatican says on sexual morality and the family when priests have to be celibate and can't get married and have children?
d) You can't trust what Jack thinks about income tax because he doesn't have a job and doesn't pay income tax.
e) Research into climate change funded by oil companies cannot be trusted, because they are just defending their own financial interests.
f) Of course the Greens keep telling us climate change will be catastrophic if we do nothing. In that way they attract more government funding and public donations.
g) 'Naturally these magistrates want to investigate my financial affairs', said the right-wing Prime Minister. 'That's because they're all a bunch of Communists'.

(Free responses)

4.4 The slippery slope

In Germany ... extreme opponents of genetic engineering fire-bombed a Max Planck Institute because it was conducting genetic research on petunias. They argued that as genetic modification was sure to lead to eugenics, and as this had been practised by the Nazis, such research was sure to lead to Nazism.

(Taverne 2005: 5, edited)

The slippery slope argument is so frequent that it has acquired a good number of popular names, including 'the thin end of the wedge', 'opening the floodgates', 'once we start allowing . . .' and the 'Camel's Nose':

There is an old saying about how if you allow a camel to poke his nose into the tent, soon the whole camel will follow.

The slippery slope argument draws upon the assumption that something that is not necessarily wrong in itself is nevertheless evaluated as bad because it could slide towards or could turn into or could open the door to something that is wrong. It is clearly invalid if it is meant to be a point of logic, since if two phenomena are separate there is no logical reason to consider them as equivalent. The camel may well not like what it sees in the tent and look for excitement elsewhere.

But if it is taken as a perception about people's psychology, the slippery slope argument may often appear to have considerable validity. By making exceptions to a rule, the psychological reasoning runs, one may well weaken respect for the rule or encourage people to look for other exceptional cases.

TASK 4: *Slippery slopes*

Which of the following slippery slope arguments would you consider to have some validity or force? Do you agree with the arguments they propose to some extent yourself? (Free responses)

a) Voluntary euthanasia will lead to involuntary euthanasia, with doctors killing people without asking for permission first.
b) If you legalise soft drugs, more people will later move on to hard drugs.
c) If we permit nudity on beaches, why not in other public places?
d) The more immigrants we allow in, the more of their family members they will also later bring in.
e) If we allow nationalists to campaign against immigration, sooner or later this will lead to verbal and physical attacks against immigrants.

This famous poem follows the form of the slippery slope:

> [On the Nazi rise to power]
>
> They came first for the Communists, And I didn't speak out because I wasn't a Communist;
> Then they came for the trade unionists, And I didn't speak out because I wasn't a trade unionist;
> Then they came for the Jews, And I didn't speak out because I wasn't a Jew;
> Then . . . they came for me . . . And by that time there was no one left to speak out.
>
> ('First they came . . .', Pastor Martin Niemöller, 1892–1984)

In political argument, the slippery slope is frequently found in relation to discussions on freedom of speech and censorship, that is, whether and how much to limit freedoms of expression. It is found on both sides. On the side of libertarianism, of complete freedom of speech:

> This idea that any opinion, legitimately expressed, can be dismissed on the grounds that it is offensive to an individual is the foundation of a new and terrifying censorship and censorship is the foundation of tyranny.
>
> (Peter Hitchens, Oxford Union Debate, 2015)

But also on the side of censorship, on limiting freedom of expression, for example, if we allow Holocaust denial or newspapers to publish cartoons offending religion, where will it lead to?

This second viewpoint was made explicit in one newspaper opinion piece:

> A fractional loss of liberty entailed in penalising the expression of neo-Nazi views or Holocaust denial seems a small price to pay compared to what can follow if the far right is shielded all the way into power.
>
> (*Guardian* 2008)

To which a reader was moved to reply:

> Perhaps we in Britain take democracy for granted because the Far Right and the Far Left have not posed a significant threat up to now. And extremists have not posed a threat *because* we allow

them the freedom to speak their minds – and show us what poisonous little reptiles they are. For much of the last century governments in Europe have restricted freedom of speech and their countries have often been plagued by political extremists. Perhaps there is an intimate connection between those two facts?

(*Guardian* 2008, original emphasis)

4.5   (False) binary opposition (false dichotomy, the excluded middle[2])

A typical example of the false dichotomy might be: 'We must deal with crime on the streets before improving the schools'. Such statements exclude the possibility of a middle ground: why can't we do some of both at the same time? And perhaps improving schools will also help reduce crime.

We are all familiar with opposites (also referred to as antonyms), and we will look at them again in Unit 5 when we discuss **oxymorons** like *bittersweet*, or *radical moderate*, but it may be useful to think in more detail about the relationship between items which are presented as in opposition.

First of all, only items which are considered to be related in some way are treated as opposites or antonyms: *dog* and *philosophy* are very different but we would not usually consider them to be opposites, whereas *big* and *small* are easily recognised as opposites because they both refer to size.

Second, we can identify three distinct types of antonym:

Gradable antonyms are words that mark two extremes on a cline, for example:

hot _____ *cold*
What other terms could you add between *hot* and *cold*?

Complementary antonyms could be considered the 'real' opposites because they are not gradable and are mutually exclusive, for example *dead–alive*: things cannot be dead and alive at the same time. Another example is *present–absent*.

Converse antonyms describe different perspectives on relationships or activities, for example *husband–wife*. The existence of a husband invokes the existence of a wife. Another example is *lend–borrow*.

TASK 5: *Antonyms*

Can you add some more examples for each type of antonym? (Free responses)

1) Gradable antonyms:
2) Complementary antonyms:
3) Converse antonyms:

In political language, how do you think the terms 'left' and 'right' are used – as gradable, complementary or converse antonyms?

You may have noticed that it is quite difficult to think of examples of complementary antonymy. In persuasive language, what often happens is that pairs of phenomena, of ideas, of policies, etc. are presented as exclusive when they are not. For example, newspapers or politicians may present incitement to hatred and freedom of speech as binary oppositions, as in the *Guardian* headline 'Hate speech v free speech' (2007). Public debates, such as those organised by the Oxford Union Debating Society or the Intelligence Squared Association (which has branches in the US, UK and Australia) are generally deliberately framed so that speakers take opposing points of view. For example, in 2015 the Oxford Union Debating Society held a debate on the proposition 'the right to free speech always includes the right to offend', with two speakers arguing that it does and two arguing that it does not. In these instances, the binary opposition is used to create what is sometimes called a *false dilemma*, defined as assuming there are only two alternatives when in fact there are more. For example, assuming atheism is the only alternative to religious fundamentalism, or being a traitor is the only alternative to being a 'my country right or wrong' patriot. Another famous example comes from the post-9/11 political discourse when President Bush said:

> Every nation, in every region, now has a decision to make. Either you are with us or you are with the terrorists.
>
> (Bush 2001)

This opposition was, in reality, first used by Hillary Clinton a week before George W. Bush when she declared 'Every nation has to either be with us, or against us. Those who harbor terrorists, or who finance them, are going to pay a price'. The phrase also has Biblical connotations; Jesus is reported as saying 'He who is not with me is against me' (Matthew 12:30). The creation of 'them' (negatively evaluated) and 'us' (positively evaluated) is a particularly pervasive binary opposition in persuasive discourse, including and especially in bipartisan (two-party) democracies like the US and the UK (Unit 3.2.1). This sort of binary opposition excludes the alternative positions of being against both sides, or the middle ground of having some sympathy with both sides.

It is important to remember that binary oppositions are very often cultural creations, sometimes called 'non-canonical antonyms'. In these instances, the opposition is created by the speaker. For instance, what would you consider to be the 'opposite' of 'America'?

Now consider the following:

- I love Denmark. But we are not Denmark, we are America. (Hillary Clinton 2015)
- We are not America. We are Afghanistan. (Hamid Karzai, President of Afghanistan, 2012)
- We are very roughly the same size as America and we are a great country like America – but we are not America. (Julia Gillard, Australian Prime Minister, 2010)

We can assume that each of these speakers had a different idea of what 'America' means and so was constructing a very different opposition in each case.

Another well-known example of binary opposition comes from 1983 when the Conservative (or 'Tory') Party used the following slogan on their campaign posters, alongside a picture of a young black male:

Labour say he's black.
Tories say he's British.

The two parts of the phrase are parallel and the speaker (the Conservative Party) creates an opposition between two seemingly disassociated words, *black* and *British*.

Q3

What message do you think the Conservative Party was trying to convey?

But this type of persuasion is also criticised, in an article in the *Guardian* in 2005 this comment was made:

Yet the most alarming feature of the media-dominated universe is that it presents the world in terms of opposites and polarises every issue into extreme positions.

We can also distinguish between different 'triggers', that is, syntactic frames which alert us to the construction of an opposition in a text. These triggers are particularly salient when we are dealing with *non-conventional* oppositions; that is, those instances where the speaker is constructing an opposition in order to make an argument. We can identify these 'bespoke' oppositions through a range of triggers, as illustrated in Table 4.1, taken from Davies (2012: 50–51).

Table 4.1 Summary of this study's syntactic frame categories and their functions as triggers

Category	Common syntactic frames, triggers	Canonical textual example	Noncanonical textual example	Function(s)
Negated opposition	X not Y; not X,Y	The government was elected to create **unity** in this country and *not* create **division**.	**Clotted cream not ruptured spleen.**	Emphasizes already inherent mutual exclusivity in canonical examples, and constructs mutual exclusivity in noncanonical ones. Often expresses preference for one state over another. Often combined with the contrastive "but" (e.g., *not X but Y*).
Transitional opposition	X turns into Y; X becomes Y	. . . *turn* the many decent, honourable and **law-abiding people** . . . *into* **criminals**.	**Villages** are *turning into* **weekend rest centres or dormitories for commuting TV executives and merchant bankers**.	*Transformation* from one state to a canonical or noncanonical opposite.
Comparative opposition	more X than Y; X is more A than Y	Dr Higgs was a lot *more* **right** *than* **wrong** . . . . . . **reward** is *more* **effective** *than* **punishment**.	. . . the marchers seemed more **bemused** *than* **offended** . . . . . . *more* **important** *than* the fate of **Labour** is the fate of **mankind**.	Measures X against Y by comparing them either *directly* (using the same relations of equivalence and difference) or *indirectly*, judged against another scale of equivalence and difference.
Replacive opposition	X rather than Y; X instead of Y; X in place of Y	Wanting to be **happy** *rather than* **sad**, I accepted . . . (Jones 2002:79)	There has been speculation that Mr Michael may propose introducing **a licensing system** *rather than* an **outright ban** . . .	Expresses an alternative preferred or nonpreferred *option* to that which it is opposed.

(Continued)

Table 4.1 (continued)

Category	*Common syntactic frames, triggers*	*Canonical textual example*	*Noncanonical textual example*	*Function(s)*
		. . . the whole concept of managing by **punishment** *instead* of **reward** . . . (Jones 2002: 90)	*In place* of a **charismatic leader**, they have the **belief that politicians are lying**.	
Concessive opposition	X but Y; despite X, Y; while X, Y; although X, Y; X, yet Y	[Unlikely to conjoin individual canonical lexical items unless expressing simultaneously contradictory states, e.g., "I was **happy** *but* also **sad**".]	There was plenty of **passion** *but* the marchers remained **good-natured**.	Creates contrast between two conjoined phrases or clauses, often relating the *unexpectedness* of what is said in one clause in view of the circumstances described in the other clause.
			Despite **the numbers, the march was peaceful**.	
			While it was true that **militants** . . . were out in force, the heart and mind of the protest was **ordinary people**.	
Explicit opposition	X contrasted with Y; X opposed to Y; the distinction/ division/ difference/ between X and Y; X against Y	Being **young** and keen as *opposed* to being **old** and keen . . . (Jones 2002:90)	The **professionally-produced placards** . . . *contrasted with* **cobbled-together banners**.	Where a linguistic item within the syntactic frame makes an explicit metalinguistic reference to either a presupposed or a constructed contrast between X and Y.

Table 4.1 (continued)

Category	Common syntactic frames, triggers	Canonical textual example	Noncanonical textual example	Function(s)
		. . . the *division* between **gay** and **straight** . . . (Jones 2002:81) This blurred *distinction* between **fact** and **fiction** . . . (Jones 2002:81)	The **Liberty** and **Livelihood** March began ostensibly *divided into* **two** camps . . . "**House music** *against* **war**"	
Parallelism	[No specific frames. Relies on repetitive structures]	You are as **young** as your *faith*, as **old** as *your* **doubts** (Jones 2002:56)	. . . *they can walk over our* **lands** *but they can't walk over* **us**. *Leave* **us** *to* **our cow s*** *** and we will *leave* **you** *to* **your city bull***t**.	Repetition of a range of syntactic structures within which specific lexical items are foregrounded, inviting the addressee to relate them as oppositions. Often combined with other syntactic triggers such as "but" or other more canonical oppositional items. Often contain canonical oppositions which in Jones's (2002) terms makes the second X/Y pair examples of "ancillary antonyms."
Binarized option	whether X or Y; either X or Y	Is she a **good** mommy or a **bad** mommy (Murphy et al. 2009:2162)	*whether* Mr Blair still treats those hundreds of thousands of people as an **irrelevant minority**, or accepts that this time, **the countryside really has spoken**	Offers and/or creates a choice between two mutually exclusive options.

Source: Published in: Davies 2012. Copyright © 2012 SAGE Publications

---

Q4

Can you think of any other examples of issues that are presented as binary oppositions?

As mentioned above, in 2015, the Oxford Union Debating Society held a debate on the proposition 'the right to free speech always includes the right to offend'. Do you agree or disagree? Why?

Here are some other propositions which have recently been debated in this 'for or against' format at the Oxford Union (OU) or at one of the Intelligence Squared (IS) Associations:

Choose one and decide what debating points you would make to persuade an audience and 'win' the debate:

Democracy is not always the best form of government (IS, US)
Immigration is good for Britain (OU)
Europe is failing its Muslims (IS, UK)
All nuclear weapons are morally indefensible (OU)
Religion harms society (OU)
Monogamy equals Monotony (IS, US)

But are these really all binary issues, with no middle ground? To test this, imagine you were invited to speak for a side *opposing* the view that you hold. What different arguments might each side put forward? (Free responses)

TASK 6: *Kwame Nkrumah and Ghana*

Read/watch the following speech given by Kwame Nkrumah who became the first Prime Minister and President of Ghana. It makes repeated use of negated opposition. Identify examples of this and consider what rhetorical effect the repetition has.

https://tinyurl.com/PiP-Q5

4.6 False parallels (odd couples)

Another common rhetorical tactic or trick is to link two different phenomena together and imply they are very similar, for instance:

The BBC defended recent episodes of *EastEnders* after more than 250 people complained about scenes of sex and violence
(Daily *Mail* 2006)

Film sex and violence [are] fatally eroding society
(*London Evening Standard* 2007)

But what do scenes of sex and scenes of violence have in common?

The following is from an MTV interview with Bryan Singer, the producer, and Tom Cruise, the protagonist, of the film *Valkyrie* about a plot to assassinate Hitler:

> MTV: Did the fact that you, Bryan, are Jewish, and you, Tom, are a Scientologist affect your decision to make this film? These are two sometimes-persecuted groups. I would think that would inform wanting to make a film about killing Hitler.

Q5

What is the parallel being made here? How might it be considered highly questionable?

By this means it becomes possible to transfer the negative associations of something very bad onto something else which may well not necessarily strike everyone as bad. The following is somewhat similar:

> Let's just say that global warming deniers are now on a par with Holocaust deniers [. . .]
>
> (Ellen Goodman, *Boston Globe* 2007)

Q6

What does the refusal to recognise a well-documented historical event, the Holocaust, probably the most brutal and cruel episode of the last century, have in common with scepticism about a current scientific theory, however widely accepted? Why does Ms Goodman make this parallel? What is she trying to imply about the morality of people who are sceptical about global warming?

4.7 Causation or correlation? (*Post hoc ergo propter hoc*: 'after this, therefore because of this')

Cause and effect would seem to be simple matters, although there are different types of cause and effect. The sun *causes* (contributes to causing) plants to grow, smoking often *causes* cancer (but not always), winning an election *causes* in the sense of having the effect of allowing a political party to form a government. But just because two events happen at the same time or two phenomena co-exist at the same time does not mean that one necessarily causes the other. Relationships between them can be tenuous, complex or even non-existent.

For instance, proportionally, more middle-class people than working-class people vote Conservative than Labour. Would we say that being middle-class *causes* people to vote Conservative?

People who believe in astrology are also more likely to use so-called 'alternative medicine' than people who do not believe in it. Does the belief in astrology *cause* people to use alternative medicines?

Did the September 11th atrocity *cause* the invasions of Afghanistan and Iraq?

And finally, a famous instance of causational fallacy. The cock crows as the sun rises. Does the crowing *cause* the sun to rise?

4.7.1 Two phenomena can be linked by a third factor

Many seemingly causal relations are in fact simply both being brought about by a third outside factor (as belief in astrology and in alternative medicine are often brought about by a particular anti-science mindset). This is especially important in medicine. In 1998 the British medical journal the *Lancet*, published an article claiming that the administration of the triple vaccination against measles, mumps and rubella (known as the MMR vaccination) correlated with an increased risk of autism in young children. The media began – and continued for years – to talk of a 'link' (a word which does not distinguish between correlation or causation):

Scientists fear MMR link to autism

New American research shows that there could be a link between the controversial MMR triple vaccine and autism and bowel disease in children.

(*Daily Mail* 2006)

And many parents, fearing that the triple vaccine indeed was likely to *cause* autism, refused to have their children vaccinated. The result was major outbreaks of the diseases in the UK, Europe and America, in which several children died. Later research that included a major study involving over 95,000 children, published in 2015 in the *Journal of the American Medical Association*, found no evidence whatsoever of a causational link. The truth is that autism, when it does manifest itself in young children, manifests itself at the same age as when the vaccines are administered, around one year. The relation between the administration of the vaccine and the occasional onset of autism is one of pure correlation, with each being affected by an unrelated third factor, the age of the child. Unfortunately, the scientific research has not halted the so-called anti-vaccination – or anti-vaxxers – campaign, which has even become a political and ethical 'pro-choice' movement. Proponents of vaccination, doctors and scientists, are accused of wanting to ban people's freedom to choose and of being in the pay of the pharmaceutical industries (see, for example, the website ageofautism.com). The result is that children worldwide continue to be at higher risk of infection by these diseases.

Q7

The following is an extract from a speech in the UK Parliament. What are the two phenomena which are related and what is the third factor that may be causing both?

I come now to the subject of drug testing. We fully support attempts to make the criminal justice system more effective at tackling the causes of offending behaviour and at challenging the behaviour of offenders. It has been established that much criminality is related to drug misuse, and an effective response needs to be developed: As I said earlier, however, in statistical terms *correlation* does not prove – or even imply – *causation*. Many repeat offenders lead chaotic lives, as do many drug users: The chaotic life style may cause the crime, rather than the drug use per se.

(Mrs Jackie Ballard, MP for Taunton, 2000)

4.7.2 Two phenomena might simply be coincidence

Compare the following rather fatuous statement:

> Since the 1970s, both the atmospheric CO_2 level and the use of recreational drugs has increased sharply.
>
> Hence, atmospheric CO_2 causes people to take drugs.

to the central tenet of man-made climate change:

> Since the 1970s (the 1950 and 60s were periods of global cooling), both the atmospheric CO_2 level and global temperatures have increased.
>
> Hence, higher levels of atmospheric CO_2 causes global warming.

Common sense tells us the first is coincidence, but as for the second, experimental evidence supports the CO_2 hypothesis. Nevertheless, in complex matters it can be very difficult to distinguish whether two phenomena are linked causally or coincidentally or through a third factor influencing both.

In politics, it is common to give credit or blame to incumbent officials for events that occur while they are in office but over which they have little, if any, control, as when the leader of Britain's Conservative Party, David Cameron, attributed the global financial crisis which began in 2007 to the policies of the British Prime Minister, Gordon Brown:

Financial crisis: David Cameron blames Gordon Brown for Britain's 'broken economy'

David Cameron has broken an uneasy truce over the financial crisis, blaming Gordon Brown for breaking Britain's economy with policies that now 'lie in ruins'.

(Daily Telegraph 2008)

4.7.3 Multiple causation

Indeed, complex events like the global financial crisis generally have more than one cause and are not the fault of a single individual. Nevertheless, simplifying the cause of an event can be a useful strategy in political argument. Few economists predicted the 2007 financial crisis, and even now there are radically conflicting explanations of how it came about – and who is to blame. Banks lent far too much money, creating debt; governments failed to regulate the banks, indeed the US governments under Clinton and Bush encouraged banks to lend; private citizens borrowed more money than they could afford; economists failed to warn of the dangers of so much debt. Here is just one reported economist's opinion, from before the crisis broke:

Dan McLaughlin, an economist, appeared on the radio to pour scorn on those concerned about our increasing debt. He believes that worrying about our profligate borrowing is unnecessary and silly. We should remember that McLaughlin is not any old economist. He is chief economist at the Bank of Ireland.

(Times 2005)

TASK 7: *Causation or correlation?*

Do you think the following pairs of events are linked by major causation, minor causation or just by correlation and coincidence? (Free responses)

1) As justification for reducing financial assistance to students the UK government has argued that going to university increases earnings. Are the higher earnings of graduates caused by going to university?
2) Reading newspapers is correlated to an increased interest in politics. Does reading newspapers cause an increase in people's interest in politics? Does a particular interest in politics cause people to read newspapers? Or is there some third factor which causes both?

3) Being fat causes global warming, say scientists

Being overweight is bad for the environment as well as your health, according to a study out today. Researchers found that overweight people were likely to be more responsible for carbon emissions than slim people because they consume more food and fuel.

4) Early cannabis abuse 'leads to heroin addiction'

Taking cannabis as a teenager really does pave the way to heroin addiction in later life, say scientists. Researchers have found that cannabis acts as a 'gateway' drug, because exposure during adolescence primes the system to crave the chemical stimulation of hard drugs.

5) Living in chic Chelsea leads to a longer life

Those living in Kensington and Chelsea in London have cause to celebrate, after statistics have shown both men and women from the area have the highest life expectancy in the UK.

6) Generous state benefit allowances encourage women to become single mothers, research has found. The EU-wide study showed a close correlation between the number of single mothers and the level of benefits. The UK had by far the highest proportion of young single mother households – 8 per cent.

7) Debbie Wolf claims she is one of Britain's growing army of 'sliders' – people who believe their presence causes havoc with household appliances, radios and light bulbs. Street lamps flicker when she passes, TVs change channels when she walks into a room and she causes electronic clocks to go crazy.

(all from the *Daily Mail*)

Further reading

Jeffries, L. (2010) *Opposition in Discourse: The Construction of Oppositional Meaning*, London: Bloomsbury Publishing.
Leith, S. (2012) *You Talkin' to Me? Rhetoric from Aristotle to Obama*, London: Profile.

Case studies

Davies, M. (2012) 'A new approach to oppositions in discourse: The role of syntactic frames in the triggering of noncanonical oppositions', *Journal of English Linguistics* 40(1): 41–73.
Plug, H.J. (2010) 'Ad-hominem arguments in Dutch and European parliamentary debates: Strategic manoeuvring in an institutional context', in C. Ilie (ed.) *European Parliaments under Scrutiny: Discourse Strategies and Interaction Practices* (*Discourse Approaches to Politics, Society and Culture*, 38), Amsterdam: John Benjamins, 305–328.

Keys and commentaries

TASK 1: *ad hominem 1*

The ad hominem is in the accusation that her critics' 'minds had been bought'. In this way, she avoids having to address their criticisms.

TASK 2: *ad hominem 2*

In the following with which group is Prince Charles associated?
The British aristocracy.

How is this group brought into ridicule?
By talk of its rediscovering medieval chivalry, jousts, castles and armour.

What is the real object of criticism and how does the *ad hominem* argument attack it?
The real object of criticism is a presumed unjustified opposition to modern farming techniques. The *ad hominem* depicts Charles and the British aristocracy as outdated and capricious (note the irony in 'Prince Charles has rediscovered organic peasant farming').

Q3

The Conservatives intend to imply that Labour does not consider ethnic minorities to be truly British.

TASK 6

In the speech we see powerful oppositions set up throughout. One of the most frequent forms for opposition is the simple category of negated opposition (x not y) and, more commonly (not x but y). You might have identified the following examples of this category:

1) The right of a people to decide their own destiny, to make their way in freedom, is not to be measured by the yardstick of colour or degree of social development. It is an inalienable right of peoples which they are powerless to exercise when forces, stronger than they themselves, by whatever means, for whatever reasons, take this right away from them.
2) Thus may we take pride in the name of Ghana, not out of romanticism, but as an inspiration for the future.
3) What our ancestors achieved in the context of their contemporary society gives us confidence that we can create, out of that past, a glorious future, not in terms of war and military pomp, but in terms of social progress and of peace.

4) And while yet we are making our claim for self-government I want to emphasise, Mr Speaker, that self-government is not an end in itself. It is a means to an end, to the building of the good life to the benefit of all, regardless of tribe, creed, colour or station in life.
5) We must not follow blindly, but must endeavour to create.

However, there are also multiple other forms of opposition in the text as the speaker sets out persuasively the differences between their past and possible futures, as seen in the following extract:

The heroes of our future will be those who can lead our people out of the stifling fog of disintegration through serfdom, into the valley of light where purpose, endeavour and determination will create that brotherhood which Christ proclaimed two thousand years ago, and about which so much is said, but so little done.

Another strong thread of opposition concerns the speaker's plans for the future and what others (especially the beneficiaries of the speech) might consider to be the future. Thus, he anticipates potential criticisms through the opposition. In this regard, we might notice the repetition of *repudiate*:

For we *repudiate* war and violence. Our battles shall be against the old ideas. . .

We *repudiate* the evil doctrines of tribal chauvinism, racial prejudice and national hatred.

We *repudiate* these evil ideas because in creating that brotherhood to which we aspire, we hope to make a reality, within the bounds of our small country, of all the grandiose ideologies which are supposed to form the intangible bonds holding together the British Commonwealth of Nations in which we hope to remain. . .

Q5

It is absurd to compare any persecution that Scientology may or may not suffer to that undergone by Jews throughout the last 2000 years. Moreover, Jewish people have good reason to hate the memory of Hitler and National Socialism, the theme of the film, whereas Scientology did not even exist until the late 1970s.

Q6

Free response. Ms Goodman obviously feels very strongly about climate change scepticism.

Q7

The two phenomena are drug abuse and criminality. However, the first does not necessarily cause the second, in the view of the speaker. Both the drug abuse and the criminality could occur because of the chaotic lifestyle of the individuals in question.

Notes

1 Let the buyer beware. In other words, it is the potential buyer's – in politics, the public's – responsibility to examine carefully the goods – and the arguments – on offer before committing themselves.
2 That is, no middle ground, no middle way is recognised between two extreme positions.

5 The rhetoric of liberty, freedom, emancipation

Freedom is always unfinished business.

(Anonymous)

In this Unit, we will look at the sorts of rhetorical devices that help make a political speech memorable and exciting to an audience. These include:

Binomials
Bicolons
Tricolons (or 'three-part list')
Contrasting pairs
Oxymorons

What they have in common is the appeal to the human fascination for **creative repetition** and **creative contrast,** similar to our fascination for rhythm in music. They exploit what Jakobson (1960) called the 'poetic' function of language, playing with the sounds and rhythms of language because it is pleasing to us. In a political context, the poetic function can be allied with ideas to produce a striking effect on the audience. A skilful speaker can, as it were, set ideas to music.

TASK 1: *Creative repetition*

a) Read the following (and watch it via the link) and pick out the elements that are repeated. What dramatic effect is being created? What is this advertisement implying about the *ethos* (Unit 1.2), that is, the credentials of the candidate being proposed, and what is it implying about his or her adversary? Who do you think the candidate is?

US Campaign TV advertisement, 2008

It's 3 a.m. and your children are safe and asleep. But there's a phone in the White House and it's ringing.

> Something's happening in the world. Your vote will decide who answers the call, whether it's someone who already knows the world's leaders, knows the military, someone tried and tested and ready to lead in a dangerous world.
> It's 3 a.m. and your children are safe and asleep. Who do you want answering the phone?
>   https://tinyurl.com/PiP-Task1

b) Read the following and pick out the elements that are repeated. What dramatic effect is being created? What does the speaker imply about his or her adversaries? Who do you think the candidate is?

> We will be a country of generosity and warmth. But we will also be a country of law and order.
> Remember: All of the people telling you that you can't have the country you want, are the same people that wouldn't stand – I mean, they said ******** doesn't have a chance of being here tonight. Not a chance! The same people. Oh, we love defeating those people, don't we? Love it, love it, love it. No longer can we rely on those same people in politics and in the media, who will say anything to keep a rigged system in place. Instead, we must choose to Believe In America.

5.1 Binomials and bicolons

Binomials are semi-fixed phrases which are very common in the language in general, in both literal and figurative forms; for example, *salt and pepper, man and wife, one and all*. They have been defined as 'two or more words or phrases belonging to the same grammatical category, having some semantic relationship and joined by some syntactic device such as *and* or *or*' (Bhatia 1994: 143). In actual fact, as can be seen from instances like *by and large* and *time and again*, the two parts do not even need to belong to the same grammatical class. They sometimes have an extra, idiomatic meaning: *by and large* means 'generally' and *time and again* means 'very often'. They also frequently have some phonological similarity to emphasise the parallelism; for example, rhyme as in *hire and fire*.

Binomials are strikingly popular in legal language: *law and order, assault and battery, aid and abet, full faith and credit* (the order of binomials is generally irreversible – do you notice anything about the way the two items are ordered?). They are also quite a common feature of political language: *government and Parliament, political and monetary* (union), and also of finance: *stocks and shares, industrial and commercial* (companies).

Bicolons are expressions containing two parallel phrases and thus tend to be rather more extended than binomials. They are common in the Bible, since Hebrew poetry was based on the couplet:

They shall run and not be weary
They shall walk and not faint

(Isaiah 40:31)

and upon the high mountain, and upon all the hills that are lifted up.
(Isaiah 2:14)

They can be found in political rhetoric too:

[. . .] whether you are citizens of America or citizens of the world
(Kennedy 1961)

With confidence in our armed forces, with the unbounding determination of our people, we will gain the inevitable triumph – so help us God.
(Roosevelt, after the attack on Pearl Harbor, 1941)

TASK 2: *Binomials and bicolons*

In the following extract from a speech by Nelson Mandela on his release from prison in 1990 we find a skilful interplay of several binomials and bicolons. You might like to look for them:

The South Africa so many have sacrificed so much to achieve is within sight. Together let us walk this last, long gruelling mile to reach a non-racial, non-sexist society, where all our people will be equal before the law [. . .] Together we have it in our power to defeat those who continue to kill to maintain the old order. We have it in our power to transform our country into the peaceful and prosperous homeland of all our people. Let us work together to achieve these goals. Let us vow never to celebrate another Christmas in chains.

We have a right to be free, and we shall be free!
(Mandela 1990)

5.2 The three-part list (or *tricolon*)

Like the bicolon, the tricolon employs parallelism. As the name implies, it consists of three parallel items. The simplest kind of *three-part list* or *tricolon* is the repetition of three words or phrases (we are indebted to Beard 2000 for this and several other examples in the following sections):

Maggie, Maggie, Maggie / Out, Out, Out.
> (Popular chant at protests against Margaret (Maggie)
> Thatcher's government in the 1980s)

My government, if elected, will have three main priorities:
Education, Education, Education.
> (Blair 1996)

But most tricolons consist of a set of three phrases, each of which has a similar lexical and syntactic structure but accommodating a degree of variation, as in the following promise by the US presidential candidate Trump to bring industry back to America:

American cars will travel the roads, American planes will soar in the skies, and American ships will patrol the seas.
> (Trump 2016)

Each phrase begins with the adjective *American*, followed by a mode of transport – *cars*, *planes*, *ships* – followed by *will* and a verb of movement – *travel*, *soar*, *patrol* – along or through a physical medium in the plural – *the roads*, *the skies*, *the seas*. In the following, the same speaker uses both the simple repetition type – *we will win* – together with the more complex three variations type of tricolon: *we don't win with [variation]*:

Our country that we love so much doesn't win anymore. We don't win with the military we don't win with healthcare. We don't win with trade [. . .] If I'm elected president, we will win, and we will win, and we will win.
> (Trump 2016)

In addition, there can be many different kinds of elegant variations, for instance:

It is a riddle wrapped in a mystery inside an enigma.
> (Churchill 1939)

Churchill was speaking about Russian foreign policy and his tricolon calls up the image of the Matryoshka, the Russian doll. McCain instead summons up an image of endless lines of gravestones, testimony to the many sacrifices he is discussing:

One cannot go to Arlington [military] Cemetery and see name upon name, grave upon grave, row upon row, without being deeply moved by the sacrifice made by those young men and women.
> (McCain 2008)

The parallel structure builds up an expectation that the three items are related. But this expectation can also be exploited to create surprises as, for example, in:

> There are lies, damn lies and statistics.
>> (Attributed to Disraeli and Mark Twain, among others)

An implicit argument is made that statistics are deliberately misleading, and are thus evaluated as bad. Professional statisticians might not agree.

In characteristic newspaper fashion this particular tricolon was reworked by the Eurosceptic *Daily Mail* as the headline:

> There are lies, damned lies and *EU* statistics
>> (*Daily Mail* 2004)

A good number of tricolons, like the one above, have a metrical pattern of crescendo, each part increasing on the last. In Shakespeare's Mark Antony's famous appeal:

> Friends, Romans, countrymen.

The first part has one syllable, the second has two and the third has three. A similar crescendo effect is seen in the United States *Declaration of Independence*:

> Life, Liberty, and the pursuit of Happiness

And the following tricolon in praise of democracy and the wisdom of crowds, attributed to Abraham Lincoln, has a logical (or pseudological) crescendo, it reads almost like a syllogism:

> You can fool some of the people all of the time
> You can fool all of the people some of the time
> But you can't fool all of the people all of the time

5.2.1 Beyond three

Sometimes one finds longer parallel structures, a kind of elegant variation on the tricolon, for example:

> First they ignore you, then they laugh at you, then they fight you. Then you win.
>> (Attributed to Gandhi)

Politics is the art of looking for trouble, finding it everywhere, diagnosing it wrongly, and applying unsuitable remedies.

(Sir Ernest Benn 1946)

Other, longer, repetitions for rhetorical effect include President J.F. Kennedy's renowned 'let them come to Berlin', part of a speech delivered in West Berlin itself in 1963 at the start of the Cold War:

There are many people in the world who really don't understand, or say they don't, what is the great issue between the free world and the Communist world.

Let them come to Berlin.

There are some who say – There are some who say that communism is the wave of the future.

Let them come to Berlin.

And there are some who say, in Europe and elsewhere, we can work with the Communists.

Let them come to Berlin.

And there are even a few who say that it is true that communism is an evil system, but it permits us to make economic progress.

Lass' sie nach Berlin kommen.

Let them come to Berlin.

(Kennedy 1963)

TASK 3: *Who said what (1)?*

One of the following tricolons was said by Nelson Mandela, one by Abraham Lincoln, one by Winston Churchill and one by Donald Trump. Who said which? (Write the name in the space alongside each.)

Government of the people, by the people, for the people. (...............)

We are one nation and their pain is our pain. Their dreams are our dreams. And their success will be our success. We share one heart, one home, and one glorious destiny. (.......................................)

Friends, comrades and fellow South Africans. I greet you all in the name of peace, democracy and freedom for all. (...................................)

This is not the end. It is not even the beginning of the end. But it is, perhaps, the end of the beginning. (..)

TASK 4: *Can you complete?*

Can you complete each tricolon and indicate who said them or where they come from?

Liberté, Fraternité, ...

Bread, peace and ....

Life, Liberty and ....

5.3 The contrasting pair (or *antithesis*)

The *contrasting pair* (or *antithesis*) is a structure containing two parts (and as such can be considered a subcategory of bicolon) which are parallel in structure but at the same time somehow opposed in meaning. One celebrated example is the statement uttered by Neil Armstrong as he became the first man to set foot on the Moon's surface:

> One small step for a man,
> one giant leap for mankind

in which the two parts have a similar structure but 'small' contrasts in meaning with 'giant', 'step' contrasts with 'leap', and 'for a [single] man' with 'for [all of] mankind'. A most unusual but effective example is the following, containing a string of contrasting binomials:

> So they [the Government] go on in strange paradox, decided only to be undecided, resolved to be irresolute, adamant for drift, solid for fluidity, all-powerful to be impotent.
>
> (Churchill 1936)

and Donald Trump chose to use a series of such contrasts to set the tone of his inauguration speech in 2017, setting the so-called political elite against 'you, the people':

> For too long, a small group in our nation's capital has reaped the rewards of government while the people have borne the cost. Washington flourished, but the people did not share in its wealth. Politicians prospered, but the jobs left and the factories closed. The establishment protected itself, but not the citizens of our country. Their victories have not been your victories. Their triumphs have not been your triumphs. And while they celebrated in our nation's capital, there was little to celebrate for struggling families all across our land.
>
> (Trump 2017)

TASK 5: *Who said what (2)?*

The authors of the following five examples of contrasting pairs are: Margaret Thatcher when first elected as UK Prime Minister; President J.F. Kennedy; Nelson Mandela after being released from political imprisonment; Hillary Clinton, when campaigning against Barack Obama for the Democrat presidential nomination; and Martin Luther King. Can you match speaker to words? (Write the name in the space alongside each.)

Mankind must put an end to war, or war will put an end to mankind. (...)

I stand before you not as a prophet but as a humble servant of you, the people [. . .] We have waited too long for our freedom. We can no longer wait. (...). Note here that one contrastive pair is followed by another.

You campaign in poetry, you govern in prose (...............................)

Ask not what your country can do for you, Ask what you can do for your country (..)

Now is the time to lift our nation from the quicksands of racial injustice to the solid rock of brotherhood. (...)

While the following is a whole series of contrasting pairs:

Where there is discord, may we bring harmony.
Where there is error, may we bring truth.
Where there is doubt, may we bring faith.
Where there is despair, may we bring hope. (...............................)

Q1

The last example ('Where there is discord . . .') is a paraphrase of an older, celebrated text. Do you know which?

Q2

It was also revisited more recently by a world statesman:

In the struggle of the centuries, America learned that freedom is not the possession of one race.

With the power and the resources given to us, the United States seeks to bring peace where there is conflict, hope where there is suffering, and liberty where there is tyranny.

Who do you think the speaker was, and what actions was he or she seeking to justify?

The contrasting pair formula is highly suitable and much used in the discourse of bipartisan democracy to contrast 'them' and 'us'; for instance (Tony Blair, quoted in Beard 2000: 54):

We are the party of practical ideas today. The Tories are the party of outdated dogma.

We are the party of the decent, hardworking majority. The Tories the party of extremes.

We are the party that can unify the nation and bring it together. The Tories are the party that divide it.

Note that this extract is also a *tricolon*; it is *three* contrasting pairs in sequence. We might also note how this kind of structure creates non-conventional antonyms of the kind discussed in the previous Unit.

5.3.1 Chiasmus

The first quotation in Task 5, 'Mankind must put an end to war, or war will put an end to mankind' is an example of **chiasmus**, a special form of contrasting pairs where the elements of the first part are switched around in the second. Other examples include:

A pessimist sees the difficulty in every opportunity; an optimist sees the opportunity in every difficulty.

(Attributed to Churchill)

The press takes Trump literally, but not seriously. Voters take him seriously, but not literally.

(Zito, *The Atlantic* 2016)

Q3

There is another example of chiasmus in Task 5. Can you find it?

5.4 Oxymorons

The last structure we will look at here is the *oxymoron*, where two apparently contradictory elements are combined in a single word, phrase or epigram; for example, *bittersweet, a deafening silence, noble savage, being cruel to be kind*. Note how, very often, the opposition between the elements is evaluative, as in the last two examples: *savage* or *cruel* are bad, while *noble* or *kind* are good. Examples of oxymorons from politics might include *radical conservative, extreme moderate* or *left-wing* (or *red*) *fascist*.

The term 'oxymoron' is often used to make an argument by negatively evaluating some entity, by suggesting that the two components are incompatible:

> Mr Adams confirmed in my presence as recently as last week that he did not, and would never, recognise British justice, which he described as an **oxymoron**.
> (Baroness Park of Monmouth, House of Lords 2005)

'British justice' is negatively evaluated and portrayed as an oxymoron because the speaker, Gerry Adams the president of Sinn Fein, feels that the British judicial system is unfair. The function is similar to that of the non-canonical opposition seen in the previous Unit in that the speaker is creating a contrast for argumentative purposes.

Similarly:

> There may be people--there may even be people in this House–who are so cynical as to suggest that business ethics is an **oxymoron**.
> (Borrie, House of Lords 1996)

The speaker is suggesting that some people – cynics as he calls them – evaluate all business as unethical. This comment from *The New Yorker* magazine:

> The United Kingdom is an **oxymoron**.
> (*The New Yorker* 2016)

followed the Brexit Referendum in which a slim majority voted to leave the European Union and served to highlight the reality of the divisions within the UK, since the leave vote was higher in England and Wales, but in Scotland the remain vote was higher.

TASK 6: *Can you explain what the use of oxymoron is doing in the examples below (all taken from UK newspapers)?*

a) To some, the radical centre may seem to be just an **oxymoron** – a political equivalent of a humble barrister, the open marriage, military intelligence. But is there substance to this increasingly influential notion? (*Guardian* 2005)

b) I don't deny Oona is ambitious – an unambitious MP is surely an **oxymoron** – but her ambitions have been focused on helping improve her constituents' lives over the past eight years. (*Guardian* 2005)

c) That there is such a thing as 'celebrity culture' – an **oxymoron** if ever there was one … (*Observer* 2005)

d) They want to continue amassing fortunes in China's booming 'socialist-market economy' – an **oxymoron** dreamed up by Peking's gerontocrats. (*Telegraph* 1993)

e) Church democracy is an **oxymoron** for Roman Catholics. The Pope decides and we obey – or face the wrath of those who run God's business address on earth. (*Guardian* 1993)

Extension task

Go to the free corpus of UK parliamentary debates at http://www.hansard-corpus.org/

Search for the term 'oxymoron' and note what contrast the speaker is trying to create.

5.5 Rhetorical figures in times gone by: liberty, freedom and emancipation

In the following sections and the next Unit we will look at the language and the messages it communicates in three of the most famous documents in US political history. One is a written work and two are speeches. Here we concentrate on the *Declaration of Independence* and Frederick Douglass's *Fourth of July* speech. The third text, Martin Luther King's Lincoln Memorial speech (*I Have a Dream*), will be analysed in Unit 7. The three have many links: they each have the pursuit of 'liberty' as one of their themes, the second and third both make explicit intertextual reference to the first, as if the authors saw themselves as natural heirs of the previous ones. All three have made a considerable contribution to the way Americans see themselves and probably how the world sees America. But they also have very different emphases.

5.6 The *Declaration of Independence*

In Unit 2, we looked at how the grammatical features of the US *Declaration of Independence* made it an effective piece of persuasive propaganda. In this section we examine some of the other language features of the document.

The *Declaration* was drafted by Thomas Jefferson, later to be acknowledged as one of the Founding Fathers of the nation, and subsequently revised by a drafting committee set up by Congress and ratified by the same in 1776. Although Jefferson says he wrote the document using 'neither book nor pamphlet' it is not entirely original and in particular contains traces of the *Bill of Rights*, composed in England in 1689, which lays out the rights of (property-owning) subjects. Although entitled *Declaration*, the actual 'declaration' comes only in the very last paragraph, the previous twenty-two – some consisting of a single sentence – are a long justification for the act of rebellion. As mentioned in Unit 2, the dispute over secession/independence, later called 'the American Revolution', was a bitter one. The British government felt the 'rebels' were disloyal, opportunistic and ungrateful, since the British had recently (1755–1760) fought a bloody and costly war in North America against the French to defend the colonists. The authors of the *Declaration*, for their part, resented the lack of consultation and outside interference in their affairs. The war itself was partly one of liberation, partly a civil war, with American colonists fighting on both sides. This explains why the overall tone of the document is both accusatory – of the King of Great Britain – and defensive, a justification of secession. When the war was over, however, the Revolution and the *Declaration* were soon seen by many Americans as part of the 'manifest destiny' of the moral and material supremacy of the nation. As Jefferson himself declared:

> Old Europe will have to lean on our shoulders and to hobble along by our side, under the monkish trammels of priests and kings, as she can. What a Colossus we shall be!
>
> (Jefferson 1816)

Although the rhetoric of freedom of the *Declaration* is inspiring, it contains more than a touch of hypocrisy. Many American black slaves joined the pro-British side, and were freed from slavery. After the end of the war, those who could not escape to British Canada were sold back into slavery by the 'freedom-fighting' secessionists. Moreover, Jefferson and many of the Founding Fathers were themselves slave-owners (see Unit 4.3).

TASK 7: *Declaration 1: Free and Independent States*

Read the final paragraph of the document.

1) Why does the language feel so legalistic?
2) How would you describe the last few words?
3) Who do you think 'the Supreme Judge of the world' is? What other lexis relating to the same topic is present?

> We, therefore, the Representatives of the United States of America, in General Congress, assembled, appealing to the Supreme Judge of the world for the rectitude of our intentions, do, in the name, and

by authority of the good People of these Colonies, solemnly publish and declare, That these United Colonies are, and of Right ought to be Free and Independent States; that they are Absolved from all Allegiance to the British Crown, and that all political connection between them and the State of Great Britain, is and ought to be totally dissolved; and that as Free and Independent States, they have full power to levy War, conclude Peace, contract Alliances, establish Commerce, and to do all other Acts and Things which Independent States may of right do. And for the support of this Declaration, with a firm reliance on the Protection of Divine Providence, we mutually pledge to each other our Lives, our Fortunes and our sacred Honor.

TASK 8: *Declaration 2: Declare the Causes*

The most celebrated segment of the document, however, is the opening.

1) Here is the first paragraph. Again, God is mentioned. How do the authors see God and their own relation with him?
2) Is the language passionate or detached? How do the secessionists refer to themselves? What motives for their actions do the authors give here? What impression do items like 'necessary', 'require' and 'impel' give the reader?

   When in the Course of human events, it becomes necessary for one people to dissolve the political bands which have connected them with another, and to assume among the Powers of the earth, the separate and equal station to which the Laws of Nature and of Nature's God entitle them, a decent respect to the opinions of mankind requires that they should declare the causes which impel them to the separation.

TASK 9: *Declaration 3: Inalienable Rights*

The beginning of the second paragraph is particularly memorable.

1) Does it contain any binomial expressions, bicolons or three-part lists?
2) Is anything implied about the actions and nature of the (British) government?

We hold these truths to be self-evident, that all men are created equal, that they are endowed by their Creator with certain unalienable Rights, that among these are Life, Liberty, and the pursuit of Happiness. That to secure these rights, Governments are instituted among Men, deriving their just powers from the consent of the governed. That whenever any Form of Government becomes destructive of these ends, it is the Right of the People to alter or to abolish it, and to institute new Government, having its foundation on such principles and organizing its powers in such form, as to them shall seem most likely to effect their Safety and Happiness.

As was said earlier, the *Declaration* has made a considerable contribution to the way Americans see themselves This is part of the reply given by Barack Obama, during the 2008 election campaign, to the question 'What does "patriotism" mean to you?' Note also the complex use of binomials, bicolons and tricolons:

> When I was a child, I lived overseas for a time with my mother. And one of my earliest memories is of her reading to me the first lines of the *Declaration of Independence*, explaining how its ideas applied to every American, black and white and brown alike.
>
> We are a nation of strong and varied convictions and beliefs. We argue and debate our differences vigorously and often. But when all is said and done, we still come together as one people and pledge our allegiance not just to a place on a map or a certain leader but to the words my mother read to me years ago: 'that all men are created equal, that they are endowed by their Creator with certain unalienable rights, that among these are Life, Liberty and the pursuit of Happiness.'
>
> (Obama 2008)

5.7 The rhetoric of anti-rhetoric: 'This Fourth of July is Yours, not Mine'

Frederick Douglass was born an African-American slave in Maryland, US, in 1818, but escaped to the northern states where he became a renowned campaigner for the abolition of slavery. In 1852, he was invited by the local dignitaries to address an Independence Day – Fourth of July – celebration in Rochester, New York, the seventy-sixth anniversary of the adoption of the *Declaration of Independence*. Few of his audience could have expected what he had to say. You can listen to a re-enactment of the full speech at: www.youtube.com/watch?v=L60475SRXkk. Note in this version, parts 7 and 8 are reversed.

'This Fourth of July is yours, not mine': Frederick Douglass, July 4, 1852 (edited)

1) Fellow citizens, pardon me, and allow me to ask, why am I called upon to speak here today? What have I or those I represent to do with your national independence? Are the great principles of political freedom and of natural justice, embodied in that Declaration of Independence, extended to us?

2) Such is not the state of the case. The rich inheritance of justice, liberty, prosperity, and independence bequeathed by your fathers is shared by you, not by me. The sunlight that brought life and healing to you has brought stripes and death to me. This Fourth of July is yours, not mine. You may rejoice, I must mourn.

3) Fellow citizens, above your national, tumultuous joy, I hear the mournful wail of millions, whose chains, heavy and grievous yesterday, are today rendered more intolerable by the jubilant shouts that reach them.

4) But I fancy I hear some of my audience say it is just in this circumstance that you and your brother Abolitionists fail to make a favorable impression on the public mind. Would you argue more and denounce less, would you persuade more and rebuke less, your cause would be much more likely to succeed. But, I submit, where all is plain there is nothing to be argued. What point in the anti-slavery creed would you have me argue? On what branch of the subject do the people of this country need light? Must I undertake to prove that the slave is a man? That point is conceded already. Nobody doubts it.

5) Would you have me argue that man is entitled to liberty? That he is the rightful owner of his own body? You have already declared it. Must I argue the wrongfulness of slavery? Is that a question for republicans? Is it to be settled by the rules of logic and argumentation, as a matter beset with great difficulty, involving a doubtful application of the principle of justice, hard to understand? How should I look today in the presence of Americans, dividing and subdividing a discourse, to show that men have a natural right to freedom, speaking of it relatively and positively, negatively and affirmatively? To do so would be to make myself ridiculous, and to offer an insult to your understanding. There is not a man beneath the canopy of heaven who does not know that slavery is wrong for him.

6) What! Am I to argue that it is wrong to make men brutes, to rob them of their liberty, to work them without wages, to keep them ignorant of their relations to their fellow men, to beat them with sticks, to flay their flesh with the lash, to load their limbs with irons, to hunt them with dogs, to sell them at auction, to sunder their families, to knock out their teeth, to burn their flesh, to starve them into obedience and submission to their masters? Must I argue that a system thus marked with blood and stained with pollution is wrong?

7) At a time like this, scorching irony, not convincing argument, is needed. Oh! had I the ability, and could I reach the nation's ear, I would today pour out a fiery stream of biting ridicule, blasting reproach, withering sarcasm, and stern rebuke. For it is not light that is needed, but fire; it is not the gentle shower, but thunder. We need the storm, the whirlwind, and the earthquake. The feeling of the nation must be quickened; the conscience of the nation must be roused; the propriety of the nation must be startled; the

> hypocrisy of the nation must be exposed; and its crimes against God and man must be denounced.
>
> 8) What to the American slave is your Fourth of July? I answer, a day that reveals to him more than all other days of the year, the gross injustice and cruelty to which he is the constant victim. To him your celebration is a sham; your boasted liberty an unholy license; your national greatness, swelling vanity; your sounds of rejoicing are empty and heartless; your shouts of liberty and equality, hollow mock; your prayers and hymns, your sermons and thanksgivings, with all your religious parade and solemnity, are to him mere bombast, fraud, deception, impiety, and hypocrisy – a thin veil to cover up crimes which would disgrace a nation of savages. There is not a nation of the earth guilty of practices more shocking and bloody than are the people of these United States at this very hour.

TASK 10: *Frederick Douglass*

In this extraordinary speech, Douglass equates 'independence' with 'liberty' and subverts and exploits some of the very basic tenets of classical rhetoric (Unit 1.2).

1) How does he establish *ethos*, that is, his credentials for speaking and to be listened to?
2) How does he employ *logos*, that is, plausibly rational argumentation?
3) He makes at least two kinds of appeals to *pathos* or emotional argument. In which parts of the speech are they found and what are the emotions he appeals to?
4) Why does he talk about the need for 'scorching irony' and 'withering sarcasm'? Irony is used to point to a contradiction in evaluation (Unit 10). What are the contradictions he is referring to?
5) Douglass employs a good number of the creative repetitions and contrasts we have met in this Unit. You might like to re-read the text and examine the use he puts them to.

Further reading

Charteris-Black, J. (2013) *Analysing Political Speeches: Rhetoric, Discourse and Metaphor*, Basingstoke: Palgrave Macmillan.

Websites to explore

www.americanrhetoric.com
www.britishpoliticalspeech.org
www.nelsonmandela.org/content/page/speeches

Keys and commentaries

TASK 1(A): *Creative repetition*

The first sentence is repeated at the beginning of the third part. The theme of the phone is repeated several times, first as ringing and second as being answered. In the second part, we find the string *something . . . someone . . . someone,* as well as the couplet *knows the world's leaders, knows the military.*

The dramatic effect created is that of anxiety, fear of an unknown danger.

The implication is that this candidate can be trusted with the security of the State and your family, and that the other candidate cannot be.

The candidate who sponsored this ad was Hillary Clinton during the 2012 Democratic Party primaries campaign. The opponent who supposedly could not be trusted with your security was Barack Obama.

It is interesting that a female candidate chose to sponsor an ad with the theme of national security. One can presume that her campaign management wanted to counter any conscious or unconscious prejudice in the public that a woman might be 'weaker' on defence issues than a man.

TASK 1(B)

We will be a country of . . .; the people, those people, the same people (×3); love it (×3).

He implies that his adversaries in politics and the media are ignorant, inept and corrupt. The speaker is Trump.

TASK 2: *Binomials and bicolons*

Binomials are indicated in *italics*, bicolons in **bold** type:

The South Africa **so many** have sacrificed **so much** to achieve is within sight. **Together let us walk** this last, long gruelling mile to reach a *non-racial, non-sexist* society, where all our people will be equal before the law [. . .] **Together we have it in our power to defeat** those who continue to kill to maintain the old order. We **have it in our power to transform** our country into the *peaceful and prosperous* homeland of all our people. **Let us work together** to achieve these goals. **Let us vow** never to celebrate another Christmas in chains.

We have a right to be free, and we shall be free!

(Mandela 1990)

Note the two overlapping bicolons: *Together let us walk/Together we have it in our power. . .* and *we have it in our power to defeat/we have it in our power to transform.* There is also the exact repetition of *all our people.*

TASK 3: *Who said what (1)?*

- Government *of* the people, *by* the people, *for* the people. (Abraham Lincoln). This is often taken as the definition of democracy.
- We are one nation and their pain is our pain. Their dreams are our dreams. And their success will be our success. We share one heart, one home, and one glorious destiny. (Donald Trump)
- Friends, comrades and fellow South Africans. I greet you all in the name peace, democracy and freedom for all. (Nelson Mandela)
- This is not the end. It is not even the beginning of the end. But it is, perhaps, the end of the beginning. (Winston Churchill). 'This' was victory in the battle of El Alamein.

TASK 4: *Can you complete?*

- Liberté, Fraternité, Egalité. (Motto of the French Revolution)
- Bread, peace and land. (Lenin, a slogan used during the October Revolution)
- Life, Liberty and the Pursuit of Happiness. (The US *Declaration of Independence*, Jefferson)

TASK 5: *Who said what (2)?*

- Mankind must put an end to war, or war will put an end to mankind. (J.F. Kennedy)
- I stand before you not as a prophet but as a humble servant of you, the people [. . .] We have waited too long for our freedom. We can no longer wait. (Nelson Mandela)
- You campaign in poetry, you govern in prose (Hillary Clinton)
- Ask not what your country can do for you, Ask what you can do for your country. (J.F. Kennedy)
- Now is the time to lift our nation from the quicksands of racial injustice to the solid rock of brotherhood. (Rev Martin Luther King)
- Where there is discord, may we bring harmony [. . .]. (Margaret Thatcher)

Q1

Margaret Thatcher's speech was a paraphrase of the Prayer of St Francis of Assisi.

Q2

President George W. Bush, seeking to explain and justify military intervention in Afghanistan and Iraq.

Q3

Ask not what your country can do for you. Ask what you can do for your country.

TASK 6: *Oxymoron*

The writer in each example wishes to say that:

a) The radical centre may not be such a contradiction as it seems.
b) Politicians are by nature ambitious, but in Oona's case, in a positive way.
c) Celebrities tend to be intellectually superficial and have little grasp of real culture.
d) The writer believes that socialism and a real market economy are incompatible, and that the Chinese leaders, 'Peking's gerontocrats', are fooling either themselves or their people.
e) The Roman Catholic Church does not permit the same freedom of expression or of belief inherent in a true democracy.

TASK 7: *Declaration 1: Free and Independent States*

1) 1) and 2) One important reason it sounds so legalistic is the extensive use by Jefferson of *binomials*. These, as we said, are typical of legal language. Here we find 'in the name, and by authority of', 'publish and declare', 'Free and Independent', 'Acts and Things', as well as 'is/are and ought to be'.

2) The final sentence, in contrast and in climax, ends with a three-part expression, a *three-part list* or *tricolon*: 'our Lives, our Fortunes and our sacred Honor'. The effect of this is quite different from the binomials. Tricolon is extremely common in politics and rhetoric in general. As we noted, the simplest kind is mere repetition: 'education, education, education' (Tony Blair). Slightly more complex is three single items in a list: 'liberté, egalité, fraternité'. The kind we have here is more complicated and elegant. The first two items on the list are very similar – 'our' plus a noun – which sets up an expectation that the third will be the same. This expectation is upset because we actually see a variation: 'our' plus an adjective ('sacred') then the noun. There is

the implication too that, by crescendo, Honor is the most important of the three pledges to be given.

3) The 'Supreme Judge' is of course, God. Other religious lexis includes 'Divine Providence' and 'sacred'.

TASK 8: *Declaration 2: Declare the Causes*

1) The authors portray God as a rational rather than a mystical entity: a Judge, one who applies 'the Laws of Nature' and is, indeed, subservient to those Laws ('Nature's God'). He is, as it were, under a contractual duty to do his job properly and grant the authors' requests.

2) It seems very detached. The metaphor 'dissolve the bands' is a rather dispassionate description of what was a bloody and bitter war. The authors refer to themselves in the third person – 'one people', 'them' and so on. No motives as yet are provided, though there is a promise to list 'the causes' of the 'separation' (rather than the more colourful and negative 'rebellion'). In fact, there is no sense of volition on the part of the authors, they are acting out of necessity rather than desire. They are implying that they really have no choice but to rebel, hence the vocabulary items 'necessary', 'require' and 'impel'.

TASK 9: *Declaration 3: Inalienable Rights*

1) 'Safety and Happiness' is a binomial, while 'to alter or to abolish it' and 'having its foundation on such principles and organizing its powers in such form' are forms of bicolons.

'Life, Liberty and the pursuit of Happiness' is one of the most famous of all tricolons. The original document draft, in fact, contained 'property' instead of 'happiness'. The rethinking has fascinated historians and political scientists ever since.

2) The implication is, surely, that the British government is just such a one as indicated, has become 'destructive of [the] ends' to which it was appointed and therefore merits rejection.

TASK 10: *Frederick Douglass*

1) The first thing you do, said Aristotle, is to establish your *ethos*, to lay out your credentials for why you should be speaking and listened to. Douglass turns this on its head right at the start (paragraph 1), and asks his audience: what are my credentials, please tell me, to be speaking at your celebration? As long as there

are black slaves in this country, as a black man, I have no cause to speak in celebration of your liberties.

2) The middle part of the speech is a set of skilful rational arguments to argue that rational argument is irrelevant – using *logos* to defeat *logos* – because the truth is that his case is self-evident (paragraph 4: 'where all is plain there is nothing to be argued'). What is needed is not the 'light' of reason, but the 'fire' of *pathos*, emotion.

3) One emotional appeal is pity for the slaves (paragraph 6), this is quickly followed by the 'thunder' and the 'storm' of anger, the 'blasting reproach' and 'stern rebuke' for those who tolerate slavery (paragraph 7).

4) The 'scorching irony' and 'withering sarcasm' is for those, including the people listening, who cannot see the glaring contra-dictions that (a) seventy-six years after the *Declaration of Independence* there is still slavery in the US, that (b) this day of *your* freedom is the very darkest day for those still in chains and (c) inviting a black man to celebrate when his fellows are enslaved is 'hollow mock' and 'deception, impiety, and hypocrisy'.

5) Free response.

6 The importance of importance marking in persuasion

I hate to put a little pressure on you but the fate of the Republic rests on your shoulders. The fate of the world is teetering and you, North Carolina, are going to have to make sure that we push it in the right direction.

(Barack Obama 2016)

6.1 The marking of importance

One striking feature of political speeches is the frequency of *importance* or *relevance* marking as a means of capturing the audience's attention, of emphasising that what is being said is both important in itself and relevant to the lives of their listeners. The aim of this Unit, then, is to examine how speakers mark the importance of what they are saying to their audience both at local and more macro levels in a particular discourse type.

Most of the examples in this Unit have been taken from the TED talks website (www.ted.com/talks). TED talks are speeches delivered, as the website tells us, at worldwide conferences, which bring together the world's most fascinating thinkers and doers, who are challenged to give the 'talk of their lives'. The talks are filmed and can be seen online or downloaded free to users in both mp3 and mp4 format. They are accompanied both by translated subtitles and by transcripts, frequently in a wide variety of languages, including many non-European languages. The speakers come from a wide variety of fields, including science and technology, economics and business, environmentalism, politics and international development. We will be concentrating, here, on talks addressing the latter two of these. Although using TED talks for examples, the points made in this Unit can be generalised to all kinds of political language. Duguid (2007), for example, shows how in interactive discourse in a political judicial enquiry both questioners and witnesses foreground information not only in order to proclaim its importance but also to refocus the discussion for strategic rhetorical advantage.

6.2 Text-oriented importance marking

One kind of importance marking is called 'text-oriented' or *endophoric* ('inward-leading') and the other is called 'real-world oriented' or *exophoric* ('outward-leading') (Thompson and Hunston 2000: 24).

The first kind, text-oriented, indicates that what the speaker is about to say (cataphoric marking, from *cataphora*, leading ahead) – or has just said (anaphoric marking, from *anaphora*, leading behind) – is a key point in the development of their talk. 'Here's the key question . . .' (from a talk given by Yasheng Huang, the Chinese economist), is a straightforward cataphoric importance marker. The second sentence in 'India will be the only country in the world to have this demographic dividend. And this is very important' (Nilekani) is an anaphoric importance marker. 'But having said that, we come to what I call ideas in progress' (Nilekani) begins with an anaphora and continues with a cataphora. 'And that's what I want to focus on' (Sarandon), 'Let me say that again' (Enriques) are also looking forward and backwards at the same time.

These markers can also sometimes be in the form of:

- suggestions/instructions to the audience, e.g. 'I think it's really important to understand that something like this is totally open' (Neuwirth)
- a personal judgment, e.g. 'Now, I believe this is an interesting way of looking at it' (Nilekani)
- include a comment on oneself, e.g. 'And here's where I begin to get worried'
- announcing the beginning of a list, e.g. 'And there are two key things it's got to do. One is it's got to do economic reform [. . .]' (Collier)

The opening sections of a talk are often introduced by a cataphoric importance marker, for example:

> What I want to do this morning is share with you a couple of stories and talk about a *different* Africa.
>
> (Okonjo-Iweala 2007)

and closing sequences might have an anaphoric reference to what has gone before:

> [. . .] and I just wanted to give that context of what's going on in their minds, not what necessarily is going on in yours.
>
> (Chang 2012)

TASK 1

Are the following excerpts anaphoric, backward-looking to something already said or cataphoric to something about to be said, or do they do both, look forwards and backwards in the text?

a) Now the problem is that we're not thinking about it in very innovative ways. (Nye)
b) And by the way, mistrust was always very important for democracy. This is why you have checks and balances. (Krastev)
c) That's cool thing number one. Cool thing number two is [. . .] (Tandon)
d) Just how important are infrastructures for economic growth? This is a key issue. (Yasheng Huang)

6.3 'Real-world' importance marking

The second kind of marking stresses how the *topic* the speaker is expounding has importance in the real world we live in. We have already mentioned how TED speakers are under special pressure to impress upon the audience the importance of their own particular work, and exophoric importance marking is by far the more common type. For example, in the following extracts speakers use the word *key* and *important* to highlight the importance of some entity:

> And then the third **key** actor is the post-conflict government. And there are two **key** things it's got to do. One is it's got to do economic reform [. . .]
>
> (Collier 2009)

> [. . .] in the modern age, where everything is connected to everything, the **most important thing** about what you can do is what you can do with others. *The* **most important bit** about your structure is your docking points, your interconnectors, your capacity to network with others.
>
> (Ashdown 2012)

Other ways of stressing importance include intensifying evaluative lexis, what Duguid calls 'positive and amplified evaluation' (2010: 120–123):

> Just look what they have done. It's an **amazing** improvement, from seven children per woman, they've gone all the way down to between four and five. It's a **tremendous** improvement.
>
> (Rosling 2012)

as well as standard emphasisers, like *extraordinary, really, truly,* and so on, often accompanied by evaluative lexis (our emphasis):

> And this is part of a **really extraordinary** phenomenon, and that is the end of the Great Divergence [between the West and the rest of the world].
>
> (Ferguson 2011)

Notable too is the employment of importance emphasisers of *uniqueness* and of *unique frequency,* such as *ever, suddenly, every, only, first, no,* and so on:

> **Suddenly** and for the **very first time,** collective defense, the thing that has dominated us as the concept of securing our nations, is no longer enough.
>
> (Ashdown 2012)

> That's what we're seeing across the bottom billion at the moment. The best growth rates they've had – **ever.**
>
> (Rosling 2012)

Recurrent too, is the use of superlatives (a form of grammatical evaluation, see Unit 2) – another kind of emphasis of uniqueness. Superlatives often appear in a lexical template like *the (single) *est [. . . .] in the world/you've ever seen,* and so on, again often alongside explicitly positively evaluated lexis, for example:

> And this is the **single** *most exciting adventure* that we have ever been on. It's the **single** *greatest* mapping project we've *ever* been on.
>
> (Enriquez 2015)

> Slowly it was dawning on me that these handbags were made by their factory, and **every single one of them** was authentic.
>
> (Chang 2012)

> The rise of English [. . .] has contributed to why India is today growing at rates it has **never seen before.**
>
> (Nilekani 2009)

The expression *the real* is used as an importance marker, functioning by contrasting one entity, behaviour, project with another – *the real* one – a reflection at the microstructure level of the false versus true contrast found as one type of talk macrostructure (Unit 3.2.2), for example:

> And so, **the real** question to pose is not, 'Can we be optimistic?' It's, 'How can we give credible hope to that billion people?'
>
> (Collier 2009)

> **The real** question is, how can markets be developed in rural Africa
> to harness the power of innovation and entrepreneurship that we
> know exists?
>
> (Gabre Mahdi 2007)

Necessity, need, and desire, wanting, are also forms of importance:

> But the problem is, we **need** more and more support for these ideas
> and cases.
>
> (McCue 2012)

> [. . .] and the **urgent need** that we have, that we all feel today, to
> redesign the flow of our institutions.
>
> (Noveck 2012)

But relevance/importance marking in these talks goes well beyond
the use of single words; often whole sentences are pointing out the
importance of the speaker's topic. Opening ('exordium') and closing
('peroration') sequences are common sites of topic importance
marking (Swales 1990). One TED talk speaker begins by openly
expressing the hope of changing the way his audience thinks about his
topic (recycling plastic):

> I hope, within the next 10 minutes, to change the way you think
> about a lot of the stuff in your life.
>
> (Biddle 2011)

and ends with the hope that he has also changed the way his audience
members actually see themselves, not as consumers but as re-users.

Yet another form of importance marking is the appeal to personal
relevance:

> And lastly, what are you going to do to be part of this partnership
> of aid, government, private sector and the African as an individual?
> (Okonjo-Iweala 2007)

> Nobody thinks there's opportunity. But I'm standing here saying
> that those who miss the boat now, will miss it forever.
> (Okonjo-Iweala 2007)

We also find topic-importance marking by the mention of 'big
numbers' as in the following talk opening:

> Let's talk about billions. Let's talk about past and future billions.
> We know that about 106 billion people have ever lived [. . .] And we

also know that most of them were or are very poor. Let's talk about the 195,000 billion dollars of wealth in the world today.

(Ferguson 2011)

Finally, we might note how the rhetorical devices (sometimes called rhetorical 'flourishes') examined in Unit 5 are also frequently used to sound momentous. A bicolon like 'the manacles of segregation and the chains of discrimination' or a tricolon like 'Life, Liberty and the pursuit of Happiness' or a contrasting pair like 'One small step for a man; a giant leap for mankind' or 'Now is the time to lift our nation from the quicksands of racial injustice to the solid rock of brotherhood' are all employed to lend importance to the topic in hand.

TASK 2(A): *The Indian economy*

Nilekani, the Indian economist, deploys two types of importance marking in this extract. What are they?

> Why does what's happening 10 thousand miles away matter to all of you? Number one, this matters because this represents more than a billion people, 1/6th of the world population. It matters because this is a democracy. And it is important to prove that growth and democracy are not incompatible. (Nilekani 2009)

TASK 2(B): *The Good News you don't Hear about Diseases*

Comment on the importance marking in the following text on global health. What special effects does the writer employ?

> Not all diseases are retreating [. . .] But overall the tropical world is seeing the same huge retreat of infectious death that happened in the temperate world during the previous century.
> And nobody seems terribly interested. Why is this? You can understand why journalists don't tell good news stories more often; their motto, after all, is: 'If it bleeds, it leads.'
> But why are public health officials not keener to blow their own trumpets? It is, after all, the hard work of dedicated professionals, backed up by millions of volunteers and funded by generous philanthropists, that is driving these contagions out.
> Here's where I turn a touch cynical. A few years ago, maternal mortality — that is, death among women giving birth — began to fall fast, having stagnated for a decade or so. The editor of The Lancet recounted how he came under co-ordinated and determined pressure

> from [campaigners] to delay publication of the news of this fall in maternal mortality because, said those pressurising him, 'good news would detract from the urgency of their cause'. Aha.
>
> (Ridley 2014)

TASK 2(C): *The Global Power Shift*

Listen to the first 2 minutes 22 seconds, or read the first four paragraphs and the first sentence of the fifth of the transcript of the beginning of the TED talk 'The Global Power Shift' by Paddy Ashdown: https://tinyurl.com/PiP-Ashdown

What effects does he use to build a sense of importance, suspense and even foreboding?

Further reading

Duguid, A. (2007) 'Soundbiters bit: Contracted dialogistic space and the textual relations of the No. 10 team analysed through corpus assisted discourse studies', in N. Fairclough, G. Cortese and P. Ardizzone (eds.) *Discourse and Contemporary Social Change*, Bern: Peter Lang, 73–94.

Partington, A. (2013) 'The marking of importance in "Enlightentainment" talks', in M. Gotti and D. Giannoni (eds.) *Corpus Analysis for Descriptive and Pedagogical Purposes*, Bern: Peter Lang, 143–166.

Keys and commentaries

TASK 1

(a) cataphoric, (b) anaphoric, (c) both anaphoric and cataphoric, (d) both anaphoric and cataphoric. Questions are clearly cataphoric in looking ahead to an answer, and an answer is generally anaphoric in looking back to the question.

TASK 2(A): *The Indian economy*

Importance marking by (a) personal relevance to his audience and (b) big numbers. Note also that he begins by asking two questions, which by their nature are cataphoric, they look forward to being answered.

TASK 2(B): *The Good News you don't Hear about Diseases*

The writer uses the evaluative intensifier *huge* to describe the retreat of tropical disease mortality. He twice draws attention to how important *he* thinks this is by asking questions: why others give it so little attention 'And nobody seems terribly interested. Why is this?' and 'But why are public health officials not keener to blow their own trumpets?', that is, to broadcast their important achievements.

To introduce his explanation, he first makes a cataphoric importance-marking, ironic self-reference (see 6.3 above), 'Here's where I turn a touch cynical'. The very final word, the exclamation 'Aha', is itself marking the importance of his supposed discovery.

TASK 2(C): *The Global Power Shift*

Both paragraphs one and two open with a suspense-building cataphoric expression, 'There's a poem . . .' and 'But what Housman understood . . .'. Notice that the poet is 'very famous' (intensifying) and the poem supposedly echoed in the brain of a famous important personage, Churchill (though no evidence is given for this). Another famous person, Mao, is mentioned later on, for no particular reason other than his general importance. Another cataphoric expression of importance is slipped into the second paragraph, 'And my message for you is . . .'.

The passage is peppered with lexis of turbulence, violence – *blood* is mentioned three times – and intense fear, *terrifying*, 'we are *condemned*'.

Ashdown also uses rhythmic devices for importance marking. He introduces short phrases to slow down the rhythm and build up suspense, e.g. 'and all too often', 'and we see it very clearly today', 'by the way' and 'ladies and gentlemen' (twice). He also uses a number of the rhetorical devices discussed in Unit 5 to maintain the slow rhythm, namely, bicolons 'the old nations, the old powers of Europe' and 'the one [World War] in the first part and the one in the second part' (which is not strictly accurate, they were both in the first half of the century), tricolons 'long, hot, silvan summers' and 'highly turbulent times, highly difficult times, and all too often very bloody times' and contrast: *stability* and *turbulence*.

Finally, he concludes his introduction with the anaphoric importance marking, 'we live at one of those [turbulent, difficult, bloody] times'.

7 Metaphors and company: the subtle persuaders

Omnis comparatio claudicat.

(Latin proverb)

Many forms of persuasive discourse contain large numbers of figures of speech largely because they are commonly used to make arguments by *comparison* or **analogy** or supposed *resemblance*. We might recall from Unit 3 that comparison/contrast was one of the major models of persuasion and was classified as one of the more rational types. However, argument by analogy is often, as we shall see, 'pseudo-rational' at best. The kinds of figures we will concentrate on here include **metaphor**, **simile** and **metonymy**.

7.1 Metaphors

The following dictionary definition of metaphor:

> A figure of speech in which a name or quality is attributed to something to which it is not literally applicable, e.g. 'an icy glance', 'nerves of steel'.

(Yerkes 1989)

highlights the 'non-literalness' of metaphors. They are, first of all, a pretence, a kind of play on words. Another definition of metaphor provides a clue as to why people indulge in metaphorical wordplay. Metaphors involve:

> understanding and experiencing one kind of thing in terms of another
> (Lakoff and Johnson 1980: 10)

Very frequently metaphors involve 'understanding and experiencing' – and communicating – something abstract in terms of something more concrete.

Metaphor is a basic part of the way we both see the world and explain it to others. For example, we often talk of making an **argument** in terms of going on a **journey**: we take *one step at a time*, if we *lose our way* we are likely to *go round in circles* and so on. Or we often talk of **ideas** or **theories** as **buildings**: *Is that the foundation for your theory?*; *his argument collapsed; we need to support the theory with solid arguments* (Lakoff and Johnson 1980). We can call these metaphors which can be realised in many ways 'general metaphors' (the term 'conceptual metaphor' is also often used).

Q1

What do you think is the general metaphor behind the following: *I've invested a lot of time in it; it's a waste of time; I saved a lot of time by planning properly; Is that worth your while?*

In recent times one much discussed metaphor is *war on terror*. Or perhaps it is better described as half metaphorical and half literal. If we look at what words collocate with the phrase *war on* we can see that there is a mix of literal, semi-metaphorical and metaphorical uses. The following were frequently cited as objects of *war on* in a US newspaper corpus from 2015:

> War on ... terror, terrorism, cancer, drugs, poverty, al Qaeda, (organised) crime, Egypt's Christians, the Islamic State, obesity, the western world

---

Q2

Which do you think are literal and which are metaphorical? (Free response)

The metaphorical expression *war on* is also used as a rhetorical weapon. In the US, conservative opponents of so-called 'planned parenthood', that is, relatively open access to contraception and abortion, have been accused by their opponents of conducting a 'war on women'. Members of the US coal industry accused President Obama of conducting a 'war on coal'. Religious conservatives are said to fear that secularists are going to conduct a 'war on Christmas' (all *New York Times* 2015).

7.1.1 How metaphors work

One traditional explanation of how metaphors function runs as follows. A certain quality (we shall call this the *basis* of the resemblance),

Table 7.1 How metaphors work

Metaphor	Target	Source	Basis of the resemblance?	Evaluation
Richard the Lion-Heart	Richard	The lion's heart	Courage, strength, etc.	Good
Sally is a block of ice	Sally	Block of ice	Coldness	Bad
Putin the Grandmaster	Putin	Chess master	Calculating	Depends on context

supposed to belong to an entity (the *source*), is re-applied or transferred to another entity (the *target*), which is usually of a very different type from the source. Finally, metaphors always express an *evaluation* (Unit 2) of the target in terms of good or bad, praise or blame, and so on, which is why they are so useful in persuasive argument. This can be seen in Table 7.1.

In the first metaphor, the source, the lion's heart, is commonly associated with strength and courage. These qualities are transferred to Richard and act as the grounds of the supposed resemblance between Richard and a lion. The two entities involved are very different in that one is human, the other an animal. Since courage is a good thing, Richard – the target – is evaluated very positively.

In the second, the source, a block of ice, is commonly associated with coolness. This quality is transferred to Sally and acts as the basis of the supposed resemblance between her and the ice. The two entities involved are very different in that one is human, the other inanimate. Note that there is a metaphor within the metaphor: the physical cold of the ice becomes the emotional coolness of the person. This is possible because we conventionally associate emotions with warmth and lack of them with cold. Since we generally appreciate the former, warmth, Sally is probably being evaluated negatively.

In the third, 'Putin the Grandmaster', politics is likened to a game of chess. Here the basis is quite complicated. Is the quality being transferred from chess its complexity, the need for great skill or the fact that there is a winner and a loser? Perhaps all three.

Try to fill in the following for the metaphor *Juliet is the sun* (from, of course, *Romeo and Juliet*).

You might have had some doubt about the precise basis of the resemblance. Are the sun and Juliet both supposed to be hot? Do they both give light? Or is it that Romeo needs them both to live? Probably all of these. What is important is that the evaluation of Juliet is most definitely good. From this, we see once again that one of the main purpose of metaphors is to express an evaluation.

Part of what makes metaphor so powerful in persuading people is that this process of comparison is not fully conscious. In recent

Table 7.2 Juliet is the sun

Metaphor	Target	Source	Basis of the resemblance?	Evaluation
Juliet is the sun				

experimental work, Hart (forthcoming) has shown that the presence/absence of different metaphors in texts affects how people evaluate the events.

Q3

Read the following extract from a conservative US politician speaking in favour of an English-only language policy (discussed in Lawton 2013).

---

1) What is the main evaluation that the speaker wants to make?
2) How many metaphors can you identify?

> When our ancestors came to America, they came to this country knowing they had to learn English to survive. Today, our melting pot has become a patchwork quilt of cultures, isolated because they cannot speak English. They aren't assimilating into our society like our ancestors did. Our current bilingual policies are shredding the common bond that has made our nation great. By making it easy for those who come to America, we have ripped the heart out of our national unity.
>
> (US Congressman Joe Knollenberg 1996)

The power of metaphor (and its danger) is that the grounds are implicit, not stated openly. This has two consequences. First, different people can interpret the same metaphor in different ways. Second, it makes the supposed resemblance more difficult to challenge or deny. It would sound perverse or at least mean-spirited to respond, 'no Juliet isn't like the sun' or 'what do you mean "like the sun"?' And yet, a metaphor is really an opinion dressed up in fine clothing (a metaphor itself). In the following, the speaker refers explicitly to the possibility of metaphor to confuse matters:

> [On Iraq] we have to make sure we are clear. We cannot use metaphors. We cannot allow the Department of Defense nor this White House [. . .] to wiggle out of the tough questions.
>
> (US Congressman Robert Scott 2003)

Having said this, however, politicians and political journalists are wily and skilled users of language and any use of colourful language, including metaphors, on the part of an opponent or interlocutor is likely to come under close scrutiny and may even be challenged in some way, as in this episode in a White House briefing:

> MR. FLEISCHER: [. . .] let me put it to you this way; the President is going the last mile for diplomacy. We shall see if the other nations on the Security Council are willing to entertain that last mile. We shall see.
>
> Q: Is the last mile 10 days long?
>
> (White House briefing 2003)

7.1.2 Metaphor and irony

Moreover, rather than challenge openly the 'truth' or appropriateness of another speaker's metaphor, one further frequent tactic is to take it and use it against them, a technique which can be very successful, as illustrated by another White House briefings question about the environment posed during the George W. Bush administration:

> Q: Ari, with respect, there are some people who don't quite see it that way, and they were out there this morning, talking about some of the rollbacks in arsenic, his reversal on carbon dioxide [. . .] *they said that the President came to town saying that he would change the climate in Washington; we didn't know that it was the actual climate that he was talking about.* (Laughter) And I'm wondering if the White House is concerned that they're giving the Democrats a very big stick with which to whack the President between now and a year November.
>
> (White House briefing 2001)

The phrase *change the climate*, originally intended metaphorically as the political climate, is reinterpreted to refer to the physical climate, the air we breathe. This is in fact a pun, that is, a play on words, and puns very often convert a metaphorical phrase into its concrete equivalent. The journalist here manages to, first of all, amuse his audience and perhaps win their support, second to make a sarcastic joke at the President's expense and, finally, to make a serious political point.

One US election campaign poster mixed metaphor and **irony** in a highly effective way. Obama was pictured looking into the distance, with a halo around his head and the caption: 'The Obamessiah'. The poster was issued by anti-Obama Republican supporters. The metaphor is of course 'Obama is the Messiah, the Saviour'. However, the evaluation of the apparent message, as in all irony, is reversed in the real, implied message, in this case from the outwardly positive to the inwardly negative. There are of course two targets to the sarcastic irony. First

Table 7.3 Political metaphors

Metaphor	Target	Source	Basis of the resemblance?	Evaluation
A puppet government				
Sunshine government				
Crusade against terror				

Obama, for his supposedly exaggerated self-belief and second, his supporters, who adulate him as divine.

TASK 1: *Political metaphors*

Complete Table 7.3.

Sport and war

Beard (2000) notes how sport and war are two areas of experience which are frequently raided to obtain political metaphors, for example:

Sport: *the gloves are off, to play ball, first-past-the-post* system, the election *front-runner*, 'it's time for America to see *a winning season* again' (Mitt Romney 2012);

War: *bombarded with questions, take flak*, election *battle*, to *marshal the troops*.

However, paradoxically, when *real* war is being discussed, we often find euphemistic (Unit 4) metaphors:

lost in action, caught in the cross-fire, collateral damage, [civilians killed when caught between fighting forces], *ethnic cleansing* [extermination, genocide], *administrative detention* [imprisonment without charge or trial], *enhanced interrogation* [torture], *military involvement, incursion* [attacking with tanks and planes], *air campaign* [aircraft bombing], *friendly-fire* [death inadvertently caused to one's own troops], *Operation Infinite Justice* [the war in Afghanistan, 2002].

Euphemistic metaphors like these are not always adopted uncritically by the media as illustrated in the story of a US attaché, Colonel Opfer, who complained to the press reporters during the Vietnam War that:

You always write it's bombing, bombing, bombing. It's not bombing. It's *air support*.

(Colonel Opfer 1974)

In the following, on the other hand, a politician complains openly about their use:

> Is it not possible to drop this absurd military euphemism 'friendly-fire'? All fire that kills or injures is hostile, even if it comes from an allied weapon.
>
> (Tony Banks, House of Commons 1992)

TASK 2: *Metaphors of anti-Americanism*

As seen above, general metaphors can be expressed in many different ways; that is, the metaphor IDEAS ARE BUILDINGS or WAR IS A SPORT, can have lots of different realisations. Look at the following sentences referring to anti-Americanism, can you group the sentences into expressions of four general metaphors? What sort of evaluation, positive or negative, does each of the general metaphors express? Which is the odd one out in these four general metaphors?

a) The Chiracs and the Schröders are riding a wave of anti-Americanism that they have done nothing to discourage. (*Telegraph*)

b) Meanwhile, the US ambassador to London has rejected suggestions that the outpouring of sympathy in Britain when the World Trade Centre fell has given way to a tide of anti-Americanism. (*Observer*)

c) This is not to deny the existence of a deep current of anti-Americanism in this Muslim country of 140 million. (*New York Times*)

d) For the time being, the new American order has generated a tsunami of anti-Americanism, with the United States perceived in some quarters as a greater threat to world peace than Al Qaeda. (*New York Times*)

e) It is a timely antidote to the more thoughtless strains of anti-Americanism prevalent today. (*Times*)

f) It's a shame, but not surprising, that the virus of anti-Americanism has infected the Olympics. (*Washington Post*)

g) British schools should devote less time to Hitler and more to understanding America – except that too many teachers are probably infected with the anti-Americanism that they ought to be working to eradicate. (*Independent*)

h) Now is a particularly bad time to embark on a dispute that will inflame anti-Americanism in Europe. (*Financial Times*)

i) But the White House knows full well that only if there is progress towards an equitable Middle East settlement and a viable Palestinian state, will one of the main factors fuelling anti-Americanism and Islamic extremism across the region be removed. (*Independent*)

j)   Some privately owned TV stations licensed by the AKP have entered
     the market with programmes using thinly disguised religious messages
     and series that fan the fires of anti-Americanism and anti-Semitism.
     (*Times*)

k)   But it is not only pessimists who believe the opposite is more
     likely: that a war in Iraq will stoke the fires of fundamentalism
     and anti-Americanism. (*Financial Times*)

l)   By using the language of advertising to undermine its principles,
     DeLillo has inspired a thousand theses, but he has also been
     bizarrely accused of anti-Americanism. (*Guardian*)

m)   His 'USA' films have incited reproachful accusations of pinko
     anti-Americanism. (*Independent*)

n)   Perhaps partly to disarm the charge of anti-Americanism, Mr. Newman
     also sang 'Follow the Flag,' which registered as an outright patriotic
     hymn. (*New York Times*)

o)   Now, after 30 years abroad, I find myself in *the dock once again
     for the thought-crime of 'anti-Americanism'*. (*Guardian*)

7.1.3 The dangers of metaphors: how a metaphor
nearly started a war

In a routine press conference held in Stockholm in 2012 to discuss the
conflict in Syria, President Obama made the following remark:

> We have been very clear to the Assad regime, but also to other play-
> ers on the ground, that **a red line** for us is we start seeing a whole
> bunch of chemical weapons moving around or being utilized. That
> would change my calculus. That would change my equation.
>
> (Obama 2012)

The warning to an opponent not to cross 'a red line' is a metaphor
with a military connotation, the implication being that military action
will be taken against the opponent if the metaphorical red line is
crossed. When evidence emerged some months later that the 'Assad
regime' had actually utilised chemical weapons, Obama was felt by
many to have placed himself in a problematic position; he either had to
carry out the threat he had made and attack the Syrian regime, an
important ally of the Russian Federation, or lose face internationally.
Secretary of State John Kerry attempted to ease the pressure by claiming
to the US Congress that the 'red line' threat had not just been drawn
by Obama but by the 'world' and by 'humanity':

> Some have tried to suggest that the debate we're having today is
> about **President Obama's red line**. I could not more forcefully state

that is just plain and simply wrong. This debate is about **the world's red line**. It's about **humanity's red line**. And it's a red line that anyone with a conscience ought to draw.

(Kerry 2013)

Indeed, he even attempted to shift responsibility onto Congress itself:

This debate is also about Congress's own **red line**. You, the United States Congress, agreed to the chemical weapons convention.

(Kerry 2013)

In the meantime Obama himself attempted to take back the original metaphor and replace it with one without military connotations, namely 'game-changer':

What I've also said is that the use of chemical weapons would be a **game-changer** not simply for the United States but for the international community.

(Obama 2013)

A solution of sorts was reached when Kerry suggested informally that if the Syrian administration surrendered its chemical weapons voluntarily then the US would not attack. The Russian diplomats agreed to organise the exercise:

In the end, a surprise diplomatic opportunity arose: following an off-hand remark from Secretary of State John Kerry that Assad could avoid airstrikes by turning over all of his chemical weapons, Russian Foreign Minister Sergey Lavrov contacted his Syrian counterpart, who got Assad to agree.

(Taddonio, *PBS* 2015)

The President was relieved at his unexpected escape from having to attack an ally of Russia, but his critics accused him of needlessly risking his own and the nation's reputation and of almost taking the country into an unnecessary war. The episode was certainly a reminder that metaphors need to be used with care and that, as Bolinger (1980) put it, language is a 'loaded weapon' (itself, of course, a metaphor).

7.2 Similes

In defining similes as used in political discourse, we can bear in mind four general attributes:

1) They exploit the analogy of two deliberately very different things in the roles of target and source.

2)   They contain an explicit lexical signal of comparison.
3)   They are often accompanied by an 'explanation' of why the source and target are supposedly similar.
4)   They are evaluative and so are often used to persuade.

First then, a simile is a statement which makes a comparison between two entities which are deliberately very *unlike*, for example:

Putin is like a shark: He has to keep moving in order to stay alive, meaning to legitimate his rule.

(*National Review* 2015)

The Chancellor is like a mugger who grabs someone's money and then wants that person to thank him for providing the bus fare to get him home.

(William Hague, UK House of Commons 2000)

In contrast, a statement such as 'India is like China, a growing economic power' would not be considered a simile, given that two similar entities, nations, are being compared.

Similes contain an overt expression of comparison, for instance: *like, is like, acts like, looks like, as, as . . . as, resembles, reminds me of, is the same as, is similar to, the same way, seems like, sounds like, is more like, gives the impression of/that*, and many more.

Just like metaphors, they evaluate, and we can analyse them in a similar way. Here are two examples from the UK House of Commons:

The Tories are **as** popular in Wales now **as** Ceaucescu was in Romania at Christmas 1989.

(Paul Flynn, Labour MP 1994)

He is **like** a bottle of port, which improves with maturity. Today he showed, as he always does, sound judgement.

(John Wilkinson, Conservative MP 2003)

In the first, a political party is evaluated negatively. In the second, an MP is praised by a member of the same party.

Similes are often used to allow the author to extend the analogy and develop the basis of the resemblance, explaining *why* x is like y:

Love has entered me **like a disease,** so stealthily I have not seen its approach nor heard its footsteps. My mind recognizes the folly of it and yet I still [. . .] burn with it, precisely as with a fever. To whom or what shall I turn in order to be cured?

(Tremain 1989: 160–161)

The distance between source (disease) and target (love) is intentionally dissonant and the author takes some time to connect the two. It is a striking evaluative statement in that it maps a bad thing onto what is generally taken as a good one – an evaluative or connotational switch – and, in fact, in the episode in question, the narrator's passion has landed him in a tricky situation.

Similes in political language function in a similar way, as in the following:

> **America** is dumb, it's **like a dumb puppy** that has big teeth that can bite and hurt you.
>
> (Johnny Depp 2003)

> 'America is described as a melting pot where people of different cultures, ethnic backgrounds and religions are galvanized to make it one great nation'. But Ms Samina Faheem believes that **America is like a big beautiful salad bowl** with each component having its own color, texture and flavor.
>
> (*American Muslim Voice* 2002)

In these, as with the 'Putin is like a shark' example cited earlier, we find the analogy asserted first: 'America . . . is like a dumb puppy', 'America is like a . . . salad bowl', with the explanations of why they are so following on. This exploits the reader's curiosity: we want to discover why.

Just occasionally the explanation comes first and the analogy comes at the end. This can provide a kind of humorous punchline ending to the argument:

> President Obama's concept of engaging Congress is giving a speech that nobody up here listens to. **If passing legislation is like making sausage,** then **this White House is like a bunch of vegetarians.**
>
> (Alex Conant, Republican spokesperson 2013)

Notice that the dramatic punchline contains two similes – 'like making sausages' and 'like a bunch of vegetarians' – where the first is necessary to prepare the listener for the negative evaluation of the second (otherwise being vegetarians would not necessarily seem a bad thing to be).

Q4

The metaphors and similes a person uses can tell us a great deal about that person.

How do you think the following very famous simile finishes? (The original is given in the Key.)

A woman without a man is like a ....

(Gloria Steinem)

What point is the speaker making?

> **Extension task**. Go to the free corpus of UK parliamentary debates at www.hansard-corpus.org/ and search for the following string: *as [j*] as a* (the [j*] tells the software that you want an adjective here). What conventional similes do you find? Choose some examples to read in more detail. How are they used to evaluate and persuade?

Table 7.4 How similes work

Simile	Target	Source	Basis of the resemblance?	Evaluation
Encyclopaedias are like gold mines				
Putin is like a shark				
America is like a puppy				

TASK 3: *Similes*

Fill in the missing parts in Table 7.4.

At this point, the reader might like to turn back to the text in Unit 1, Task 4: 'The Spin-doctor and the Wolf-pack', and review the metaphors and similes used there in the light of what we have learned in this Unit.

Making the '*right noises*'

A final word on metaphors and similes. Their evaluative potential means they have two evident functions in the language of politics. Since they present an argument, they are part of the language of persuasion. But in other circumstances, for example, during electoral campaigning, they can sometimes be employed more simply to communicate to an audience shared values (and evaluations). For instance, we find *America . . . is a shining city on a hill* (Ronald Reagan 1980), *Barack knows the American Dream because he's lived it* (Michelle Obama 2012), *this open-door immigration policy can't go on* (*Daily Telegraph* 2016), where speakers indicate that they are a certain type of person who evaluates key issues (country, family, foreigners) in a way that conforms to the audience's view of the world. We might call them *right noises* political metaphors.

To illustrate, typically when the representative of one country visits another they will be flattered in a public display of the good relations between those countries. When President Xi of China visited Australia in 2014 this is what the Labour leader, Bill Shorten, had to say:

> [. . .] it is always good for the global community when China is involved.
> Because we know that when China sets a goal, you achieve it.

When opportunity knocks, China opens the door.

When the moment comes, China meets it and masters it.

When leadership is there, China is there, the best qualified to offer it.

This is the story of modern China.

It is a proud, unfolding story – with many inspiring, buoyant, chapters yet to be written.

Now, more than ever, Mr President, yours is a nation of destiny.

A 'Chinese dream' becoming reality for millions of people.

Q5

How many metaphors can you identify in the above speech of welcome and what are their evaluations and functions?

7.3 Metonymies

Both metaphor and simile bring together two generally unconnected, and often quite dissimilar, entities. In a metonym, instead, some entity is alluded to by mention of something else connected or associated with it. One dictionary definition is:

> a figure of speech in which the name of one object or entity or concept is used to refer to another to which it is somehow related, for example, *the Crown* to indicate sovereignty, or *the bottle* to indicate alcoholic drink, to count *heads* meaning to count people.
>
> (Yerkes 1989, edited)

Sometimes this 'other entity to which it is somehow related' is actually some *part* of it. Classic examples are 'body parts' which stand for the whole person: for instance, *hand*, *heart*, *head*, and so on. Examples include *new faces*, *lend a hand*, *new blood*, *a head-count*, and so on.

Q6

Different aspects of human beings and their abilities are emphasised in each of these cases. Can you say which?

new faces

lend a hand

new blood

a head-count

Many of these occur in set expressions which combine elements of metonymy and metaphor; for example, the following all occurred in UK parliamentary debates in 2001 (the year of the 9/11 attack):

This needs to be a shared responsibility: We have chosen to stand **shoulder to shoulder** with **America** to provide global leadership in the fight against international terrorism.

How ready are British troops to stand – I borrow the phrase – **shoulder to shoulder** with **American** troops?

The Secretary of State knows that the UK and the **US** are standing **shoulder to shoulder** in respect of Afghanistan.

What progress are the Government making to ensure that the UK and the **US** stand **shoulder to shoulder** on this issue, which is also of international importance?

Thus, standing 'shoulder to shoulder' expresses cooperation or support, usually in adversity. Other such expressions include *winning hearts and minds* (gaining someone's rational and emotional support), *let's put our heads together* (joining forces to solve a problem). If you asked a friend to *lend you a hand* in solving a Sudoku puzzle, then the physical *hand* stands metaphorically for *mental intelligence*.

On other occasions the 'something else' connected to or 'standing for' an entity is simply something related to it. In politics, an important and productive set of metonyms are **toponymical**, that is, the places where political events happen are used to stand for those events themselves. Consider:

Washington this morning refused to comment on President Modi's statement that . . .

Downing Street denied all the allegations about the Prime Minister's private life . . .

Buckingham Palace distanced itself from claims over a constitutional row . . .

Washington 'stands for' the US government or someone connected to it (the President perhaps), Downing Street for the UK Prime Minister or his office, Buckingham Palace for the Queen or the Royal Family or some spokesperson for them. Notice how the vagueness, the lack of precision of the reference can be useful for the author; if, in the second example, we replaced 'Downing Street' with 'Prime Minister', the result would sound rather absurd. As it stands, it appears superficially acceptable.

This vagueness is also exploited by the Eurosceptic press in the UK who use 'Brussels' to refer to all five of the institutions of the European Union, which serves to make 'Brussels' seem more powerful and pervasive.

TASK 4: *Brussels*

Look at the examples below, what does the 'Brussels' in the headline actually refer to?

1) *Brussels* orders even landlocked countries to enact maritime laws
   They have no coastline; no international mariners ply their non-existent territorial waters. You might think that would excuse landlocked Hungary and Slovakia from implementing European Union legislation on safety at sea, but that would be to underestimate Brussels bureaucracy. (*Telegraph* 2005)

2) *Brussels* Beavers away
   Tony Blair and most of his ministers are on holiday, but our legislators are as tireless as ever. A 47-page document from the European Parliament circulated by the UK Independence Party lists more than 460 directives, regulations and decisions. (*Telegraph* 2005)

3) Hands off our pints, traders tell *Brussels*
   The European Commission has ordered the UK Government to announce a date by which it will finally replace pints, miles and acres with litres, kilometres and hectares. (*Daily Mail* 2005)

Personification is used pervasively to express evaluations. A headline such as 'Brussels says UK women are second fattest' (*Daily Mail* 2016), will not endear 'Brussels' with the largely female, British readership of the *Daily Mail* newspaper, but no European Union institution or authority actually 'said' this, because the story simply refers to statistics published in the *Eurobarometer*, a body which carries out opinion surveys on behalf of the EU, which included figures regarding the average weight of people in each EU member state.

The opposite tactic is sometimes used by pro-European groups who, instead of narrowing and identifying the EU institutions with 'Brussels', employ an opposite, widening form of metonymy and the institutions of the EU are frequently replaced with 'Europe' (Unit 10.2.3), for example:

I am amazed at the sheer ignorance, a lot of it fuelled by the anti-European press in our country, about what **Europe** is and how it works.
(Dennis MacShane, former Minister for Europe 2005)

At other times, individuals can be made to stand for institutions (**personificational** metonyms):

. . . the White House today warned **President Assad** not to make a 'final mistake' . . .

The 2012 Olympic Games were awarded to **Tony Blair** yesterday as a reward for Britain's record on multi-cultural integration.

Q7

Personificational metonymy can be very powerful in expressing points of view. Compare, for instance, the following versions of the 'same' report. What difference in points of view are communicated?

The White House today threatened to punish **Assad** for his use of chemical weapons.

Barack Obama today threatened to punish **the Syrians** for their use of chemical weapons.

TASK 5: *Metonymies*

Complete Table 7.5.

National or ethnic **stereotypes** can be partly explained as metonymies. It is, unfortunately, common practice to use 'whole' labels to refer to a part of a national or ethnic group. We sometimes read things like: 'Palestinians are terrorists', 'Americans are gullible', 'Italians are musical', when what is meant is that *some*, a *group* of, Palestinians, Americans or Italians possess this attribute or act in this way. In particular, we use national or ethnic labels to refer to the actions of governments or leaders: 'the Americans have begun bombing Baghdad', 'the Palestinians have broken the ceasefire'. All this often appears natural and justified until it happens to involve us personally. For example, a French pacifist might take offence at the wording of a piece of news as follows: 'The French have given their full support to the US military involvement in Syria'; or a taxpaying Italian might object to the wording: 'the Italians have yet again broken their promises on meeting European budget requirements'.

What we might call the 'missing quantifier', that is, not specifying whether *some*, *all*, *a few* or *many* is intended, can at the very least project an unjustified collective responsibility and, at worst, be the precursor to racist stereotyping.

Table 7.5 Metonymies

Person	Place	Role/Institution
Donald Trump	Washington	US President
....	Beijing	President of China
....	The Vatican	....
Giorgio Napolitano	Quirinale	....
....	10 Downing St	....
....	Kremlin	....
Shri Narendra Modi	....	....

7.4 A case study in metonymy: how the *Arab world* is seen and how it sees itself

Expressions such as 'the West', 'the western world', 'the Arab world', and so on, are a special kind of metonym. Who or what precisely they refer to can often seem quite vague. Sometimes they presumably stand for something like 'all those who reside in western countries' or 'all those whose mother tongue is Arabic', but they also often seem to refer to 'those immersed in western culture and thought' and 'those immersed in Arabic culture and thought'. All of which raises the question, in terms of *the West*, what does Sweden have in common with Sicily or, in terms of *the Arab world*, how much does Yemen, one of the poorest countries in the world, have in common with Qatar, one of the richest?[1]

However this may be, this case study is a three-part comparative analysis of how *the Arab world* is represented in various written media. The first comparison is political, between what is said about 'the Arab world' in two UK newspapers, the left-leaning *Guardian* and the right-leaning *Telegraph*. The second is between these UK representations and what is said about *the Arab world* by voices *from* that world, namely, two Arabic English-language newspapers, the *Daily News Egypt* and the *Gulf News (UAE)*. In a further comparison, the objective is to see if there are any changes in the representations in the UK newspapers between 2010 and 2013, given the intervening events in the Middle East and North Africa.

The first step was to prepare six lists (known as **concordances**) of all the mentions in context of the expression *the Arab world*, from the *Guardian* 2010 and the *Telegraph* 2010; *Guardian* 2013 and the *Telegraph* 2013; and the *Daily News Egypt* (DNE) 2013 and the *Gulf News (UAE)* 2013.

7.4.1 The frequency of use of *the Arab world*

> **Q8**
>
> Is *the Arab world* a purely western media concept and an outsider term (see Unit 1) or, instead, is it also used within *the Arab world* itself? See Table 7.7 in the Key section for the answer.

7.4.2 The grammar and agency of *the Arab world*

In both the UK and the Arab newspapers, the expression *the Arab world* was very frequently part of a prepositional phrase, that is, in constructions like *in . . . , across . . . , throughout, within . . . the Arab world*. It was used this way in over 44% of all mentions in the UK papers, in 60% of mentions in *DNE* 2013 and in 50% of mentions in *Gulf News* 2013. The expression, then, very often functions as part of a CONTAINER metaphor:

[. . .] continuing turbulence *in the Arab world* (*Guardian* 24 June 2013)

or as a (MEMBER OF A) CLUB metaphor:

Malhab said that Egypt would 'once again assume its rightful place *within the Arab world*' (*DNE* 20 July 2013)

The next question was how was *the Arab world* viewed in the UK papers in terms of agency; in other words, was *the Arab world* mainly 'Do-er' or 'Done-to' (Unit 2.1.1)? It transpired that it occurs as active 'Do-er' just nine times in 114 occurrences in *Guardian* 2010 (8%), and three times in thirty-eight occurrences in *Telegraph* 2010 (8%). It was much more likely to be in some way passively 'Done-to':

[. . .] the self-serving, unrepresentative governments that have, with few exceptions, ruled the Arab world since the 19th century (*Guardian* 2010)

the cable news television channel that has revolutionised the media in the otherwise heavily censored Arab world (*Telegraph* 2010)

On the other, it frequently appeared in the role of an *Audience*, one to be cajoled and placated:

Erdogan [. . .] has tried to shore up his credentials in the Arab world (*Telegraph* 2010)

Clinton courts Arab world to help on Tehran (*Guardian* (headline) 2010)

and which is especially emotional and volatile:

The Arab world has reacted with predictable fury [. . .] (*Telegraph* 2010)

In comparison, the expression *the Western world* in the UK 2010 papers performed as active 'Do-er' in around 25% of cases (more frequently than *the Arab world* but not overwhelmingly so, partly because it too is often part of a prepositional phrase). It never appears in the role of an Audience.

TASK 6: *Agency*

What role is being played by *the Arab world* in each of the following, active Do-er, passive Done-to or Audience?

a) Obama is seizing on the Biden row to send a message to the Arab world: to show that he won't be pushed around by Israel. (*Guardian* 17 March 2010)

....

b) Governments across the Arab world are under pressure to create jobs for their young unemployed and we expect this to intensify. (*Telegraph* 27 March 2010)

....

c) The chances of America being able to persuade the Arab world to recognise Israel were diminishing by the month. (*Guardian* 24 March 2010)

....

d) The deification of Nasser or any ruler is actually a chronic disease Egypt and the Arab world suffers from. (*DNE* 16 January 2013)

....

e) An international effort [. . .] to support countries in the Arab world engaged in transitions towards 'free, democratic and tolerant societies'. (*DNE* 3 August 2013)

....

f) The Arab world has inherited an unfavourable and divisive legacy. The roots of a weak private sector run deep in history. Merchants were politically weak under the Ottomans. (*DNE* 23 February 2013)

....

g) Money is flowing to al-Nusra [. . .] from benefactors in the Sunni Arab world. (*Guardian* 18 January 2013)

....

h) [Mansour stated that] the Arab world needed to listen to the king [of Saudi Arabia]. (*DNE* 17 August 2013)

....

i) The Arab world continues to struggle with employment and social equality. (*DNE* 15 March 2013)

....

7.4.3 Topics discussed in 2010, before the Arab uprisings

In terms of topics, the *Guardian* 2010 is preoccupied with *the Arab World*'s relations with Israel (mentioned forty-eight times) and with the United States (mentioned twenty-five times). The *Telegraph* concentrates on these topics much less, citing Israel and the US just five times each. Its focus is less on conflict and more on political and social conditions within the Arab world and also on Arab culture which is generally evaluated positively:

> The most beautiful poem in the Arab world and beyond is the subject of Crazy for Love: Layla and the Mad Poet (*Telegraph* 2010)

By way of comparison, when the UK papers discuss the metonymical *Western world*, the two most common topics are the economy and healthcare.

7.4.4 How *the Arab World* is reported in 2013, after the uprisings

Comparing the topics regarding *the Arab world* mentioned in the Arab newspapers to those mentioned in the UK newspapers in 2013, the former are far more varied. They include investment, economics, trade, commerce and finance, attesting to a greater interest in the economy and sphere of business in *the Arab world* than the UK papers. Other interesting topics discussed in the Arab newspapers include science, technology, research and media entities such as Facebook, Internet, networks, smartphones, as well as 'older' cultural artefacts such as cinema, films, music, books/literary/literature. The UK newspapers, in contrast, talk about little else than the conflicts which arose in *the Arab world* after the uprisings which began in 2010–2011.

The Arab newspapers are also more widely critical of *the Arab world* than the UK papers; the latter mentioned a lack of democratic rights and the unequal legal condition of women in some Arab countries. The Arab newspapers also criticise *the Arab world* for both these issues but also for a lack of employment opportunities and deficiencies in healthcare and education systems. This is, of course, perfectly natural; it is one of the main functions of the media to criticise their local world. The *Daily News Egypt* has a particularly liberal stance and campaigns for women's rights (thirty-one mentions), against the persecution of Christians (four) and other minorities (four), for freedom of expression (five) and for the abolition of the death penalty in the *Arab world* (five).

7.5 Beware of arguments by comparison–analogy–resemblance that employ metaphor, simile or metonymy

To finish this section, we might consider why the use of the devices discussed here could be misleading and even dangerous, if the reader is not aware of how analogy can be used for persuasion and manipulation.

1) They are generally unsupported by rational evidence. At the beginning of this Unit, we defined argument by analogy as 'pseudo-rational'. Why? Because they tend to hide bald assertions: X is asserted to be Y (metaphor), or X is said to be like Y (simile), on the basis of Z, as in 'Sally is (like) a block of ice (because she is cold)' and no evidence is given to prove the assertion. Who knows, perhaps Sally is really quite warm and friendly. Perhaps she is only indifferent to that particular speaker for some reason.

    Given that metaphor and simile are always evaluative too, the audience is invited, by the use of colourful language, to accept and agree with the speaker's judgement. But we must bear in mind that calling such-and-such an administration a 'puppet government' does not by itself mean it is the case. Metaphor is not a neutral description but an evaluative opinion.

2) They can have hidden meanings for particular audiences. Calling for a 'crusade' on terror (as, famously, George W. Bush did in 2001), for example, has all sorts of hidden, possibly dangerous meanings. While a western audience is used to the word *crusade* being employed with a figurative meaning and in a positive way (for example: 'crusade against cancer', 'a crusade for peace'), for a Muslim audience the word *crusade* has an extremely negative connotation. This was discussed in a White House briefing, where the spokesman was asked (note the use of the word *connotation*):

    > Q: [. . .] the President used the word 'crusade' last Sunday which has caused some consternation in a lot of Muslim countries. Can you explain his usage of that word, given the connotation to Muslims?
    >
    > (White House briefing 2001)

3) As we saw with the euphemistic metaphors above, they can be deployed to substitute and obscure plain-speaking.

4) *Omnis comparatio claudicat* (literally: 'every comparison limps'). Which parts of an analogy or comparison apply and which do not? When the poet Burns wrote 'My love is like a red, red rose. . .' presumably he did not mean it was prickly and short-lived.

Consider the various analogies for the State which have been popular in different historical periods. In the past, from the Greeks to Shakespeare, it was common to compare the State to the human body, and even today we still talk of the '*body* politic' and 'the *head* of state'.

Today, in contrast, it is common to use the analogy of the State as a company, a business, for example: *UK plc* (that is, *public limited company*), *l'azienda Italia* (Italy Co), *the business of America is business*.

Q9

How do these analogies apply and how not?

The State as a human body:

The State as a business:

How can both of these analogies be used to justify authoritarianism?

Revision exercise: *I Have a Dream*

In Unit 5 we looked at two celebrated historical documents on the rhetoric of freedom. Here is the third in this imposing series (with our editing).

I Have a Dream: by Dr Martin Luther King, Jr.

Delivered on the steps at the Lincoln Memorial in Washington DC on 28th August, 1963.

Figure 7.1 Picture of Martin Luther King

1) Five score years ago, a great American, in whose symbolic shadow we stand, signed the Emancipation Proclamation. This momentous decree came as a great beacon light of hope to millions of Negro slaves who had been seared in the flames of withering injustice. It came as a joyous daybreak to end the long night of captivity.

2) But one hundred years later, we must face the tragic fact that the Negro is still not free. One hundred years later, the life of the Negro is still sadly crippled by the manacles of segregation and the chains of discrimination. One hundred years later, the Negro lives on a lonely island of poverty in the midst of a vast ocean of material prosperity. One hundred years later, the Negro is still languishing in the corners of American society and finds himself an exile in his own land. So we have come here today to dramatize an appalling condition.

3) In a sense we have come to our nation's capital to cash a check. When the architects of our republic wrote the magnificent words of the Constitution and the Declaration of Independence, they were signing a promissory note to which every American was to fall heir. This note was a promise that all men would be guaranteed the inalienable rights of life, liberty, and the pursuit of happiness.

4) It is obvious today that America has defaulted on this promissory note. Instead of honoring this sacred obligation, America has given the Negro people a bad check which has come back marked 'insufficient funds'. But we refuse to believe that the bank of justice is bankrupt. We refuse to believe that there are insufficient funds in the great vaults of opportunity of this nation. So we have come to cash this check – a check that will give us upon demand the riches of freedom and the security of justice. We have also come to this hallowed spot to remind America of the fierce urgency of now [. . .] Now is the time to rise from the dark and desolate valley of segregation to the sunlit path of racial justice. Now is the time to open the doors of opportunity to all of God's children. Now is the time to lift our nation from the quicksands of racial injustice to the solid rock of brotherhood.

5) But there is something that I must say to my people. In the process of gaining our rightful place we must not be guilty of wrongful deeds. Let us not seek to satisfy our thirst for freedom by drinking from the cup of bitterness and hatred.

6) I say to you today, my friends, that in spite of the difficulties and frustrations of the moment, I still have a dream. It is a dream deeply rooted in the American dream. I have a dream that one day this nation will rise up and live out the true meaning of its creed: We hold these truths to be self-evident: that all men are created equal.

Questions

1) Antithesis, or contrasting pair: find one example in paragraph (1) and one in paragraph (2).

2) '... finds himself an exile in his own land' (paragraph 2) is an example of which rhetorical structure?
3) A number of metaphors are used in paragraphs (1) and (2). Analyse three of them, using Table 7.6.

Table 7.6 Metaphors in *I Have a Dream*

Metaphor	Target	Source	Grounds of the resemblance?	Evaluation
Beacon light of hope				

4) In paragraphs (3) and (4) we find an 'extended metaphor'. What is it? Underline all the vocabulary relating to this metaphor.
5) Underline in the text an example of a tricolon (the three-part list).
6) The *Declaration of Independence* is referred to twice. What are these references?
7) With which phrase is Abraham Lincoln referred to?
8) Is the language used by Dr King different from the *Declaration of Independence*? How would you describe the language?

Further reading

Charteris-Black, J. (2011) *Politicians and Rhetoric: The Persuasive Power of Metaphor*, London: Palgrave Macmillan.

Musolff, A. (2016) *Political Metaphor Analysis: Discourse and Scenarios*, London: Bloomsbury Publishing.

Partington, A., Duguid, A. and Taylor C. (2013) *Patterns and Meanings in Discourse*, Amsterdam: John Benjamins. Chapter 5: 'Metaphor'.

Case studies

Meadows, B. (2007) 'Distancing and showing solidarity via metaphor and metonymy in political discourse: A critical study of American statements on Iraq during the years 2004-2005', *Critical Approaches to Discourse Analysis across Disciplines* 1(2): 1–17. [open access]

Partington, A. (2015) 'Corpus-assisted comparative case studies of representations of the Arab world', in P. Baker and T. McEnery (eds.) *Corpora and Discourse Studies*, Basingstoke: Palgrave Macmillan, 220–243.

Vaghi, F. and Venuti, M. (2004) 'Metaphor and the Euro', in A. Partington, J. Morley and L. Haarman (eds.) *Corpora and Discourse*, Bern: Peter Lang, 369–381.

Keys and commentaries

Q1

Time is a **valuable commodity** (especially **time is money**).

Table 7.2 Key: *Juliet is the sun*

Metaphor	Target	Source	Basis of the resemblance?	Evaluation
Juliet is the sun	Juliet	The sun	Impossible to live without	Good

Q3

The speaker aims to negatively evaluate people who have recently moved to the US and does so through comparison with previous migrants. Rhetorically this functions both to evaluate and to anticipate a possible criticism of the anti-migrant stance on the basis that the US has a long history of migration.

How many metaphors can you identify?

The extract is dense with metaphors. You might have noticed the following:

melting pot (target = old migration, evaluated as good)
patchwork quilt (target = new migration, evaluated as bad)
shredding the common bond (target = bilingual policies, evaluated as bad)
ripped the heart out of our national unity (target = migration policies, evaluated as bad)

TASK 1: Political metaphors

Table 7.3 Key: political metaphors

Metaphor	Target	Source	Basis of the resemblance?	Evaluation
A puppet government	Government	A puppet show	Manipulated from above/outside	Bad
Sunshine government	Government	Sunshine/light	Transparent, open to scrutiny	Good
Crusade against terror	Operations against terrorism	Crusade	Complete dedication	Good (for the author)

Note the importance of the preposition *against*. The target is not terror but, implicitly, operations *against* terror.

TASK 2: *Metaphors of anti-Americanism*

The four main metaphors are: ANTI-AMERICANISM IS AN UNCONTROLLABLE BODY OF WATER (sentences a–d), ANTI-AMERICANISM IS A DISEASE (e–g), ANTI-AMERICANISM IS A FIRE/FLAMMABLE (h–k) and, finally, ANTI-AMERICANISM IS A CRIME (l–o).

In the first three metaphors, anti-Americanism is likened to a natural disaster, the basis of resemblance is that it is something which cannot be controlled – and, of course, it is very unfavourably evaluated. The evaluation in the metaphor ANTI-AMERICANISM IS A CRIME is a little more complex. In this case, the target is not so much anti-Americanism itself as *reactions* to potential anti-Americanism, and we can see that this reaction is negatively evaluated from 'bizarrely accused of' and 'thought-crime'. Thus, this one is the 'odd-one out' because it is not evaluating anti-Americanism negatively, more the *anti* anti-Americanism. Perhaps unsurprisingly, this metaphor was only found in the left-wing British press, which is perhaps more likely to be anti-American (Taylor 2008).

Q4

A woman without a man is like a fish without a bicycle.

What do you think we can say about the author of this simile? Gloria Steinem is a feminist and a writer on women's issues. She makes a colourful affirmation of women's ability to manage their own lives.

TASK 3: *Similes*

Table 7.4 Key: how similes work

Simile	Target	Source	Basis of the resemblance?	Evaluation
Encyclopaedias are like gold mines	Encyclopaedias	Gold mines	Places where hidden wealth can be discovered	Good
Putin is like a shark	Putin	Shark	Dangerous and in danger, has to keep moving	Bad
America is like a puppy	America	Puppy	Immature but dangerous	Bad

Q5

The dominant theme here is that China is consistently personified in this extract, starting from the positioning of the most powerful governments in the world as a *community*, with China as a member. The most striking metaphors are perhaps the tricolon in the centre which continue this motif of personification. The first of these is relatively conventionalised (*opportunity knocks*) and CHINA IS A HOST/ HOME OWNER. In the second, CHINA IS A SUCCESSFUL WORKER, and this also spills into the third in which we could interpret CHINA AS A CANDIDATE FOR WORK, praised for their qualifications. Following these, we have a fairly familiar HISTORY AS A BOOK metaphor with lexical items such *as unfolding story, chapters* and *written* activating the source semantic field. Finally, the speaker borrows the well-known *American-dream* metaphor and repackages it into the *Chinese dream* (though whose *dream* this is remains unspecified). What all of these metaphors share is a strongly favourable evaluation of the target – China. There is also a conflation of the leader and country (both are addressed as *you*) which the personification facilitates. The creativity allows the speaker to flatter the target at length without simply repeating the underlying concept of 'I value you'. The speaker may hope the use of figurative language will enable them to save face by not appearing too subservient, and gain face by establishing good relations, and perhaps also by displaying verbal dexterity.

Q6

new faces: *faces* refers particularly to people's appearance;

lend a hand: *hand* refers to someone's ability to help, primarily physically but, by further metaphorical extension, also intellectually;

new blood: *blood* is something which gives 'new life', as in *blood injection*;

a head-count: when counting *heads* we count simply the number of people present without much attention to who they are (their *faces*).

TASK 4: *Brussels*

1) European Court of Justice/Court of Justice of the European Communities – the highest court in the European Union in matters of European Community law.
2) European Parliament – the directly elected parliamentary institution of the EU.
3) European Commission/Commission of the European Communities – the body responsible for proposing legislation, implementing decisions, upholding the Union's treaties and the general day-to-day running of the Union (definitions from *Wikipedia*).

Q7

In the first, we look at the matter from the US point of view. A 'respectable' authority, the White House, quite understandably, warns an individual who is doing wrong. This is another example of what we called 'metonymic blame' (see the *Declaration of Independence*) – assigning all the guilt and responsibility to a single individual, Assad.

In the second, we see things from an anti-US viewpoint. Instead of an authoritative body we again concentrate on a single individual, Barack Obama, who is now threatening an entire people rather than its leader.

TASK 5: *Metonymies*

Table 7.5 Key: metonymies

Person	Place	Role/Institution
Donald Trump	Washington	US President
Xi Jinping	Beijing	President of China
Benedict XVI	The Vatican	The Catholic Church
Giorgio Napolitano	Quirinale	Italian President
Theresa May	10 Downing St	UK Prime Minister
Vladimir Putin	Kremlin	President of the Russian Federation
Shri Narendra Modi	New Delhi	Prime Minister of India

(Accurate at the time of going to press. By the time you read, things may well have changed!)

Q8

Is *the Arab world* a purely western media concept and an outsider term (see Unit 1) or, instead, was it also used within *the Arab world* itself? As can be seen from Table 7.7, the answer is that it decidedly *is* used within that world, in fact much more frequently than in the UK newspapers. It is far from being an outsider term (see Unit 1).

Table 7.7 How often is the term *the Arab world* used in each of the six newspaper concordances?

The Guardian 2010	114	(3.0 per million words, pmw)
Telegraph 2010	38	(0.7 pmw)
The Guardian 2013	86	(2.3 pmw)
Telegraph 2013	57	(1.0 pmw)
Daily News Egypt 2013	301	(58.2 pmw)
Gulf News 2013	373	(40.1 pmw)

TASK 6: *Agency*

What role is being played by *the Arab world* in each of the following, active Do-er, passive Done-to or Audience?

a)   Obama is seizing on the Biden row to send a message to the Arab world: to show that he won't be pushed around by Israel. (*Guardian* 17 March 2010)
     Audience: someone to be sent a message to.

b)   Governments across the Arab world are under pressure to create jobs for their young unemployed and we expect this to intensify (*Telegraph* 27 March 2010)
     Done-to: They are 'under pressure' from some unnamed Do-er.

c)   The chances of America being able to persuade the Arab world to recognise Israel were diminishing by the month. (*Guardian* 24 March 2010)
     Audience. To be persuaded to become a Do-er, but the sense is that the 'Doing' is unlikely to get 'Done'.

d)   The deification of Nasser or any ruler is actually a chronic disease Egypt and the Arab world suffers from. (*DNE* 16 January 2013)
     Done-to: the Do-er is the disease of an alleged tendency to deify leaders.

e)   An international effort [. . .] to support countries in the Arab world engaged in transitions towards 'free, democratic and toler- ant societies'. (*DNE* 3 August 2013)
     Done-to and Do-er: the 'international effort' is the main Do-er, but the Arab World is also actively 'engaged in transitions'.

f)   The Arab world has inherited an unfavourable and divisive leg- acy. The roots of a weak private sector run deep in history. Merchants were politically weak under the Ottomans. (*DNE* 23 February 2013)
     Done-to, or perhaps better, 'Receiver' of 'an unfavourable and divisive legacy'.

g)   Money is flowing to al-Nusra [. . .] from benefactors in the Sunni Arab world. (*Guardian* 18 January 2013)
     Do-er: donating money.

h)   [Mansour stated that] the Arab world needed to listen to the king [of Saudi Arabia]. (*DNE* 17 August 2013)
     Audience and Done-to: it is told that it must become a better audience, and to Do something it is currently failing to Do.

i)   The Arab world continues to struggle with employment and social equality. (*DNE* 15 March 2013)
     Do-er and Done-to: it struggles with but it is also afflicted by employment and social equality.

Q9

How do these analogies apply and how not?

The State as a human body:

The head is the 'head' of state, the arms are the people, the workers, the arteries are the circulation of goods. But what are the equivalents of the hair, the knees or the less 'noble' parts like the buttocks? States might be 'born', but they hardly get married, have sex and children and die 70–80 years later. Nevertheless, we might note that, in Imperial times, colonies were often described as 'children' of the 'mother country'.

The State as a business:

Nations 'employ' people, try to make a profit or at least balance their budgets, but can the State 'sack' its citizens when it no longer has any need of them? Most fundamentally of all, a business is owned by and responsible to a few individuals, either a family or a group of share-holders. One hopes that, in a democracy at least, the State belongs to all the people.

How can both of these analogies be used to justify authoritarianism?

All the parts of the body must work in harmony if it is to remain healthy. Any social unrest on the part of the poor and dispossessed can be depicted as a 'disease' to be extirpated. Similarly, the struggle for social justice on the part of the downtrodden can be depicted as disrupting the smooth running of the 'business' of the State.

Revision exercise: *I Have a Dream*

1) Paragraph (1): 'It came as a joyous daybreak to end the long night of captivity'. Paragraph (2): 'the Negro lives on a lonely island of poverty in the midst of a vast ocean of material prosperity'.
2) Oxymoron.
3) Free response, but here are some suggestions:

Table 7.6 Key (examples): metaphors in *I Have a Dream*

Metaphor	Target	Source	Grounds of the resemblance?	Evaluation
Beacon light of hope	Hope for us	Beacon light	A guide towards safety	Good
The long night of captivity	Our captivity	Long night	Darkness, no light of hope	Bad
To cash a cheque	Freedom	Cheque/money	They are both owed to us	Good (if paid)

4) The metaphor of SOCIAL JUSTICE IS CAPITAL (MONEY) OWED TO THE 'NEGRO' PEOPLE. For example: *to cash a check*, *signing a promissory note, the bank of justice is bankrupt.*

5) Paragraph (3): *Now is the time . . . now is the time . . . now is the time.*

6) Paragraph (3): '. . . the inalienable rights of life, liberty, and the pursuit of happiness'. Paragraph (6): 'We hold these truths to be self-evident: that all men are created equal.'

7) 'Five score years ago, a great American, in whose symbolic shadow we stand'.

8) Free response. Suggestions: the language is less legalistic and more direct and emotional. It has a greater concentration of metaphors and stirring images ('the fierce urgency of now', paragraph (4)). Dr King preaches against violence, the Founding Fathers of the US take the use of violence for political gain for granted.

Note

1 In a corpus study of British press reporting, Baker, Gabrielatos and McEnery (2013) find that *world* is the second most frequent term to appear after the word *Muslim*. They find that *Muslim world* is consistently used to suggest a homogenous group and most frequently used in connection with *the West* which is similarly presented as a homogeneous group.

8 Questions and responses

Journalist: *WVMT [a local radio station] in Burlington reports that you thoughtfully pointed out that their protest banner was posted backwards and you also told them, 'the hardest part of my job is knowing what not to say'. And my question: How could you tell them this when you so often do not say with such evident skill?*

(Laughter)

White House spokesman: *Well, in keeping with the spirit of not saying anything, Les, let's go to Dave.*

(Laughter)

8.1 Institutional discourse

Political language is one form of **institutional discourse**. Most types of *spoken* institutional language, i.e. interrogation in court, doctor–patient interviews, political interviews, etc., take the form of questions and responses.

We will use the word *response* rather than *answer*, following Harris (1991). A response is defined as whatever follows a question. Only a response which fully satisfies the questioner can be called an answer.

TASK 1: *Question–response in institutional discourses*

Fill in Table 8.1. Think of your own example for the final row.

Table 8.1 Participants in institutional discourse

Type of discourse	Who asks the questions?	Who responds?
Political interview		
	Lawyer	Witness
Press conference		
Police interview		
	Doctor	
Job interview		

8.2 From deference to hostility

Once upon a time, until around forty years ago, it was the policy of the BBC to avoid all forms of political controversy. British journalists, both print and broadcast, were generally very careful to be polite to the point of deference when interviewing important people, including politicians.

Clayman and Heritage (2002: 49–50) report a parody of this kind of interview (with light editing):

Interviewer: Sir, would you say that your visit to Timbuktu had been worthwhile?

Politician: Oh, yes certainly.

Interviewer: Ah, good. Could you say what topics were discussed, sir?

Politician: No, I'm afraid not. These talks were of a highly confidential nature, you understand, and you wouldn't expect me to reveal anything that might prejudice our future relations.

Interviewer: No, of course not, sir. Well, sir, you must be very tired after your talks and your journey – may I ask, sir, are you going to take it easy for a while now – a holiday perhaps?

Politician: Ah, if only one could. But you know a minister in Her Majesty's Government can never take a rest. They're waiting for me now.

Interviewer: Well, thank you very much, sir.

More recently, partly due to the advent of commercial television companies (that is, companies not financed by the State), the relationship between the press and politicians in the UK has changed slowly but radically. Nicolas Jones, a British political writer and BBC journalist, explains that nowadays:

> production teams are anxious to demonstrate that their editorial standards have not been compromised and that they do not shy away from posing tough and embarrassing questions.
>
> (Jones 1996: 21)

It is not difficult to find instances on British television of hostile questioning of powerful individuals and we will examine an extended sequence at the end of this Unit. The potentially aggressive stance was perhaps best summed up by a newspaper editor who said that the aim of the interview is to ask and answer the following question: 'why is this lying bastard lying to me?' (Louis Heren).

In US circles too, such as the White House press briefings, questioners can be less than kind (Barry is a government spokesman):

Q: Barry, let me ask you this, when you say that you have no view of the possible testimony of Monica Lewinsky, does that mean that in the daily meetings that you attend at the higher levels in the White House, no view was expressed of her coming testimony? Or does it mean that you were told to express no view of her testimony?

(Laughter)

However, we should not assume that hostility is the unmarked or normal attitude in all contexts or cultures. For instance, the expectations of how a politician will be treated in a UK daytime TV chat show are quite different from those of a programme dedicated to current affairs. The former are often interpreted as an opportunity for the politician to address their affective rather than competence face (Unit 3). There are also different expectations across different cultures. For instance, Jiang (2006, listed in the reading below) found that requests in Chinese press conferences were more likely to involve asking for simple official government comment than in US press conferences, where they were more likely to involve asking for clarification or confirmation, or indeed contesting government versions. Similarly, Du and Rendle-Short (2016) analyse questions posed in press conferences with representatives of the Chinese government. They found differences in the level of deference and adversarialness in questions asked by two groups of journalists: those from mainland China and those they classify as coming from countries with greater press freedom. Compare the function of the preface (the preamble to the actual question) in these two examples from their data (both are translated from Mandarin):

1) Premier Wen, a lot of social problems have cropped up in the course of rapid economic development in China, one of them is the wealth gap. To address problems facing agriculture, rural areas and farmers is on top of your agenda. But some experts say unless farmers are granted the right to use land, or are allowed to own land, it is impossible to solve the problems they face. Do you think it is possible to give them land ownership?

2) Hello Premier. The housing issue has always been a hot topic among the Chinese society. During this year's two sessions, many members put forward their suggestions and views on this topic. I would like to ask what will be the new ideas and measures of the government on this issue?

(Du and Rendle-Short 2016: 54)

In the first, we can see that the questioner has built a case for authority (*some experts say*) which suggests that 'yes' would be the preferred response. However, this was against current government policy and thus the respondent was being presented with a question designed to elicit a 'yes' answer but which would damage the speaker if they were to reply 'yes'. In contrast, in the second example, the preface asserts the importance of the topic only and then the question is open, offering the spokesman an opportunity to present their *new ideas* (the importance of open and closed questions is discussed further in Unit 8.4).

8.3 Difficult questions, difficult answers

8.3.1 Assertions and presuppositions

Some questions are more difficult for a politician to answer than others. But some questions can actually be *dangerous* for a politician to answer, and the most difficult of all are those in which the dangers are somehow hidden. In order to analyse the hidden dangers in political questions, we need to appreciate the notions of **assertion** and **presupposition**. Consider the following:

> We have to wake up to the danger now. How long are we going to allow a madman like Kim Jong-un to keep stockpiling nuclear weapons?

The first part of the utterance contains the assertion that we have to wake up to a danger. An assertion is something, a fact, an opinion, an exhortation (as here) which is stated openly and overtly. The rest of the utterance contains a number of *presuppositions* (each of which may or may not be true). These include:

- Kim Jong-un is collecting nuclear weapons;
- he has been collecting them for a while ('*keep* stockpiling');
- 'we' have the power to stop him ('How long are we going to *allow* . . .').

A still more basic presupposition is that there exists a male (because 'mad*man*') human entity named 'Kim Jong-un', and that he is mad. A presupposition, then, is a notion, which is to some degree implicit, that is, it is either implied as or taken for granted as existing or being true. The fact that the entity called 'Kim Jong-un' is a 'madman' is somewhere between an assertion and a presupposition: it is stated fairly openly but is embedded, that is, hidden away, grammatically (compare the difference between 'a madman like Kim Jong-un' and the more transparent 'Kim Jong-un is a madman').

Q1

These are the opening questions of two recent interviews by BBC journalist Jeremy Paxman:

(1) [to US author and right-wing commentator Ann Coulter]: Your publishers gave us Chapter 1 [of your upcoming book]. I've read it. Does it get any better?
(2) [to the then leader of the UK Green Party Natalie Bennett]: What is the nuttiest thing in your Manifesto, do you think?

What are the hostile presuppositions in each of the questions?

In March 2017, the official Twitter account of the BBC Asian Network tweeted the following question, which caused much controversy:

(3) What is the right punishment for blasphemy?

What are the presuppositions in the question and why do you think it caused such consternation?

The use of presupposition is, of course, by no means always hostile. In normal talk we obviously presuppose a lot of information when communicating because otherwise our conversations would be extremely repetitive. When analysing political discourse, we need to use our knowledge of the context and the response turn in order to see which presuppositions are shared and which are disputed. In political questioning – interviews, press conferences, etc. – criticism is often hidden in the question's presuppositions (see Q1 and Q2). Furthermore, although interviewers may ask such tough questions to try and tackle evasive politicians, it is also the case that these difficult questions can actually force the politician to be evasive. In the following example, if the Prime Minister gives either of the structurally preferred answers, 'yes' or 'no', he is admitting to wrecking the British economy:

> Q: Since the chairman of the Royal Bank of Scotland has publicly apologised for wrecking his bank, will the Prime Minister apologise to the nation for wrecking the British economy?
> (Peter Tapsell, House of Commons 2008)

Questions like this, where either a 'yes or a 'no' answer would be damaging to the speaker, are popularly known as 'do you still beat your wife?' questions.

Q2

Assertions and presuppositions

What are the dangers for the interviewee (in both cases it is Boris Johnson, newly appointed UK Foreign Secretary in 2016) in the following questions posed at a televised press conference? Which question uses assertion and which relies on presupposition?

---

1) Q: Can I give you the opportunity to apologise to the world leaders you may or may not have been rude to over the past 12 months, and ask what your strategy is to build trust?
2) Q: You have an unusually long history of wild exaggerations and, frankly, outright lies that, I think, few foreign secretaries have prior to this job. And, I'm wondering, how Mr Kerry and others should believe what you say considering this very, very long history?

Extension exercise: To analyse presuppositions in more detail, and help us to identify them, it is useful to become familiar with different kinds of *presupposition triggers*. Presupposition triggers are words or phrases that signal that some information is being presupposed by the speaker. The following are some common triggers:[1]

- Factive verbs, e.g. *realise, know, ignore, regret*. These kinds of verbs presuppose that the embedded clause is true. For example, in *she realised she had broken the law* and *she didn't realise she had broken the law*, the information which stays unchanged is that she did actually break the law.
- Implicative verbs, e.g. *manage, remember*. These kinds of verbs are also interesting because even when negated, some information remains unaffected. E.g. *He didn't manage to become Prime Minister* and *He managed to become Prime Minister* both presuppose that he *tried* to become Prime Minister.
- Change-of-state verbs, e.g. *stop, continue*. Like the first set, these also presuppose that the second part (the complement) is true. Compare *he has stopped lying to Parliament* and *he has not stopped lying to Parliament*.
- Iteratives, e.g. *again, anymore, return*. These also function in a similar way, as in *The Chancellor is lying again* and *The Chancellor isn't lying again* both presuppose that she did lie at one point.
- Temporal clauses, e.g. *before, while, since*. These function in a similar way to the previous set. Compare *Before becoming President, she was very honest* and *Before becoming President, she was not very honest*. In both cases, the information that stays

the same is what is asserted in the first part; that she became president.
- Cleft sentences, e.g. *It wasn't me who leaked the report.* In this case, what is presupposed is that someone else did leak it.

All of these give us 'clues' to the presence of presupposed information and one of testing for this, as we have just seen, is by using negation and checking what information remains the same, following the negation.

TASK 2: *Presupposition triggers*

What triggers can you identify in the following questions from the UK House of Commons and House of Lords, and what information is being presupposed? Notice how the presuppositions are clustered together in these questions to make them more hostile. ('Misleading the house' is a way of saying that the politician has lied to the Parliament. As so often in political discourse, the speaker is constrained by the rules governing the interaction; in this case, they cannot say 'lied' because it is considered unparliamentary language.):

1) I should be grateful if the Minister would apologise for misleading the House: such examples show why people have lost faith in the government and why the government's assertions about taxes and benefits are simply not believed any more.
2) William Waldegrave was criticised for being involved in misleading the House.
3) I would never suggest that the Prime Minister would deliberately mislead the House, but I suggest that it is even more worrying that he did not realise that he was misleading the House.
4) How can the Secretary of State get away with misleading the House in such a vile way?
5) The Czechs are looking forward to participating: The hon. Gentleman must stop misleading the House continually by insisting that our partners in the new Europe [. . .] will not have the full right to participate in the intergovernmental conference on the same basis as the United Kingdom.

TASK 3: *Matching questions and responses*

The following questions are all from White House press conferences. Can you match the questions with the responses listed below? What are the dangers for the spokesperson in each case? The first has been completed as an example.

Questions

1) Q: On Korea – what are you planning to highlight tomorrow? Will the President – has there been any consideration of the South Korean request that the US consider lifting sanctions?

2) Q: The Senator from Virginia, John Warner, says the lack of a US exit strategy [from the war] puts the US on the brink of disaster right now.

3) Q: Mike, can you fill in the details on the reprimand that Hazel O'Leary got from Leon Panetta? And does the President intend to talk to her about this?

4) Q: If Gerry Adams can't, in effect, deliver something from the IRA, at least a commitment to peace, then what exactly is the US trying to do in talking with him?

5) Q: Do you think that the practical effect of what you did in October by putting in the monitors and trusting the existing ruler has tied NATO's hands?

6) Q: The White House supposedly refuses to intervene to try to resolve the tobacco dispute. Is that true?

7) Q: But as it's retested again in the District Court using those new criteria, will the White House continue to say that it is complying?

8) Q: Did the phone call mean that they've kissed and made up?

Responses

A) MR MCCURRY: Absolutely, because they are [. . .]

B) MR MCCURRY: We have not intervened at any point in the process. We have monitored the discussions the parties are having and we hope [. . .]

C) MR MCCURRY: We don't accept the premise of that question because he has been an important contributor in the discussions that have occurred to date and we hope he will remain so.

D) MR LOCKHART: If you persist in believing that they needed to kiss and make up, I'll let you go on with this. But I think I've addressed that several times.

E) MR MCCURRY: Well, there has not been a request by the Republic of Korea to lift sanctions on North Korea. There have been some suggestions that President Kim Dae Jung has an interest in raising that issue and exploring it with President Clinton during their state visit tomorrow.

F) MR MCCURRY: He is wrong that there is no exit strategy. We have a mission plan with clear mission objectives [continues].

G) MR LOCKHART: Mara, it's not a question of trusting the existing ruler. If we trusted him, why would we put in monitors? We put in monitors to verify the agreements we've made.

H) MR MCCURRY: No, I can't because that's not the nature of the conversation she had with Mr Panetta. Mr Panetta met with Secretary O'Leary yesterday to review her upcoming testimony on the Hill, to give her support for the job she's been doing [continues with praise of Secretary O'Leary]

1 – E The question presupposes that South Korea (the Republic of Korea) has made such a request, which, according to the podium, is not the case.

2 –

3 –

4 –

5 –

6 –

7 –

8 –

8.4 Question structure

The grammatical structure of the question may also be manipulated by those asking questions, in order to make them more coercive or controlling. Generally speaking, closed *yes/no questions* are more limiting than open *wh questions*. Compare:

Q: Prime Minister, did you ever discuss or approve a change in the rules of engagement for British police to shoot to kill, shoot in the head, policy? Do you think an apology is appropriate to Brazil or the family of the Brazilian who lost his life? (to Blair in 2005)

Q: What is the hardest thing you've done, and what does it say about your capacity to lead? (to Obama in 2007)

Although the question structure is not the only difference in these two questions, it is clear that the second question gives the politician much more room to present himself positively than the first. In the next example, by drawing attention to the structurally preferred answer of yes/no the interviewer manages to negatively evaluate the interviewee as uncooperative and/or evasive:

> PAXMAN: Do you accept any responsibility at all?
> BLAIR: No, I've said what I've said, and I feel desperately sorry for his family [. . .]
> PAXMAN (interrupting): So, you don't accept any responsibility.
> BLAIR: Well it's not a question of not accepting responsibility [. . .]
> PAXMAN (interrupting): It's a question to which you could give a yes or no answer.

The limiting function of yes/no questions may also be strengthened by the use of *tag questions*, that is, when a declarative is followed by a short question (an auxiliary verb and a pronoun):

> Q: (to Blair) Ten years ago, we did a television interview and you said to me – and the quote has been used many, many times since then – 'people think I'm a pretty straight kind of guy'. They don't think that now, do they?

The tag question allows the interviewer to make a clear assertion – in this case that people no longer think Tony Blair (UK Prime Minister at the time) is 'pretty straight', that is, honest – while fulfilling the institutional necessity of asking a question. As Gibbons states, 'the more information included in the question, the greater the questioner's control of the information, so the answerer can contribute less new information' (2003: 101).

Another restricting question type is the *negative interrogative* which is also coercive because it leads the answerer towards a preferred answer, and, similarly, it is frequently used as a 'vehicle for assertions' (Heritage 2002):

> Q: People will look at the Prime Minister and just say, 'Here is a man who breaks his promise.' Why does he not admit that the reason he will not have a referendum is that he is scared of losing it? Does he not understand that if he breaks his promise on this, no one will trust him on anything else?
> (Cameron to Brown, the Prime Minister, House of Commons 2007)

A final category of leading questions that we will consider here are *agreement statements* in which the questioner explicitly invites the interviewee to agree with him/her, usually on a potentially embarrassing proposition:

> Q: In the last few days, members of the Prime Minister's Cabinet have called for the trade unions to be given more money, more power, and in some instances both. Does the Prime Minister agree that they are all wrong?
>
>> (Cameron to Blair, the Prime Minister,
>> House of Commons 2007)

When asked by a hostile questioner, agreement statements generally allow the display of information and force the answerer to disagree, as illustrated in the example above where it is highly unlikely that the Prime Minister will (publicly) agree that his cabinet colleagues are wrong.

8.4.1 Repetition and interruption

Another tactic which may be employed by the interviewer is *repetition*; by repeating the question the questioner can highlight evasion or make the respondent seem evasive. Famously, in an interview in 1995 Jeremy Paxman, an interviewer who has earned the nickname of the 'grand inquisitor', asked Michael Howard, then Home Secretary, the same question twelve times. We can see the same strategy in the following extract between Paxman and Chloe Smith, a government minister:

> Q: When were you told of this change of plan?
> R: Well, as a minister in the Treasury and indeed dealing with fuel matters this has been under consideration for some time
> Q: When was the decision taken?
> R: As I say it's been under consideration for some time
> Q: When was the decision taken?

Similarly, *interruption* may be used to challenge the interviewee, or answerer. By interrupting, the interviewer asserts control and negatively evaluates the interviewee's response as uninformative or unimportant, a kind of *delegitimisation* of the interlocutor.

A special form of interruption is finishing the other person's answer before they themselves can (known as 'other turn completion'). In the following episode from a White House press briefing, the journalists have just been complaining to the spokesperson, Mr Fleischer, about the lack of opportunity to question the President (George W. Bush) directly:

> MR. FLEISCHER: – and I understand that you would like him to take questions in the form of a news conference. I assure you we take a look at this often, and –
>
> Q: And say no. (Laughter)

To summarise then, the following is a list of some of the questioning techniques which are often used to put the interviewee under pressure:

1) Hide a potentially controversial or dangerous proposition as a presupposition.
2) Yes/No questioning, including asking for a straight 'yes or no'.
3) Ask tag questions.
4) Use a negative interrogative.
5) Cite the interviewee's own words (or those of a close colleague).
6) Ask for agreement to a dangerous proposition.
7) Repeat the question.
8) Interruption and finishing the other's turn.
9) The 'have you stopped beating your wife?' question, where responding either 'yes' or 'no' means admitting to wrongdoing (another form of presupposition).

However, we should remember that there are risks for the interviewer too when they use these strategies. If the interviewer is seen as being too hostile, they will be accused of lacking 'neutrality'. For instance, in an interview with the Conservative politician Boris Johnson, the interviewer, Andrew Marr, interrupted on multiple occasions and the two battled over the topic direction quite overtly, as shown in the extract below.

> Q: Let's move on to tipper trucks just for a second. We need to move on, we've got a lot to cover.
> R: Well, I'm going to tell you what I'm going to cover.
> Q: No, guess what? It's not the Boris Johnson show, it's the Andrew Marr show – I get to ask the questions.

The Spectator (a conservative magazine) reported this interview with the headline 'Andrew Marr accused of EU bias over Boris Johnson interview'. In research into reactions to political interviews in Israel, Kampf and Daskal (2013) found that members of the public were more likely to complain about overly hostile interviews than overly deferential ones.

8.5 Taking responsibility (or not): *attribution* and *neutralism* in questions

In many cases, where the criticism in a question is particularly acute, or perhaps where one speaker is contradicting another, the ideas or opinions in the question are often ascribed to another *source*, especially other authorities (for example, by quoting from the press, other agencies, including governmental ones, other politicians, and so on):

> Q: Mike, two publications today, the *Post* and the *Times*, both used the word 'paranoia' to describe the way the President feels

about the issues that are raised by current accusations and past accusations.

(White House press briefing, 1998)

This is the journalistic phenomenon known as *attribution*. It enables the interviewer to appear to maintain a neutral stance with respect to both the interviewee and their own questions. To emphasise that the neutrality of the interviewer is an artifice, Clayman (1992) employs the term *neutralism* to describe it. He points out that it is normal, in American and British contexts, for interviewees to acknowledge and acquiesce to the adversarial, even hostile, stance of their interlocutor. He claims that it is, in fact, constructed and maintained collaboratively. This means that there is a default, or normal, assumption on the part of interviewees that 'the interviewer's own opinions are not at issue' and interviewees 'regularly decline to implicate interviewers or hold them responsible for what was said' (1992: 196), even when what was said was critical and potentially damaging. There can, however, be exceptions (from Harris 1991: 81; *pits* are coal-mines):

Interviewer: What's the future if uneconomic pits continue to be around – won't that in the end undermine the mining industry?

Trade Union Leader: Well, as you know Miss Chalmers, it must be that you're listening to your own propaganda because for the last 40 minutes I've been explaining to you that the NCB in Britain is the most efficient and technologically advanced industry in the world.

In such cases, however, the interviewee risks appearing particularly irascible and unreasonable. It is generally more advisable to acquiesce to the adversarial style of interviewing at least and respond to the question rather than attack the questioner.

Q3

How adversarial – with or without attribution – do you consider the questioning in political interviews in your country? How would politicians in your country react to hostile questioning? (Free response)

8.6 *Primary* and *secondary* sources

The following question contains a double attribution:

Q: Joe, the *New York Times* reports the Pentagon declaring that the captured Yugoslav lieutenant is 'a prisoner of war'. But last week, I re-call your telling us, it's not a war, it's a conflict.

(White House press briefing, 1999)

The *New York Times* in such cases is known as the *secondary* source, reporting the supposed words or opinions of a *primary* source, the Pentagon.

There are a number of what we can call *attributing expressions* in the above example: *reports*, *declaring* and *telling us*. In general, there are a variety of such expressions including *quote* (*quotes*, *is quoted*), *says* (*saying*, *said*) and *is quoted* or *reported as saying*.

TASK 4: *Attribution*

Find the primary and secondary source in the following. Underline the attributing expressions.

1) Q: The President is quoted in the *Washington Post* this morning as saying that the Democratic controlled Senate is not interested in the security of the American people.

Primary: ; Secondary:

Attributing expressions:

2) Q: The *New Zealand Star Times* quoted General Schwarzkopf as saying in Auckland that the NATO bombing mistakes, as he termed them, in Yugoslavia, are, in his words, inexcusable.

Primary: ; Secondary:

Attributing expressions:

3) Q: I'm quoting you. 'The President is not under any medical treatment for any psychiatric or mental condition.'

Now, that being the case, isn't the sole alternative what *Reuters* News Agency quoted Angie Dickinson saying in Hollywood: Clinton has a very horny appetite?

First paragraph:

a) Primary: ; Secondary:

Attributing expressions:

Second paragraph:

b) Primary: ; Secondary:

Attributing expressions:

4) DAVID FROST: [. . .] but Gordon Brown is quoted today as saying that I will decide if the five points are met.

Primary: ; Secondary:

Attributing expressions:

You will have noted how in (4) the secondary source is, in fact, not specified. This is very common practice. We often find attributing expressions like *there are reports that* Mr Such-and-such *has criticised* [. . .], Mr Such-and-such *has been quoted as saying*, and so on. Often *both* sources are left unspecified:

> DIMBLEBY: [On the BBC Today programme] Britain's Chief Drugs Commissioner, Keith Halliwell, goes public about all those reports that his job is on the line.

Who says his job is on the line (in danger)? Where can we find such reports? Perhaps the interviewer is inventing or at least exaggerating. We just cannot say and cannot check.

Q4

What do you think might be the dangers for the audience when the sources of an attribution are not specified? (Free response)

There are numerous different types of sources for facts and opinions. These include:

- press agencies
- prestigious newspaper reports
- tabloid newspaper reports
- politicians on the same side as the interviewee
- politicians on the opposing side
- government agencies and officials
- unnamed sources

TASK 5: *Quoting from sources*

When a questioner quotes from one of these sources, which do you think are liable to cause the interviewee the greatest difficulties? Look at the real-life episodes from the White House briefings below to help you decide.

In this first episode, the *Star* is a US tabloid:

> Q: A former White House steward named Mike McGrath was quoted today as having said that he was required to leave the President alone with —
> MR MCCURRY: Wait, in the *Star*, right?

Q: That's in the *Star*, correct.

MR MCCURRY: I don't have any comment on stories in which people are paid to provide information.

The spokesman (Mr Joe Lockhart) is a Democrat:

Q: Joe, some Republicans have said the Chinese espionage scandal is at least partially responsible for President Clinton and congressional Democrats reversing course on the issue of missile defense. How do you respond to that [. . .]?

MR LOCKHART: It's not. That is an example of the kind of partisan shot that I was talking about the other day.

In the next, the source is not named:

Q: Some are saying that by attacking a residence, whether he was there or not, this was an assassination attempt.

MR LOCKHART: Well, as Wolf said, probably the — some are saying that, the same 'some' that Wolf referenced, and those 'some' are still wrong. Try again.

In the final episode, the questioner suggests there is disagreement in the government ranks:

Q: Joe, there was a report in the *Los Angeles Times* this morning that Secretary of State Albright was disappointed with the formulation that you and the President have enunciated, that there would have to be either an explicit or implicit agreement from Belgrade before a force could go into Kosovo.

MR LOCKHART: Not that I'm aware of. I'm not aware of any disappointment. I'm not aware of any disagreement on what that policy is.

8.7 Fighting back

Read the following and then look at the question below.

George Negus: Why do people stop us in the street almost and tell us that Margaret Thatcher isn't just inflexible, she's not just single-minded, on occasions she's plain pig-headed and won't be told by anybody?

Margaret Thatcher: Would you tell me who has stopped you in the street and said that?

Negus: Ordinary Britons [. . .]

Thatcher: Where?

Negus: In conversation, in pubs [. . .]

Thatcher (interrupting): I thought you'd just come from Belize

Negus: Oh this is not the first time we've been here

Thatcher: Will you tell me who, and where and when?

Negus: Ordinary Britons in restaurants [. . .]

Thatcher (interrupting): How many?

Negus: [. . .] in cabs

Thatcher: How many?

Negus: I would say at least one in two

Thatcher: I'm sorry, it's an expression I've never heard. Tell me who has said it to you when are where

Negus: These are people we obviously meet in passing [. . .]

Thatcher (interrupting): But you obviously cannot say who or where

Negus: They tell us, yes, we have a tough Prime Minister but she's a little bit pig-headed. She won't be told by anybody.

Thatcher: Isn't this interesting. Even the tone of voice you are using is changing from what you used earlier

('*60 Minutes*', *Channel 9, Australia* 1981.
See https://tinyurl.com/PiP-Thatcher)

Q6

The interviewer opens with a highly confrontational question. It contains an accusation which borders on a personal insult of being 'plain pig-headed', attributed very vaguely to 'people'. How precisely does Mrs Thatcher 'fight back' against this interviewer?

We have already seen in some of the extracts in the sections above ways in which interviewees can respond to tricky or aggressive questioning. One is to dismiss the source of a reported attributed proposition as unreliable:

MR MCCURRY: I don't have any comment on stories in which people are paid to provide information.

or obviously prejudiced against you:

MR LOCKHART: That is an example of the kind of partisan shot that I was talking about the other day.

Other tactics include interrupting the questioner, if you can, to disrupt the narrative they are trying to create. Correcting the interviewer's factual information can be highly effective:

> PM Blair: Let me correct the right hon: Gentleman: Crime did not fall under the Conservatives – it doubled.
>
> (House of Commons Hansard 2000)

as can criticising their aggressive style and lack of competence. The interviewer here asks if the interviewee would like to withdraw her previous comments about the 'widows of 9/11':

> Ann Coulter: No, I think you can save any of these 'do you want to withdraw' questions, but you *could* quote me accurately. I didn't write about the '9/11 widows', I wrote about *four* 9/11 widows cutting campaign commercials for John Kerry and using the fact that their husbands died on 9/11 to prevent anyone from responding.
>
> (*BBC Newsnight* 2006)

Finally, asking for more details, as Thatcher does insistently in her interview with Negus can also be highly effective.

The interviewee may also make use of the same strategies as the interviewer, for instance, drawing on authoritative sources (especially 'the public'), or using repetition to try and assert their story. Particularly in non-live interviews, the politicians may be trying to ensure that their '**soundbite**' will be picked up by the media and so make extensive use of repetition. However, this can carry its own risks, as in the non-live interview with the then leader of the Labour Party Ed Miliband, which you can watch here: https://tinyurl.com/PiP-Miliband

---

Q7

How many repetitions do you notice?

Finally, however, as reported in 8.5 above ('it must be that you're listening to your own propaganda'), openly accusing the interviewer of prejudice is a high-risk strategy which can easily backfire. The 'rules' of interview engagement and the convention of neutralism allow the interviewer to be oppositional and the interviewee is normally well advised not to lose their calm.

8.8 Who is talking? One *above* you or one *of* you?

Another important tool in the 'fight back' is how the politician chooses to present themselves in their responses. If we imagine the Prime Minister or president of a country, they can speak from their multiple different identities: as the leader of the government, as the leader of a political party, as a politician, as a citizen of that country, as a member of a particular religion, as a man/woman and many, many more. At different points, it will be strategically useful for the speaker to emphasise these identities too. Sometimes, speakers will explicitly state who they are speaking as (their *footing* in Goffman's 1981 terms), as illustrated in the examples below from debates in the UK Parliament:

1) **Speaking as a GP working in the community,** I know how difficult it is to get specialists to go out to nursing homes, or to have someone admitted to hospital from a nursing home when they need more specialist care, because they are no longer a priority for that hospital trust: Those barriers need to be broken down.

2) **Speaking as a member of the black community,** I do not wish to be blamed for a rise in crime: What every black person wants, as much as any white person, is what every taxpaying member of our community wants – a police force that is fair and equitable.

3) My Lords, **speaking as a lonely elderly person** who is aware that her birthday cards have gone astray, may I ask the Minister what he considers normal? Does he consider it normal that, when a parcel is delivered, the postman no longer rings the bell but simply leaves a card? [. . .] will he ensure that more attention is paid to the efficiency of the Post Office as it works at present?

In these three examples, we can see that the speaker claims a particular identity, or *ethos* (Unit 1), in order to strengthen their argument. It is a model of authority (as discussed in Unit 3), in this case, one which makes them more competent to speak on the topic than their interlocutors who may not share this identity (see 'competence face', Unit 3). For each different example, discuss how the footing strengthens their argument.

Speakers may also strategically swap between identities or 'who is speaking' in order to align with their interlocutors and/or different audiences. Pronouns, particularly 'I' and 'we', have been much studied in political discourse analysis. Here, we will focus on 'we' in order to think about who the speaker is including (and also, often by implication, *excluding*).

TASK 6: *Who is 'we'?*

Look at the following examples and consider who is included (and excluded) from the 'we':

1) Do you want to see that happen? And with Alaskans' love and care for **our** environment and **our** lands and **our** wildlife, Alaskans

are saying yes because **we** believe that it can be done safely, prudently, and it had better be done ethically also. Yes, **we** want to see that drilling. So hopefully the rest of America can understand that also. (Sarah Palin)

2) I see the United States as being a force for good in the world. And as Ronald Reagan used to talk about, America being the beacon of light and hope for those who are seeking democratic values and tolerance and freedom. I see **our** country being able to represent those things that can be looked to as that leadership, that light needed across the world. (Sarah Palin)

3) The piece **we**'ve been pushing for, Barack and I during the campaign, as you'll recall, is that **we** needed an economic recovery package **we** thought back in September, October, November. And **we** still think we really very badly need it. (Joe Biden)

4) Michelle and I talk about it, and **we** decide is there somebody that **we** should – there are some people **we** should talk to who know more about the real estate market in Kenwood – because **we** had never purchased a house before. (Barack Obama)

These examples all come from research by Proctor and Su (2011) in which they analysed pronoun use by the candidates for the 2008 US elections. In this study, the analysis of pronouns was principally used not to understand the dynamics of the interview but the more general positioning of the candidate. Among other trends they found that Biden (the successful Democrat candidate for vice-president) identified himself strongly with Obama (44% of 'we' references), whereas his Republican equivalent, Palin, never used 'we' to refer to herself plus her presidential candidate, John McCain. Of the candidates for the Democrat nominations, they found that Hillary Clinton primarily used 'we' to refer to herself plus the government (44%). In contrast, Obama (the successful candidate) used 'we' mostly to refer to himself plus his campaign crew (35%), followed by himself plus Americans (18%).

The use of 'we' to include all potential voters is a powerful tool to emphasise common ground. Shifts in footing may also be a way of trying to enhance affective face; for instance, when a politician includes their interviewer in the 'we'. However, we should not assume that these strategies are always successful. When the UK Conservative Party adopted the campaign slogan 'we are all in this together' to signal that the pain of economic cuts would be shared by everyone in the country, the message was repeatedly challenged in the non-Conservative media, generating headlines such as the following:

We are not all in this together: Ministers will be largely untouched by the cuts they are introducing.

(*New Statesman* 2010)

They're all in it together! Tory rich list are big winners from 50p cut: David Cameron, Boris Johnson – and George Osborne himself – will reap Budget rewards

(*Independent* 2012)

Millionaire George Osborne may say we're all in it together, but he is in a different bit of 'it' to the rest of us.

(*Mirror* 2012)

Another way that a speaker may signal who they are 'speaking as' is through the *style* that they use. All speakers naturally use different styles of language in different contexts (think of someone you know well having a phone conversation – can you guess who they are speaking to from the way they are speaking?). In order to persuade, speakers may change their style both consciously and unconsciously. In a study of political discourse in Trinidad and Tobago, Esposito (2016) describes how Kamla Persad-Bissessar (who became Prime Minister in 2010) positions herself as 'one of the people' through explicit footing moves such as the following:

You can trust me, you can trust me with your children, because I too am a mother and a parent.

(Persad-Bissessar 2010)

And, perhaps more subtly, through her use of Trinidadian English Creole. In fact, throughout the researcher's dataset, the politician switches from standard English to Trinidadian Creole exclusively when she is talking about her opponent:

He re-shuffled his cabinet and pretended not to hear the cry from his own party to give Dr Keith Rowley the Ministry of National Security. Instead, he put Keith in the doghouse and end up firing him. And he doh want Keith tuh talk. Not at all. Having put him in the PNM doghouse, he now trying to muzzle him! Buh wait, all hell will break loose soon [. . .] yuh ever hear ah plot hound muzzle ah Rottweilier?!!

(Persad-Bissessar 2010)

In this context, as in many, style-switching serves an affective and strategic purpose; here it helps her to assert an identity other than the distant politician, and sets up a frame which allows the impoliteness acts to be more appealing to an audience. If we think back to the discussion of face in Unit 3, we can see that moving to a less formal and solidarity-driven style helps the politician prioritise their *affective* face.

The ability to style-switch successfully is often associated with the nebulous qualities of 'authenticity' and 'relatability'. In many countries, politicians are praised and criticised for their ability to style-switch. For instance, Hillary Clinton's accent appears to have changed considerably over her career and changes depending on the situation (see, for example, the clips here: http://tinyurl.com/ljktn4q).

Although we have discussed footing or 'who is speaking' with reference to responses here, it is of course also very important to the questioners. As we discussed above, the political interviewer may seek to take up a position of neutrality and they will display that by 'speaking as' a professional (just doing my job).

Review exercise

Watch the video and read the transcript of an interview between Jeremy Paxman and Tony Blair available on the BBC website: https://tinyurl.com/PiP-Paxman

Focus on the first twelve questions and responses (adjacency pairs). What can you say about the interview style with reference to all the features discussed in this Unit? (NB you may find it easier to analyse this item if you copy the first section into Word or print it so you can highlight the different features).

Further reading

Bull, P. and Fetzer, A. (2006) 'Who are we and who are you? The strategic use of forms of address in political interviews', *Text & Talk* 26(1): 3–37.
Jiang, X. (2006) 'Cross-cultural pragmatic differences in US and Chinese press conferences: The case of the North Korea nuclear crisis', *Discourse & Society* 17(2): 237–257. (This case study also includes a detailed system for categorising responses which could be useful for your own analysis.)
Partington, A. (2003) *The Linguistics of Political Argument: The Spin-Doctor and the Wolf-Pack at the White House*, London: Routledge.

Keys and commentaries

TASK 1: *Question–response in institutional discourses*

Table 8.1 Key: participants in institutional discourse

Type of discourse	Who asks the questions?	Who responds?
Political interview	Interviewer (journalist)	Politician
Examination of witness	Lawyer	Witness
Press conference	Journalist	Spokesperson
Police interview	Detective	Suspect
Medical interview	Doctor	Patient
Job interview	Personnel officer	Job applicant

Q1

The hostile presupposition in (1) is that the first chapter of her book is poor and in (2) that the Green Party Manifesto has several 'nutty', i.e. crazy, proposals. In (3) the presuppositions are, first, that so-called 'blasphemy' is a crime and, second, there should be some form of punishment for it. The controversy was heightened by the context of the question, namely, the desire of the government of Pakistan, where 'blasphemy' is a crime punishable by death, to control the 'blasphemous' content of Facebook.

Q2

Dangerous presuppositions

1) In the first, particularly damaging presuppositions are that there is an existing lack of trust (triggered by 'rebuild') and that the politician has done something wrong (triggered by 'apologise').
2) In the second, the questioner begins with the open assertion and their negative evaluation of the politician, namely, that Johnson is untrustworthy. The second part, which contains the actual interrogative, then embeds these assertions ('this very long history') so that they become presuppositions. The structurally preferred response from the politician is one that addresses 'how they should believe what you say', not the issue of past lying.

TASK 2: *Presupposition triggers*

In the examples regarding the face-threatening act of accusing a colleague of lying we see a range of different techniques being used to package up and 'smuggle in' this information. In the first, we have an example of a factive verb (*apologise*) which presupposes that the Minister did mislead the house. This example is then followed up with a second presupposition, that people have indeed lost faith in the government and, furthermore, that their assertions are not believed. The second uses an emotional factive (more transparently also labelled as a verb of judgement) (*criticise*) in which the focus is on the reception of the act of lying, not whether or not Waldegrave did so. The third also makes use of a factive verb (*realise*) and shifts the focus to the target's knowledge of his actions, not whether or not he committed the act of lying. In the fourth example, we have an implicative verb as the trigger (*get away with*) where the focus is again on the reception of the act of misleading (was he punished or not) and the actual act if lying is presupposed. Finally, in the fifth example we have a change-of-state verb (*stop*) which presupposes that the act of misleading has already started.

TASK 3: *Matching questions and responses*

1 – E The question presupposes that South Korea (the Republic of Korea) has made such a request, which, according to the podium, is not the case.

2 – F The question presupposes that the US has no exit strategy. The podium disagrees and claims it does have one.

3 – H The presupposition is that Mr Panetta reprimanded Ms O'Leary (and perhaps that the President needs to do the same). The podium claims that, on the contrary, he praised her.

4 – C The presupposition is that, since Mr Adams has no influence with the military IRA, there is no point in using him to talk to them. The podium contradicts this and suggests that he does have influence.

5 – G The questioner presupposes that 'putting in monitors' is equivalent to 'trusting the existing leader' (note the use of 'and' to imply this equivalence). The podium contradicts this and states that 'putting in monitors' implies the opposite, *not* trusting the existing leader.

6 – B The expression '*refuses* to intervene' implies a deliberate decision not to intervene and expresses an unfavourable evaluation. The podium instead evaluates the non-intervention favourably and adds that the White House is not immobile but is doing something active, i.e. 'monitoring' the situation.

7 – A The expression '*continues* to say' implies considerable doubt that what is being said is true. The podium counters this by emphasising the truth of the White House's statements.

8 – D The presupposition is that, if there is a need to 'kiss and make up', there must have been a previous falling out. The podium denies this is the case. The phone call was between President Bill Clinton and Senator Jackson: the questioner is clearly making fun of them.

TASK 4: *Attribution*

1) Primary: *The President*; Secondary: *The Washington Post*.
   Attributing expressions: *is quoted* [. . .] *as saying*.

2) Primary: *General Schwarzkopf*; Secondary: *The New Zealand Star Times*.
   Attributing expression: *quoted* [. . .] *as saying, as he termed them, in his words*.

3) (a) Primary: *The podium*; Secondary: *The journalist*.
   Attributing expressions: *I'm quoting*.
   (b) Primary: *Angie Dickinson*: Secondary: *Reuters*.
   Attributing expressions: *quoted*, *saying*.

4) Primary: *Gordon Brown*; Secondary: *Unspecified*.
   Attributing expressions: *is quoted* [. . .] *as saying*.

TASK 5: *Quoting from sources*

When a questioner quotes from one of these sources, which do you think are liable to cause the interviewee the greatest difficulties?

The spokesperson has the biggest problems with statements quoted from other government officials, such as Secretary Albright, since their statements cannot be ignored. On the other hand, the spokesperson finds it easier to dismiss allegations coming from the tabloid press as inconsequential and those coming from opposing politicians as cheap, 'partisan shots'.

Q6

How precisely does Mrs Thatcher 'fight back' against this interviewer?

She first of all refuses to accept the question at face value and challenges the assertion that 'ordinary people say she is plain pig-headed'. She does this by responding to the question with questions of her own, asking for more precise details of the very vague attributed source, namely 'people' ('who, when and where'). When an interviewer cannot provide details demanded of them, they risk appearing either unprepared, that they are fabricating, inventing a narrative or even that they are prejudiced against the interviewee.

She also manages to successfully interrupt the interviewer on several occasions, which disrupts his attempt to create his narrative, his negative portrayal of her personality.

The insertion of the information 'I thought you'd just come from Belize', carries the implication that the interviewer cannot have heard recently from 'ordinary Britons', and that he is, therefore, fabricating a hostile narrative. From then on, the interviewer is on the defensive. When he returns to the posing the question again, the wording is radically toned down: she is no longer *inflexible* but *tough* (often thought to be positive in a leader) and not '*plain* pig-headed' but '*a little bit* pig-headed'. But once more she refuses to accept the assertion and instead comments on the interviewer's altered 'tone of voice'. Not responding to a question but commenting on it assumes a position of authority and the power to set the rules of the interchange and is another way of delegitimising an interlocutor. Note the difference between this more subtle stratagem and openly accusing the interviewer of malice or prejudice.

Q7

You probably identified a large number of repetitions. What this clip really reveals is how the interview process has changed as the news media move towards short clips or soundbites. We can safely assume that Miliband never expected the whole section to be broadcast and was trying to control the content of the chosen short clip.

TASK 6: *Who are 'we'?*

In the first example, we can see that the identity Palin is prioritising here is her local nationality; being Alaskan. In fact, the paper showed that she often claimed nationalism as an identity. Here, what is interesting, given that she is running for Vice-President of the US, is that she opposes that group to 'the rest of the America'; that is, those who would be voting for her. In the second example, in contrast, she refers to 'our country', presumably including herself plus all potential voters in that 'our'. In the third example, Biden is including just himself and Obama in the 'we', thus here the pronoun has a much more restricted scope. The last example is also very restricted, referring to just Obama himself and his wife, Michelle. This was typical of his discourse in these interviews where he spoke as a member of a married couple more frequently than any of the other candidates.

Review key

As you will have noted, the interview style is aggressive and we can identify many of the features discussed in this Unit. The interviewer, Mr Paxman, tries to impose a certain narrative, in which Mr Blair is evaluated unfavourably, to force the Prime Minister to admit his mistakes.

Paxman opens the interview by asking Blair if there is anything he would like to apologise for, thus introducing immediately the *presupposition* that Blair has done something wrong, and more specifically something wrong which has affected the viewers. There are a number of bald *assertions*, in which Paxman challenges Blair, such as 'when you wrote in the foreword to the dossier "that the threat from Saddam was serious and current", it wasn't'.

The majority of the questions are *closed* in structure, that is to say they invite a yes/no answer and, therefore, limit the potential for Blair to assert an alternative narrative – one in which he is evaluated more positively, in which he can enhance his face. More specifically, there are a number of *tag questions* such as 'When you told parliament that the intelligence was "extensive, detailed and authoritative", that wasn't true *was it?*', or 'Well therefore it's not extensive, detailed and authoritative *is it?*'. These two examples are coercive because the information is already contained in the question, and they attempt to enforce a specific response, namely, 'no'. In order to reject the assertions and still stay within the preferred grammatical response of yes/no, Blair would have to very directly disagree with Paxman, which can be dangerous in front of an audience, because in this way *he* may appear to be the one who is being aggressive or uncooperative. In another example of a tag question, 'but you know *don't you* that just two weeks before you made that statement, the Joint Intelligence Committee said that "intelligence remains limited"?', the tag 'you know don't you' is embedded within the phrase. There is also an instance of what we termed *agreement statements* in the second question that Paxman asks: 'But *do you agree* that there is a trust issue, and that you can't any longer say, look at me, I'm a pretty straight kind of guy?', which attempts to coerce Blair into agreeing with two propositions which are highly damaging to him.

The question above also illustrates the way in which *attribution* is used; in this case Paxman is citing Blair's own description of himself as a 'pretty straight sort of guy', which we mentioned earlier. Towards the end of the extract, Paxman again refers to Blair's own words, saying, 'Well, so when *you wrote* in the forward to the dossier "that the threat from Saddam was serious and current", it wasn't'. Another damaging source is introduced in the following sentence: 'And indeed your *own* Chief of Staff, Jonathan Powell, had said that the dossier did nothing to demonstrate a threat' where the proximity of the source to the interviewee is emphasised with *own* and where the use of *your own* implies either disagreement among government officials (an accusation the press always delights in) or that Blair is so incompetent he does not know what his own staff think or say. As noted previously, citing sources close to the interviewee makes it much more difficult for him or her to reject the information.

You probably also noted the use of interruption, for example, in:

BLAIR: Of course intelligence always is limited but –
PAXMAN: Well therefore it's not extensive, detailed and authoritative is it?

And there is also an example of the special type of interruption mentioned earlier in which one person finishes another's utterance (other turn completion) – usually in order to portray the first speaker negatively in some way, perhaps by offering a very blunt synthesis of the speaker's presumed intent:

BLAIR: No, they weren't wrong in what they reported at the time, they were absolutely right. But later it transpired that –
PAXMAN: It wasn't true.

Clearly, Blair was not about to finish the sentence with 'it wasn't true'. By adding his own turn completion Paxman manages to interrupt Blair and also to impose his own narrative onto Blair's utterance – a narrative which creates a direct and almost ridiculous opposition between 'they weren't *wrong* [. . .] they were absolutely *right*' and 'it wasn't *true*'.

Note

1 If you would like to see some more kinds of triggers, you could start with the page from the free Stanford Encylopedia of Philosophy: https://plato. stanford.edu/entries/presupposition/

9 Humour, irony and satire in politics

Castigat ridendo mores.

(Anon. 16th Century)

The one thing the Devil cannot stand is laughter.

(Martin Luther)

I have never made but one prayer to God, a very short one:
'O Lord, make my enemies ridiculous'.

(Voltaire)

9.1 Politics and humour

Politics and humour enjoy a close relationship on a number of levels. As we saw in Unit 8, aggressive political interactions such as the UK Prime Minister's Questions are often treated as humorous entertainment by the viewing media and public. Humour is, of course, a tool used for *evaluation*, both positive and, more commonly, negative evaluation. Some political jokes are simply about politics itself:

> The problem with political jokes is that they usually get elected.
> (Harry Kate 1990)

But it can also be more closely targeted and can be used both *by* and *against* those in power. It is used to evaluate those in power and by those in power to evaluate each other.

As regards the first, used by those in power, humour – barbs, witticisms and jokes – at the expense of a political opponent of a group has always been a part of political rhetoric. In democratic systems, it plays a role in the 'us against them', 'our good ideas contrasted with their bad ideas' kind of rhetoric described in Unit 3. Politicians use humour to attack, criticise or simply gain a rhetorical advantage over rivals, as Voltaire says above, to make their enemies seem ridiculous. Examples from history are plentiful:

> The trouble with our Liberal friends is not that they're ignorant; it's just that they know so much that isn't so.
> (Ronald Reagan 1964)

As regards the second, humour being used in the media to mock politicians, entire TV comedy shows have been dedicated to this aim; for example, *Saturday Night Live* in the US or *Spitting Image*, *Have I Got News for You* or *Mock the Week* in the UK. Humorous publications like *Private Eye* in the UK and *Charlie Hebdo* in France also attack politics, politicians and the media too when it fails to do its job of scrutiny. Indeed, this ability to employ targeted humour greatly increases the media's power.

9.1.1 Humour and subversion

Many commentators have discussed the *subversive* power of humour, how it allows 'the little person', the powerless, to gain some small revenge at the expense of the powerful. In totalitarian states, of course, humour at the expense of the regime is generally forbidden. Raskin (1985), however, presents a collection of jokes which circulated in the pre-1989 Soviet bloc nations. These very often implied discontent or criticisms of the system rather than of individual politicians, for example:

> A group of students from East Germany are all killed in a car crash. They discover that hell, too, is divided into an eastern and western sector. Given the choice, those who see themselves as ideologically sound opt for the eastern hell. A fact-finding delegation arrives from the western hell; they complain: 'Conditions on our western side are terrible; we've been boiled in oil three times already and roasted half a dozen times. How are things with you, in the eastern hell?' 'Fine', is the answer. 'They've run out of fuel'.
>
> (Adapted from Larsen 1980: 94–95)

The humour arises from a reversal of *evaluation*: the renowned inefficiency of the East German communist state suddenly and ironically becomes a good thing (see section 9.2).

However, even in environments where free speech within limits is tolerated, political humour thrives – there is still a human need to dress down those with power. In fact, many stand-up comics in western countries earn their living almost entirely from political jokes. Generally, however, these tend to have as their target individual politicians rather than the system itself. There are various categories. The politician may be depicted as very unpopular:

> President Richard Nixon is visiting an elementary school one day.
>
> In one of the classes, they're in the middle of a discussion about words and their meanings.
>
> The teacher asks Nixon if he'd like to lead the discussion of the word 'tragedy'.
>
> He agrees to do so and asks the class for an example of a tragedy.

One little boy stands up and says, 'If my best friend who lives on a farm, is playing in the field and a runaway tractor comes along and runs him over and kills him, that would be a tragedy'.

'No', says Nixon, 'That would be an accident'.

Next a little girl raises her hand and says, 'If a school bus carrying forty children went off a cliff, killing everyone inside, that would be a tragedy'.

'No, I'm afraid not', says Nixon. 'That's what we would call a great loss'.

The room goes silent for a while as no other children volunteer.

Nixon looks around the room and says a little testily, 'Isn't there anyone here who can give me an example of a tragedy?'

At last, a little boy at the back of the class raises his hand and says, 'If a private jet carrying you, Mr Nixon, was struck by a missile and blown to smithereens, that would be a tragedy'.

'Fantastic!' shouts Nixon, 'That's exactly right. And can you tell me why that would be a tragedy?'

'Well', says the boy, 'Because it sure as hell wouldn't be a great loss and it probably wouldn't be an accident either'.

or vastly over-ambitious:

Donald Trump, Vladimir Putin and Barack Obama were having a meeting on the Air Force One aeroplane when it crashes. They ascend to heaven, and God's sitting on the great white throne. God addresses Barack first.

'So, Mr Obama, what do you believe in?'

'Well, I believe in democracy, the Constitution and the right of every American child to become President, just like I did. And, of course, I believe in you, Lord'.

God thinks for a second and says: 'Okay, I can live with that. Come and sit at my left'.

God then addresses Vladimir. 'Now Mr Putin, what do you believe in?'

'I believe in Mother Russia, the strength of the Russian people, and, of course, I believe in you, Lord'.

God thinks for a second and says: 'Okay, that sounds good. Come and sit at my right'.

God then addresses Donald. 'Well, Mr Trump, what do you believe in?'

'I believe you're sitting in my chair'.

or perhaps downright stupid:

> The White House secretary is giving the President his daily briefing on Iraq. He concludes by saying, 'And yesterday, three Brazilian soldiers were killed'.
>
> 'OH NO!' Bush exclaims. 'That's terrible!'
>
> His staff is stunned at this sudden outward display of emotion, nervously watching as the President sits, head in hands, practically sobbing.
>
> Finally, Bush looks up and asks, 'Just how many is a brazillion, anyway?'

And sometimes it is the politician's supporters who are delegitimised by an accusation of stupidity, as in the following poster slogan:

> Vote Trump 2016: Because Thinking is Hard [...]

Humour also becomes a way for politicians to respond to their interlocutors and express criticism in less direct ways. As, for instance, when Obama referenced Trump's obsession with his birthplace in an interview with Jay Leno in 2012:

> This all dates back to when we were growing up in Kenya. We had constant run-ins on the soccer field, he wasn't very good and resented it. When we finally moved to America, I thought it would be over.

Similarly, in an awkward press conference with the US and UK foreign secretaries, John Kerry and the notoriously gaffe-prone Boris Johnson (who, among other things, once likened Hillary Clinton to Lady Macbeth and accused Barack Obama of disliking Britain), the *Atlantic* reported how the former, when asked if he had ever come across anyone quite like the latter, used humour to indirectly (and diplomatically!) criticise his counterpart's lack of past diplomacy:

> Kerry played the seasoned diplomat. He noted that the U.S. ambassador to the EU was a friend of Johnson's from Oxford. He 'told me this man is very smart and capable'.
>
> Johnson's response: 'Fantastic, I can live with that. Phew! We can stop there'.
>
> 'It's called diplomacy', Kerry replied to laughter.
>
> (*The Atlantic* 2016, lightly edited)

9.1.2 Self-deprecating humour and affective face

Humour can also be used by politicians, not to attack others but to gain popularity for themselves. We saw in Unit 3 how politicians, especially in US politics, need to project affective as well as competence face, and one common and effective way to do so is to portray a sense of humour and, in particular, to show the ability to 'take a joke'. In the US, official gatherings are organised where top politicians are expected to make and take jokes about each other in front of an audience of press people and, of course, the TV and online audience, such as the Annual White House Correspondents Dinner, the Alfred E. Memorial Dinner and the President's Farewell Dinner in the final term of office (many of these are available online).

Just as prized is the ability to make humour directed against oneself, known as self-deprecating humour, displaying the affective quality of modesty as well as good humour. Abraham Lincoln understood this when, not known for his good looks, he quipped, when accused of being 'two-faced' (that is, hypocritical):

If I had two faces, do you think this is the one I'd be wearing?

And in the following, Ronald Reagan (1986) jokes about politicians' reticence to face press interrogation:

Before I refuse to take your questions, I have an opening statement.

TASK 1

Here is an interesting humorous exchange between a White House press secretary and a journalist. How does each participant employ self-deprecating humour (a journalist is only expected to ask one question at a time so that all the journalists in the room can take a turn)?

Q: I do not have two questions, only a two-part question [. . .]
Podium: You can stand at the podium if you keep up language like that. (Laughter)
Q: I could never fill those shoes, Ari.
Podium: Do you have a question I can evade? (Laughter)

The butt or target of the joke does not necessarily have to be the joke-teller, it can be someone on their 'side'. Presidential candidates are expected to give humorous after-dinner talks at charity dinners. A few weeks before the example below, Donald Trump's wife, Melania, had been attacked in the US press for giving a speech that allegedly plagiarised one given by Michelle Obama a few months earlier. Trump begins his anecdote by returning to an old theme of his, the US media bias against him, in front of an audience consisting largely of those very journalists:

> Oh this one's gonna get me in trouble. Not with Hillary. The President told me to stop whining but I really have to say the media is even more biased this year than ever before. Ever. You want the proof?
>
> You know Michelle Obama gives a speech and everyone loves it, it's fantastic. They think she's absolutely great.
>
> My wife Melania gives the *exact same* speech and people get on her case, and I don't get it! I don't know why! (Laughter)
> (The Alfred E. Memorial Dinner 2016)

Trump – or his speechwriter – skilfully substitutes one narrative, that you don't copy other people's speeches, with another, that my wife's speech was just as good as the President's wife's speech. The appreciative press laughter also includes a certain relief that they were not, after all, the butt of the joke. The person who he *will* be in trouble with turns out to be his wife, an allusion to domesticity which constitutes, of course, a deliberate projection of 'normal guy' *ethos*.

9.2 Irony and sarcasm

9.2.1 Irony

There are a number of different definitions and theories of ***irony***: it has been the object of much attention since Aristotle and today there are several disciplines which take an interest in irony studies, including psycholinguistics, literary criticism, conversation studies and, here, political discourse analysis.

Irony, as understood in English-speaking countries at least (the everyday or lay understanding may differ in other cultures, Taylor 2016), is constructed by speakers or writers when they put together two narratives which they propose as radically different, oppositional, perhaps even incompatible with each other.

There are two very distinct forms of irony, *explicit* and *implicit* irony, which work in rather different ways but share the same basic common mechanism of the manipulation of a double narrative. In the first, *explicit irony*, the speaker spells out both narratives and frames them as being in a conflictual relationship by using some form of explicit signal of irony: *ironically, it's ironic that, it is an irony that*. The following are examples from White House Press briefings:

Q: [. . .] You cited two precedents: one, the Kosovo situation and the other, the second is Desert Fox. Both of those were actions taken under the previous administration. The President, going back to the campaign, was very critical and even disdainful of the foreign policy of that administration. Is that not somewhat **ironic** and even a little *hypocritical* that you're citing –

Q: Ari, can I go back to the United Nations sanctions question, and I guess follow up on Bill's question about the French role, especially the Russian role. These are countries that fought sanctions in the past, and now seem to want to keep them. Do you not see something, at least **ironic**, and maybe *cynical*, about this?

The first of these can be paraphrased in terms of a pair of allegedly conflicting narratives:

N1: The President (George W. Bush), before he came to office, said military intervention was bad.
N2: The President is now saying military intervention is good.

In other words, he has reversed his own *evaluation* to suit his purposes. The strategic discursive or rhetorical function, in other words, is to accuse the President of inconsistency or even double standards.

The second example can be similarly analysed into contrasting narratives:

N1: The French and Russians first fought sanctions.
N2: They now support them.

They too have reversed an evaluation (they first said sanctions were *bad*, now they are saying they are *good*), and once more the rhetorical point of the utterance is to accuse them of duplicity.

The two narratives are not necessarily constructed by the same speaker. In many cases a second speaker challenges the proposition in a first speaker's narrative and offers one of his or her own:

Q: [. . .] what does he say to his critics [. . .] who say that the government has succumbed to protectionist pressures [. . .]?
MR. FLEISCHER: I think that's kind of an **ironic** statement for people to make, given the fact that this is one of the most free-trading Presidents we've seen.

The first narrative was meant as a criticism, the responding narrative contests this by reversing the evaluation: 'the President is not a protectionist [bad], he's for free-trade [good]'. The question also contains two damaging attributed assertions (attributed to some vague group 'his critics') that the President has (a) 'succumbed' to 'pressures' and (b) changed his policy. The podium denies both assertions.

TASK 2: *Explicit irony*

Read these two episodes where a speaker frames an assertion as *ironic*. In each case, what are the two narratives which are constructed, and what evaluations are attached to them?

1. LISA MONACO: So this is the challenge, Charlie, [. . .] and it's a brutal irony, actually, when you think about it. ISIL is a group who is dedicated to rejecting modernity. That's their apocalyptic vision. And what they use is one of the greatest innovations that the United States has brought to the world [. . .]
    CHARLIE ROSE: [. . .] the Internet.

    (Charlie Rose Show 2015)

2. MARK HALPERIN (on Governor Jeb Bush's campaign for the US Presidency): Well, [he has to campaign] as a reformer. He talked today about changing Washington. There are a lot of ironies in this candidacy. One, of course, he wouldn't be in this position if his name weren't Bush and yet the name Bush and the association with his family is the thing that's most holding him back.

    (Charlie Rose Show 2015)

In the second form of irony, *implicit* irony, only one of two narratives is actually spoken and this is named the '*dictum*', while the second one is implied and so named the '*implicatum*'. The speaker wishes to suggest that there is a radical mismatch between the evaluation expressed in what is actually written or said (the '*dictum*') and the evaluation which is really intended (the '*implicatum*'). Very often, the *implicatum* is the exact opposite of the *dictum*:

> [Politician X] is a genius! He's managed to upset both the trade unions *and* big businesses.

The politician in question is clearly not being evaluated as a genius but as completely inept. In general, the *dictum* is almost always positive and the *implicatum* negative. This is because, as we have mentioned, the principal function of irony is to criticise.

Irony, then, is the reversal of evaluation. It often employs quite elegant and surprising turns of phrase, as in the much quoted:

> America's allies – always there when they need you!

which clearly reverses the more usual sentiment that friends (and allies) should be there when *you* need *them*.

TASK 3: *implicit irony*

The following is a particularly subtle episode of implicit irony. What are the two narratives and how is the evaluation in the first narrative (that of the questioner) reversed in the second (by the podium, Mr Fleischer)?

Q: The Associated Press reports that on Sunday in Middlebury, Vermont, where you gave a speech and were given an alumni achievement award, there were around 500 protestors.

Ari Fleischer: Oh no, there were more than that.

(White House press briefing 2002)

9.2.2 Sarcasm

Mr Attlee is a modest man who has a great deal to be modest about.

(Winston Churchill 1954)

Sarcasm can be defined as 'an overtly aggressive type of [implicit] irony with clearer markers/cues and a clear target' (Attardo 2000: 795); in other words, a particularly straightforward kind of verbal irony, with a clear 'victim'. Others might refine the definition of the difference between irony and sarcasm by pointing out that the *speaker* generally sees what he or she says as ironic (and, therefore, 'elegant') while the *victim* sees the same utterance as sarcasm (and, therefore, crude and hurtful). In his sarcastic comment about Mr Attlee, Churchill skilfully and suddenly reverses the evaluation of 'being a modest person' from good to bad. But it is doubtful whether Mr Attlee saw the funny side.

Q1

In the following, there are actually two victims targeted by the questioner. Who are they and what are they accused of?

Q: Barry, let me ask you this. When you say that you have no view of [her] possible testimony, does that mean that in the daily meetings that you attend at the higher levels in the White House, no view was expressed of her coming testimony? Or does it mean that you were *told* to express no view of her testimony? (Laughter)

(White House press briefing 1998)

Rhetorical questions, too, can often be vehicles of sarcasm:

I suspect that there are many members on the Opposition benches who might be familiar with an 'unscrupulous boss'. A boss who doesn't listen to his workers? A boss who requires some of his workers to double their workload? Maybe even a boss who exploits the rules to further his own career? Remind him of anybody?

(UK PM Theresa May to Jeremy Corbyn, leader of the opposition, 2016)

If you were Osama bin Laden, would you go on satellite transmission just now?

(White House press briefing 2002)

Taylor (2016) notes that sarcasm is not always judged to be a bad thing. She observed how participants in online forums sometimes referred to their own behaviour as 'sarcastic' and portrayed it as a justifiable response to some other person's aggressive verbal behaviour towards them. Politicians too may pride themselves on their ability to display aggression in a way that is considered both acceptable and entertaining.

It may also be viewed as entertaining by those who are not the target, as in the following instance from the UK House of Lords:

I have to thank the noble Lord, Lord Carlile of Berriew, for his colourful combination of irony and **sarcasm**, which I so often enjoyed listening to when he was a Member in another place.

(House of Lords 2003)

9.3 Definitions of *satire*

Humour in politics is often associated with *satire*: Satire is a work 'in which wickedness or folly is censured' (Johnson 1755). It is a written or spoken form 'in which human or individual vices, follies, abuses, or shortcomings are held up to censure by means of ridicule, derision, burlesque, irony or other methods' (Encyclopedia Britannica, www.britannica. com/art/satire). Various mock satirical 'newspapers' or news TV are available online; for example, *The Onion* satirises current affairs from a US perspective, *The Daily Mash* and *NewsThump* from a UK angle.

In the terms adopted in this book, satire is also a means of *persuasion*. A person, behaviour or state of affairs is criticised (evaluated unfavourably) in the hope of persuading an audience that something has to change.

Moreover:

- In political satire, individuals or groups who possess **power, authority** or at least **influence** can be satirised, i.e. it is possible to satirise a Prime Minister or an opinion-maker (and celebrities seem to be fair game) but not the local newsagent. The latter can, of course, be ridiculed but this would not be classifiable as satire. Political ideas can also be satirised, depicted as a kind of sub-set of human folly.

- It differs from simple criticism in making an **indirect** attack on its object.
- Satire depends on the comparison of two worlds, one real and one invented.
- It frequently uses **humour** as a vehicle for its criticism, though this can often be bitter and sardonic in form.
- It frequently employs **parody**, that is, the imitation of a certain style of speaking or writing. Some TV shows use impersonations, a form of parody, of famous political personalities.
- It frequently indulges in **exaggeration**, also known as **hyperbole**.
- Some observers claim it has a **'moral' aspect**, that it uses criticism in the attempt to bring about improvement, to change the world for the better. However, most modern satire is performed for entertainment (and, therefore, often for commercial gain) and rather than a *moral* effect it produces a 'moral superiority' effect, it encourages the audience to feel more virtuous and more intelligent than the object of the satire.

Satirical writing works by constructing a fictional, often fantastic, world which, in important aspects, runs parallel to the real one. Or, rather, the satirist's perception and projection of the real world. Satire is a challenging – and, therefore, rewarding – genre. The reader has to recognise the aspects of the real world being called into play through the prism of the invented, fictional one. It therefore requires that the reader be already well informed. But a further task is then demanded. From the nature of the events recounted in the fictional world, the reader must deduce not only who or what is being 'held up to censure', but also why. In other words, the message or 'point' of the satire.

9.3.1 Satire's long history

Satire has a long history. Its twin fathers are generally taken to be Horace and Juvenal (and so it was often known as *italum acetum*, the Italian 'vinegar'), the former an exponent of a more comic form, the latter a darker and angrier one. Both veins surface regularly throughout literary history. In Roman times – and many others, of course – criticism of authority was a highly dangerous activity and satire presumably developed as an attempt to avert social and legal pressures (namely torture and execution) by approaching the target indirectly. In other words, when authority prohibits direct criticism and dissent, it paradoxically fosters techniques of indirectness that will make the attack less visible but more effective: for example, irony, humour and *parody*. It is itself nicely ironic that the devices that render satire acceptable at the same time sharpen its point.

Perhaps the best-known political satirist ever to write in English was Jonathan Swift, most famous for *Travels into Several Remote Nations of the World. In Four Parts. By Lemuel Gulliver* (1726), better known as *Gulliver's Travels*. One of the best-known episodes is Gulliver's account of the 'Wars of the Eggs', that is, the wars between the Big-Endians (those who broke their eggs at the larger end) and Little-Endians (those who broke their eggs at the smaller end), which gave rise to 'six rebellions [. . .] wherein one Emperor lost his life, and another his crown'.

The more intelligent among his readers would have recognised the allusion to the real world and the wars of religion between Catholics and Protestants which had utterly ravaged Europe in the previous century.

Satire, then, frequently offends some target, but it can also offend against what we might call 'good taste'. Almost as famous as *Gulliver's Travels* is another satire by Swift, entitled *A Modest Proposal for Preventing the Children of Poor People from Being a Burden to their Parents, or the Country, and for Making them Beneficial to the Public* (1729), generally referred to more simply as *A Modest Proposal*. The 'proposal' was to fatten up the undernourished children of the poor and sell them as food to the rich, which would: combat overpopulation and unemployment, spare poor families the expense of bringing up children while providing them with some extra income; improve the culinary experience of the wealthy and contribute to the overall economic well-being of the nation. Swift was obviously employing the absurd, but not all his readers saw the funny side.

More recently, in January 2016, the journalist David Aaronovitch wrote a satirical opinion article in *The Times* similarly entitled 'A Modest Proposal', this time about how to solve the crisis of migrants arriving on European shores. Since Europeans and their politicians have reneged on their promises and good intentions, he argues, all that was left was to use Europe's navies to sink the refugee boats, as a humanitarian gesture. Judging from comments 'below the line' of the article, many readers failed to understand the satirical intent:

> Murder as a former of population movement control – even 'The Trump' [Donald Trump] has not gone so far.

> I really can't believe David is proposing such an inhuman solution to this problem

> You are sick, Mr Aaronovitch

> Sounds a good idea to me

and even if they did understand the intent, some still considered the proposal to be in bad taste:

> The original Swift piece was termed a Juvenalian satirical essay – this is more of a juvenile satirical rant with gratuitous rudeness.

A reminder both that people's sense of humour can differ radically and that recognition of satire depends on context. Some readers who failed to recognise the satirical intent may have remembered the infamous 2015 opinion piece on the same topic in the *Sun*, Britain's best-selling newspaper, titled 'Rescue boats? I'd use gunships to stop migrants'. Indeed, the difficulty of performing satire at the time of writing has been a topic of much discussion among stand-up comedians and writers of satire. For instance, the producers of the popular US programme 'South Park' commented in February 2017 that they would no longer try and write satire about the US administration because 'it's tricky and it's really tricky now as satire has become reality. [. . .] What was actually happening was way funnier than anything we could come up with'.

The best-known satire of modern times is probably *Animal Farm* (published in 1945) in which the author, the libertarian socialist George Orwell, attacks what he sees as the betrayal of the Soviet Revolution by the highly illiberal Stalin. Inspired by the slogans 'Four legs good, two legs bad' and 'All animals are equal', a group of farmyard animals overthrow and chase off their exploitative human master (Farmer Jones) and set up an egalitarian society of their own – the *Animal Farm* of the title. Eventually the animals' intelligent and power-loving leaders, the pigs, led by a certain Napoleon, subvert the Revolution and form a dictatorship whose bondage is even more oppressive and heartless than that of their former human masters. The parallels with the real world of the time are not hard to draw.

9.4 *Animal Farm* (George Orwell, 1945)

Q2

Animal Farm contains one of the most celebrated quotes of modern literature. Can you complete the following:

All animals are equal

But ....

(Don't worry if you can't complete it, you will find the answer in the following text.)

TASK 4: *Animal Farm*

Read this extract:

1) YEARS passed. The seasons came and went, the short animal lives fled by. A time came when there was no one who remembered the

old days before the Rebellion, except Clover, Benjamin, Moses the raven, and a number of the pigs [. . .]

2) As for the others, their life, so far as they knew, was as it had always been. They were generally hungry, they slept on straw, they drank from the pool, they laboured in the fields; in winter they were troubled by the cold, and in summer by the flies. Sometimes the older ones among them racked their dim memories and tried to determine whether in the early days of the Rebellion, when Jones's expulsion was still recent, things had been better or worse than now. They could not remember. There was nothing with which they could compare their present lives: they had nothing to go upon except Squealer's lists of figures, which invariably demonstrated that everything was getting better and better [. . .]

3) And yet the animals never gave up hope. More, they never lost, even for an instant, their sense of honour and privilege in being members of Animal Farm. They were still the only farm in the whole county owned and operated by animals [. . .] And when they heard the gun booming and saw the green flag fluttering at the masthead, their hearts swelled with imperishable pride, and the talk turned always towards the old heroic days, the expulsion of Jones, the writing of the Seven Commandments, the great battles in which the human invaders had been defeated [. . .] It might be that their lives were hard and that not all of their hopes had been fulfilled; but they were conscious that they were not as other animals. If they went hungry, it was not from feeding tyrannical human beings; if they worked hard, at least they worked for themselves. No creature among them went upon two legs. No creature called any other creature 'Master.' All animals were equal.

4) One day in early summer Squealer ordered the sheep to follow him, and led them out to a piece of waste ground at the other end of the farm [. . .]. It ended by their remaining there for a whole week, during which time the other animals saw nothing of them. Squealer was with them for the greater part of every day. He was, he said, teaching them to sing a new song, for which privacy was needed.

5) It was just after the sheep had returned, on a pleasant evening when the animals had finished work and were making their way back to the farm buildings, that the terrified neighing of a horse sounded from the yard. Startled, the animals stopped in their tracks. It was Clover's voice. She neighed again, and all the animals broke into a gallop and rushed into the yard. Then they saw what Clover had seen.

6) It was a pig walking on his hind legs.

7) Yes, it was Squealer. A little awkwardly, as though not quite used to supporting his considerable bulk in that position, but with perfect balance, he was strolling across the yard. And a moment later, out

from the door of the farmhouse came a long file of pigs, all walking on their hind legs. Some did it better than others, one or two were even a trifle unsteady and looked as though they would have liked the support of a stick, but every one of them made his way right round the yard successfully. And finally there was a tremendous baying of dogs and a shrill crowing from the black cockerel, and out came Napoleon himself, majestically upright, casting haughty glances from side to side, and with his dogs gambolling round him.

8) He carried a whip in his trotter.

9) There was a deadly silence. Amazed, terrified, huddling together, the animals watched the long line of pigs march slowly round the yard. It was as though the world had turned upside-down. Then there came a moment when the first shock had worn off and when, in spite of everything – in spite of their terror of the dogs, and of the habit, developed through long years, of never complaining, never criticising, no matter what happened – they might have uttered some word of protest. But just at that moment, as though at a signal, all the sheep burst out into a tremendous bleating of:

'Four legs good, two legs better! Four legs good, two legs better! Four legs good, two legs better!'

10) It went on for five minutes without stopping. And by the time the sheep had quieted down, the chance to utter any protest had passed, for the pigs had marched back into the farmhouse.

11) Benjamin felt a nose nuzzling at his shoulder. He looked round. It was Clover. Her old eyes looked dimmer than ever. Without saying anything, she tugged gently at his mane and led him round to the end of the big barn, where the Seven Commandments were written. For a minute or two they stood gazing at the wall with its white lettering.

12) 'My sight is failing', she said finally. 'Even when I was young I could not have read what was written there. But it appears to me that that wall looks different. Are the Seven Commandments the same as they used to be, Benjamin?'

13) For once Benjamin consented to break his rule, and he read out to her what was written on the wall. There was nothing there now except a single Commandment. It ran:

ALL ANIMALS ARE EQUAL
BUT SOME ANIMALS ARE MORE EQUAL THAN OTHERS

Fill in Table 9.1 by indicating what the elements of the fictional world correspond to in the real world.

Table 9.1   Animal Farm

Fictional world	Real world
The farm	Russia/the Soviet Union
The farmyard animals	
The humans	
The pigs	The new communist elite
	Stalin
Squealer	
The sheep	
The dogs	

What would you say was the main point or message of the extract above?

TASK 5: *Revision: rhetorical figures in Animal Farm*

1) Paragraphs 2 and 3 contain a large number of binomials and bicolons. Underline as many as you can.
2) Underline the tricolon in paragraph 3.
3) Find a bicolon and a tricolon in paragraph 9.
4) Underline the contrasting pair in paragraph 2.
5) Walking on two legs is a sort of metaphor (or perhaps metonym). A metaphor for what?

How does it work?

9.5 Modern satires

The following two texts are taken from the SatireWire.com website.

TASK 6A: *High School Students Demand Wars in Easier-to-Find Countries*

Read the text.

1) We find not one but two objects of criticism in the satire. What are they?
2) A very frequent technique used by satirists is parody. The writer here parodies the slang speech of US high-school students. Can you find any of the elements of slang being parodied?

HIGH SCHOOL STUDENTS DEMAND WARS IN EASIER-TO-FIND COUNTRIES

'How Come No One Fights in Big Famous Nations Anymore?' They Ask.

1) Washington, D.C. (SatireWire.com) — A delegation of American high school students today demanded the United States stop waging war in obscure nations such as Afghanistan, Kuwait, and Bosnia-Herzegovina, and instead attack places they've actually heard of, such as France, Australia, and Austria, unless, they said, those last two are the same country.

2) 'People claim we don't know as much geography as our parents and grandparents, but it's so not our fault', Josh Beldoni, a senior at Fischer High School in Los Angeles, told the Senate Armed Services Committee. 'Back then they only had wars in, like, Germany and England, but we're supposed to know about places like Somalia and Massachusetts'.

    'Macedonia', corrected committee Chairman Carl Levin of Michigan.

    'See?' said Beldoni.

3) Beldoni's frustration was shared by nearly three dozen students at the hearing, who blamed the US military for making them look bad:'I totally support our soldiers and all that, but I am seriously failing both geography and social studies because I keep getting asked to find Croatia or Yemvrekia, or whatever bizarre-o country we send troops to', said Amelia Nash, a junior at Clark High School in Orlando, Fla. 'Can't we fight in, like, Italy? It's boot-shaped'.

TASK 6B: *Greenpeace will now oppose everything*

As already mentioned, satire frequently also resorts to exaggeration. Read the following text.

How does the exaggeration work?

GREENPEACE WILL NOW OPPOSE EVERYTHING

1) Amsterdam (SatireWire.com) — Known for its long-standing opposition to whaling, logging, strip mining, genetically modified food, nuclear power, the chemical industry, wars, corporations, politics, and weapons, the activist group Greenpeace today announced that as of 12:01 this morning, it will just oppose everything.

2) 'It's all bad, it all needs to stop', said a Greenpeace spokesperson, who added the group will no longer send out action alerts calling for opposition to specific issues, but will instead issue daily alerts to all members that read, 'No' in 37 different languages.

Supporters of Greenpeace may well fail to appreciate the intended humour of the second text. It is an important observation that we will tend to appreciate satire we agree with, while satire which attacks our own views will be experienced as hurtful or frivolous.

Finally, another important feature of much satire is the use of irony, which has been called the 'engine' of satire. In particular, in *dramatic irony* we find one party acting 'in the dark' while the audience/readers are 'in the know'. The clearest examples are found when a participant in a drama – a play or film, say – acts in accordance with a certain reading of the way things are which, at some point, turns out to be significantly in contrast with the way things really are. The audience and sometimes other participants in the drama are, on the other hand, in possession of the real facts, the correct reading of events. One of the most famous dramatic ironies occurs in *Othello*: we, the audience, know that Desdemona is a faithful and loving wife and that Iago is an envious mischief-maker. The tragedy arises from Othello's reversal of evaluations, his belief that Iago is a faithful friend and Desdemona an unfaithful spouse. Some of Shakespeare's comedies too are great exercises in dramatic irony. In *Twelfth Night* the young woman Viola, disguised as a man named Cesario (although only we the audience know the truth), is sent by the Duke Orsino, her master, with whom she is secretly in love (again, we know it but he does not), to plead his love for the Lady Olivia who promptly secretly falls in love with the fascinating, smooth-tongued Cesario (yet again, we are in the know but Cesario/Viola is not). Such equivocations make this one of Shakespeare's most successful comedies.

Extension task

What are the most well-known sources for political and social satire in your country? You might want to think about website blogs, radio shows, TV shows, print publications, Twitter feeds, and so on. Find an example and analyse it in terms of who is targeted in the satire and what kind of evaluation is offered. Then reconsider the list from section 9.3 and note whether these apply to the text you have chosen to analyse. (Free responses)

Further reading

Partington, A. (2006) *The Linguistics of Laughter: A Corpus-Assisted Study of Laughter-Talk*, London: Routledge.

Young, D. (2004) 'Theories and effects of Political Humour', in K. Kenski and K. Jamieson (eds.) *The Oxford Handbook of Political Communication*, Oxford: Oxford University Press. Available at: https://tinyurl.com/PiP-Young

Other resources

www.funny-jokes-quotes-sayings.com/funny-political-quotes.html

Keys and commentaries

TASK 1: *Self-deprecatory humour*

The journalist first pretends to be ingenuous by calling his two questions one question in two parts. He knows full well this will be seen by all as impish cleverness. The podium, Mr Fleischer, in saying 'You can stand at the podium if you keep up language like that' both compliments him on his cleverness and at the same time makes a self-deprecatory joke that it is usually podiums who use trick language. The journalist then both feigns self-deprecatory modesty and deference in declaring he could never be as talented as the podium is, but also makes the more barbed inference that the podium's special talent is in using tricky language. The podium follows the mood and plays in a self-deprecatory way with his own – and that of politicians in general – reputation for evading a straight answer.

TASK 2: *Explicit irony*

1.

> N1: ISIL evaluate modernity and America as bad, morally evil even.
> N2: ISIL use 'evil' modern, western inventions such as the Internet.

The critical evaluation is that ISIL lives by double standards, and perhaps that they delude themselves.

2.

> N1: Jeb Bush is able to compete for the Presidency only because of his belonging to a famous family, which has provided two recent Presidents.
> N2: Jeb Bush's popularity and his credentials as an 'outsider' and a reformer are severely hampered by his coming from a family so closely associated with 'Washington' and the levers of power.

In the first narrative the evaluation of belonging to 'a famous family' is evaluated as positive, while in the second it is evaluated as being simultaneously negative. There is a degree of negative evaluation of Jeb Bush's abilities since he is dependent on his name. Above all, this is an example of 'irony of fate', when life, the world, destiny works both in favour and against the protagonist (though the combined result of these workings is almost always, as here, negative).

TASK 3: *Implicit irony*

> N1 (questioner's narrative): There were 500 people protesting against you, and this is bad.

N2 (podium's narrative): No, there were many more than 500 people protesting, and this is good.

In the questioner's narrative, a conventional one, to have a large
number of people protesting against you is a bad thing. The podium
rather cleverly reverses the evaluation to: the more people who turn
out to protest against you, the more important you are.

Q1

Satire

The immediate victim is the podium who is portrayed as a subordinate
who must do as he is told. The second victim is the administration,
given the implication that it is capable of being closed and secretive.

Q2

ALL ANIMALS ARE EQUAL

BUT SOME ANIMALS ARE MORE EQUAL THAN OTHERS

The sentence is a comment on the hypocrisy of governments that
proclaim the absolute equality of their citizens but give power and
privileges to a small elite.

(Hirsch, Kett and Trefil 2002)

Table 9.1 Key: Animal Farm

Fictional world	Real world
The farm	Russia/the Soviet Union
The farmyard animals	The Russian/Soviet people
The humans	The western countries that opposed the Revolution
The pigs	The new communist elite
Napoleon	Stalin
Squealer	The Minister of Information (or Propaganda)
The sheep	The Communist Party members
The dogs	The secret police

TASK 4: Animal Farm

The message is that the communist elite have betrayed the hopes of
the people and the promises they made to them by steadily becoming
as uncaring as the regime they replaced and as exploitative as the
capitalists they fought against.

TASK 5: *Revision: rhetorical figures in* Animal Farm

1)   Binomials and bicolons in paragraphs 2 and 3 (examples):

Binomials: *honour and privilege*; *owned and operated by animals.*

Bicolons: *they heard the gun booming and saw the green flag fluttering at the masthead; If they went hungry, it was not from feeding tyrannical human beings; if they worked hard, at least they worked for themselves.*

2) Underline the tricolon in paragraph 3:

the expulsion of Jones, the writing of the Seven Commandments, the great battles in which the human invaders had been defeated.

3) Find a bicolon and a tricolon in paragraph 9:

Bicolon: *of never complaining, never criticising.*
Tricolon: *amazed, terrified, huddling together.*

4) Underline the contrasting pair in paragraph 2:

in winter they were troubled by the cold, and in summer by the flies.

Walking on two legs is a sort of metaphor (or perhaps metonym). A metaphor for what?
Power.

How does it work? *The pigs raise themselves above the other animals both physically, by walking on two legs, but also metaphorically, by seizing power. The evaluation of the metaphor in the context of this work is, of course, bad.*

TASK 6A: *High school students demand [. . .]*

1) The propensity of the United States to go to war and the ignorance of modern high-school students on foreign matters.
2) The frequent use of intensifiers, e.g. *but it's so not our fault* (paragraph 2), *totally* (paragraph 3), *seriously* (paragraph 3).

The frequent interjection of 'like': *Back then they only had wars in, like, Germany and England* (paragraph 2), *Can't we fight in, like, Italy?* (paragraph 3).

The addition of the suffix '-o': *bizarre-o* (paragraph 3).

TASK 6B: *Greenpeace Will Now Oppose Everything*

3) The exaggeration begins in the very long list of the activities Greenpeace is supposed to be opposed to (paragraph 1). It is reinforced by the precision in the numbers quoted – '12.01', '37 different languages'. The most important element is, of course, the sheer absurdity of being opposed to 'everything'.

10 The language of election and referendum campaigns

Throughout this book we have examined the language of political campaign speeches and campaign slogans. In this Unit we review some of the aspects we have covered so far by looking at some of the most recent English-language campaigns, the 2016 US presidential elections and the two UK referendums, the first in 2015 over Scotland leaving the UK, the second in 2016 over the UK leaving the European Union.

10.1 The US presidential election campaign of 2016: the most divisive ever?

On the 12th November, just a week after the election result was known, a BBC Radio 4 programme (available at: https://tinyurl.com/PiP-divisive) asked the question, 'Was this the most divisive US election ever?':

> The Clinton–Trump race has been extraordinary. Two of the most unpopular presidential candidates ever have slugged it out through a bitter campaign. They are both – for different reasons – deeply polarising figures.

Hillary Clinton, the BBC claims, 'is viewed with suspicion by Americans who have turned against what they regard as "the elite"', while Donald Trump, it says, 'has exploited crudely divisive, sexist, even racist, rhetoric'.

Then, as regards the language 'tone', the claim is:

> The tone of the contest has been ugly. But there is historical precedent for much of this – divisive policy positions on slavery or the famous attack ads of the 1960s.

But the question the BBC suggests we ponder is:

> How should we view this campaign compared to the candidates, rhetoric, policies and media climate of past elections?

There was no shortage of hyperbolic interventions, perhaps none more so than this apocalyptic one, from the then still President, Barack Obama to a rally in North Carolina:

> I hate to put a little pressure on you but the fate of the Republic rests on your shoulders. The fate of the world is teetering and you, North Carolina, are going to have to make sure that we push it in the right direction.
>
> (Obama 2016)

Note how Obama uses *you* and *we*. Many of the exchanges between the candidates were indeed 'ugly'. Perhaps the two most memorable were Trump nicknaming his opponent 'crooked Hillary' and Clinton calling half of Trump's supporters 'a basket of deplorables'.

But the BBC's question is whether these exchanges were substantially worse than those in any previous contest. The 'crooked' insult is strongly reminiscent of the 1960 Kennedy Democrat campaign slogan against Richard Nixon, 'would you buy a used car from this man?', in a land where a 'used-car dealer' is a metonymic symbol for someone who cheats you. And insulting the opponent's supporters is nothing new either. In the 2012 election, the Republican candidate, Mitt Romney, suggested that the large majority of Democrat supporters belonged to 'the 47% of Americans who pay no income tax' who, therefore, he was taken as implying, made no contribution to the public welfare.

But delving further back still, the BBC came across far more toxic insults and attempts at delegitimising an opponent than those of 2016. In the 1800 campaign between John Adams and Thomas Jefferson, the former's campaign referred to Jefferson as 'the Anti-Christ', while the latter's campaign spoke of Adams's 'hideous hermaphroditical character which has neither the force and firmness of a man, nor the gentleness and sensibility of a woman'. In 1828, candidate Andrew Jackson's wife was repeatedly labelled a prostitute. More divisive still was the duel in 1804 between the Vice-President Aaron Burr and Andrew Hamilton, one of the Founding Fathers. Hamilton was shot dead. And finally, the election of Abraham Lincoln in 1860 prompted seven southern states to form the Confederate States of America, leading directly to the US Civil War, which surely qualifies it as the most divisive US election ever.

10.1.1 Campaigning on social media

As well as being deeply divisive, the election was distinctive for the role of social media. While this has been important in previous elections too, there was far greater participation in 2016. In a Pew

Research Center survey (2016) at the time of the election campaign, it was found that the following were the sources most used for getting information about the election (in order of frequency):

- cable news
- social media
- local TV
- news websites/apps
- radio
- network nightly news
- late-night comedy
- local papers in print
- national papers in print
- issue-based websites
- candidate or campaign website

Among 18–29-year-olds, social media was the main source of information. Therefore, we now turn our attention to campaigns on social media, and, more specifically, the micro-blogging service Twitter. When a user tweets, they have the option of adding hashtags which function to add some kind of information about the tweet itself. As Zappavigna (2015) reports, 'while often thought of as topic-markers, hashtags are linguistically multifunctional and able to per-form different types of interpersonal meanings in social media texts'. That is to say, a given hashtag can both indicate what a topic is about (e.g. #Election2016) but also the speaker's evaluation and affiliation. For instance, the hashtag #NotMyPresident, which has been popular since Trump's election, indicates that users do not agree with his behaviour and/or policies, but also that they wish to publicly align themselves with others who feel like this.

TASK 1A: *Investigating popular political hashtags*

If you have access to Twitter, look at the trending topics today. How many of these relate to politics? Who is using the hashtag? Does it involve promoting one idea/party or opposing another? Does it involve representation or affiliation or both? (Free response)

TASK 1B: *Popular political hashtags*

In Unit 3 we examined positive and negative campaign slogans. The following were the nine most-used Twitter hashtags relating to the US elections in 2016. Would you classify them as positive or negative (Unit 3.2.1)? Who do you think used these hashtags – Clinton, Trump or Sanders supporters?

1) #MakeAmericaGreatAgain #MAGA
2) #BlackLivesMatter #BLM
3) #FeelTheBern
4) #ImWithHer
5) #NeverTrump
6) #CrookedHillary
7) #BasketOfDeplorables
8) #DeleteYourAccount
9) #LockHerUp

The context to each is discussed in the Key, but it is particularly interesting to note that the four most popular were all positive campaign hashtags. These are then followed by a series of five negative campaign hashtags. Thus, we see that both are effective in gaining adherents, but the in-group marking is more often employed.

Other popular campaign slogans included: 'When they go low, we go high', 'I'm with you, the American people', 'Stronger together', 'Fighting for us', 'Drain the [Washington] swamp', 'CNN sucks'. Which slogans do you think were used by the Democrats and which by the Republicans?

The most popular political tweet of 2016 overall was from Clinton's account and contained a quote from her concession speech: 'To all the little girls watching…never doubt that you are valuable and powerful & deserving of every chance & opportunity in the world' which was retweeted 666,000 times and received 1.2 million likes.

10.1.2 Campaign metonyms

Certain metonyms (Unit 7.3) appeared again and again in the campaign. For instance:

1) Washington DC
    Negatively evaluated. It can be used to stand for either corrupt, self-serving government, or the right-wing concept of 'big government', that is, too much official interference in the lives of 'ordinary people'.
2) Wall Street
    Negatively evaluated. It stands for the world of high finance and especially 'the banks', and is associated with the financial crash of 2007 and the misery it brought to so many 'ordinary people'.
    'Wall Street cannot continue to be an island unto itself, gambling trillions in risky financial decisions while expecting the public to bail it out' (Sanders).
3) Main Street
    Positively evaluated, especially when in contrast with *Washington* or *Wall Street*. It has two meanings, first, 'normal America'

outside of Washington and, second, small businesses, especially retail businesses, that is, the kind of shop one would find on 'every town's Main Street'.

'"Main Street Patriots" Plan Week of Pro-Trump Rallies' (CBS).

4) Blue collar and white collar
'Blue-collar workers' are manual workers, 'white-collar workers' are office workers or so-called professional people; the 'blue' refers to hard-wearing denim clothing, 'white' to more refined cotton shirts. And thus 'blue-collar states' are those with a preponderance of manufacturing labour, and 'white-collar states' are those where most jobs are not in industry or agriculture.

TASK 2: *Political metonyms*

Fill in the gaps with either *Washington, Wall Street, Main Street* or *blue collar*.

a) Do Not Let This Chance Slip Away. You have one magnificent chance to deliver justice for every forgotten man, woman and child in this nation. The arrogance of .... will soon come face to face with the righteous verdict of the American voter. (Trump)

b) The Battle for .... America: Remembering the Forgotten Men who have to live with .... policies. (*Breitbart*)

c) We simply cannot afford four more years of an economic philosophy that works for .... instead of ...., and ends up devastating both. (Obama)

d) .... voters launch hand grenade into .... (*The Hill*)

e) John Kasich balances his .... roots and his ties to .... (*New York Times*)

REVISION TASK: *Trump's victory speech*

Watch or read Donald Trump's victory speech, 'Binding the wounds of division' (available at: https://tinyurl.com/PiP-Trump).

i. What are his main themes?
ii. Evaluation: who does he praise? (Unit 2)
iii. Look at his use of the pronouns, *I, you, we, us,* etc. How is each used? What overall effect does he want to achieve? (Unit 8)
iv. Trump is famous for his liberal use of hyperbolic language including intensifiers (*totally, incredibly*) and highly charged

evaluative items (*magnificent*, *huge*, *carnage*). Can you find any examples here? Are they mostly positive or negative in evaluation? (Unit 2)

  v. Look for examples of creative repetition and contrast. (Unit 5)

 vi. What sort of personality and qualities (*ethos*) does he attempt to project? What logical or pseudo-logical arguments (*logos*) does he employ? And what appeals to emotion (*pathos*) does he use (Unit 1)?

vii. Find a couple of examples of *chiasmus*. (Unit 5)

viii. Does Trump use any metaphors? (Unit 7)

Binding the wounds of division

1) I've just received a call from Secretary Clinton.
2) She congratulated us — it's about us — on our victory, and I congratulated her and her family on a very, very hard-fought campaign. I mean, she — she fought very hard.
3) Hillary has worked very long and very hard over a long period of time, and we owe her a major debt of gratitude for her service to our country.
4) I mean that very sincerely. (APPLAUSE)
5) Now it's time for America to bind the wounds of division; have to get together. To all Republicans and Democrats and independents across this nation, I say it is time for us to come together as one united people.
6) It's time. I pledge to every citizen of our land that I will be president for all Americans, and this is so important to me.
7) For those who have chosen not to support me in the past, of which there were a few people... (LAUGHTER)
8) ... I'm reaching out to you for your guidance and your help so that we can work together and unify our great country.
9) As I've said from the beginning, ours was not a campaign, but rather an incredible and great movement made up of millions of hard-working men and women who love their country and want a better, brighter future for themselves and for their families.
10) It's a movement comprised of Americans from all races, religions, backgrounds and beliefs who want and expect our government to serve the people, and serve the people it will.
11) Working together, we will begin the urgent task of rebuilding our nation and renewing the American dream. I've spent my entire life and business looking at the untapped potential in projects and in people all over the world. That is now what I want to do for our country.
12) Tremendous potential. I've gotten to know our country so well — tremendous potential. It's going to be a beautiful thing. Every single American will have the opportunity to realize his or her

fullest potential. The forgotten men and women of our country will be forgotten no longer.

13) We are going to fix our inner cities and rebuild our highways, bridges, tunnels, airports, schools, hospitals. We're going to rebuild our infrastructure, which will become, by the way, second to none. And we will put millions of our people to work as we rebuild it.

14) We will also finally take care of our great veterans.

15) They've been so loyal, and I've gotten to know so many over this 18-month journey. The time I've spent with them during this campaign has been among my greatest honors. Our veterans are incredible people. We will embark upon a project of national growth and renewal. I will harness the creative talents of our people and we will call upon the best and brightest to leverage their tremendous talent for the benefit of all. It's going to happen.

16) We have a great economic plan. We will double our growth and have the strongest economy anywhere in the world. At the same time, we will get along with all other nations willing to get along with us.

17) We'll have great relationships. We expect to have great, great relationships. No dream is too big, no challenge is too great.

18) Nothing we want for our future is beyond our reach.

19) America will no longer settle for anything less than the best.

20) We must reclaim our country's destiny and dream big and bold and daring. We have to do that. We're going to dream of things for our country and beautiful things and successful things once again.

21) I want to tell the world community that while we will always put America's interests first, we will deal fairly with everyone, with everyone — all people and all other nations. We will seek common ground, not hostility; partnership, not conflict.

22) And now I'd like to take this moment to thank some of the people who really helped me with this, what they are calling tonight a very, very historic victory. [. . .]

10.1.3 Gendered evaluation

Another feature which made the 2016 US election quite distinctive was the extent to which gender featured in the evaluations of the presidential candidates. It was the first US election in which a woman was running for the role of president and this became part of the discourse of the race. At the end of the election campaign, the US weekly, *Newsweek* concluded (echoing in some ways the BBC report discussed above) that:

There have been some nasty presidential campaigns in the 250 years of American politics. John Quincy Adams's backers tarred

Andrew Jackson's wife as a bigamist; and Thomas Jefferson's opponent claimed he was dead. But there has never been a campaign that so clearly and (often viciously) split along gender lines.

(*Newsweek* 2016, edited)

This may have been anticipated, given that it was the first campaign with a female presidential candidate nominated by a major party. Gender became a campaign issue in a number of (overlapping) guises. First, some voters declared outright that they would not vote for a woman. Interestingly, one piece of research indicated that for male voters this correlated with a perceived threat to their economic status as men. In the study, a sample of possible voters were asked whether they would support Clinton or Trump. Before this question, half the male voters were asked who earned most in their household – the intention being to remind them of the traditional gender role – of the male as chief provider (or 'breadwinner'). In the results, men in the first group preferred Clinton over Trump, 49 to 33. However, those in the second group, who were reminded about economic gender roles, preferred Trump over Clinton, 50 to 42 (reported on the LSE blog at https://tinyurl.com/PiP-LSE). Second, Trump had a history of making sexist remarks including the infamous brag about sexual assault (see the *Daily Telegraph*'s list for an overview of comments: https://tinyurl.com/PiP-sexism). Third, as we discuss here, candidates were evaluated in gendered ways, both overtly and covertly.

In Unit 3 we discussed ***competence face*** and ***affective face***. In any election campaign, both will become salient: the politician is expected to appear both authoritative and able to lead the country (competence face), and yet also to appear to be 'one of the people', someone the voting population can relate to (affective face). This is always a difficult balancing act, but particularly so for women in which context it is frequently talked about as 'the double bind' of gender. In the double bind you are required to fulfil two incompatible demands simultaneously. How this plays out for women in politics is summarised very succinctly in the following piece:

Women running for office are subject to two demands: Be a good leader! Be a good woman! While qualities expected of a good leader (be forceful, confident) are similar to those expected of a good man, they are the opposite of those expected of a good woman (be gentle, self-deprecating).

(*Washington Post* 2016, edited)

As the author continues, the female politician can either conform with the 'good woman' stereotype and risk appearing under-confident (for a leader). Or she can conform with the 'good leader' stereotype and risk appearing too aggressive (for a woman). Clinton was much criticised for not being 'likeable' enough, and that 'likeability' clearly relates to gender expectations of 'nice' behaviour.

TASK 3: *Identifying gendered evaluations*

1) Look at the following evaluations of Clinton taken from news headlines. What aspect is being evaluated?

   a) Assange says Clinton has been 'eaten alive by her ambitions' (*Daily Mail* 2016).
   b) Trump's claim that Clinton lacks the 'physical stamina' to be president (*Washington Post* 2016).
   c) Hillary Clinton tries warmth as US voters go cold (*Financial Times* 2016).
   d) Hillary Clinton's charisma deficit is a common problem for female leaders (*Quartz* 2016).
   e) Hillary Should Play Up Her Feminine Side (*Newsweek* 2015).
   f) Hillary Clinton talks more like a man than she used to (*Washington Post* 2016).
   g) TRUMP: Hillary Clinton is 'trigger-happy and very unstable' (*Business Insider* 2016).
   h) Hillary Clinton's lack of empathy has her limping to the finish line (*Guardian* 2016).
   i) Hillary Clinton ripped as 'scheming, robotic liar' by Catholic bishop after WikiLeaks dump (*Washington Post* 2016).
   j) Donald Trump calls Hillary Clinton 'shrill' (*The Boston Globe* 2016).

2) In a comparison of the top 100 collocates (words which have a strong statistical connection) of *Donald Trump* and *Hillary Clinton* in the NOW Corpus (see corpus.byu.edu) of news articles from 2016 only one of the two candidates had collocates which referred to age and clothing. Which candidate and why?

3) Go to Google images and search for *Hillary Clinton memes* and then *Donald Trump memes* (memes are typically images, videos, short texts, etc. which creators consider humorous and share online). This will show you the visuals which were shared and used in unofficial campaigning on social media. Compare the memes that you see. In what ways do any of them specifically draw on gender?

   This kind of negative gender evaluation can be considered as another form of attempted *delegitimisation*, in this case, trying to undermine the *ethos* and political legitimacy of an adversary on the simple basis of their being a woman.

10.2 Referendums

Unlike national general elections which are meant to be held periodically every, say, five years (UK, Cyprus, France, Ireland, Italy, Luxembourg and Malta) or four years (US and most other European Union countries) or three years (Australia), a referendum is called to ask the voting population to decide on a matter felt to be of particular and overriding constitutional or social importance. Instead of electing representatives to be sent to the relevant Assembly, the electorate is asked to either accept or reject a particular proposal, in other words, a binary choice, for or against.

In the United States there is no provision in the Constitution for the holding of nationwide referendums and, in fact, none have ever been held. National referendums are also rare in the United Kingdom and only two had ever been called before 2014. The first was held in 1975 over the proposal of whether the country should stay in the European Economic Community (known more colloquially as 'the Common Market'), the precursor to the European Union. Backed by all the major political parties, the proposal to remain passed with the support of 69% of the vote. In the second, held in 2013, voters were asked if they wanted to abolish the existing majoritarian or 'first-past-the-post' system of electing Members of the House of Commons and replace it with the so-called 'alternative vote' system, a preferential voting system in which voters rank the candidates in order of preference rather than voting for a single candidate. The proposal was overwhelmingly rejected, with 68% voting against.

In recent years two extremely important referendums have been called in Britain and constitute the topic of this section. These are the so-called 'Scottish Referendum' in 2014 and the 'European Union' Referendum of 2016.

Q1

Some countries do not envisage referendums, others reserve them for constitutional matters, while others also hold referendums over social issues. Italy, for example, held a referendum over the legalisation of divorce in 1974 and another on rights to the interruption of pregnancy (sometimes called abortion) in 1981. In your own country, which of the following questions would you envisage as questions to be put to a referendum vote? Are there any issues you would like to see put to a referendum in your country? (Free responses)

same-sex marriage;
the legalisation of certain recreational drugs;
if a member of NATO, membership of NATO;
the legalisation of capital punishment;
if a member of the European Union, important changes to the EU constitution, continued membership of the EU.

10.2.1 The 2014 Scottish Referendum: background

A national referendum was held in Scotland on the 18th September 2014 on the question of whether the country should remain part of the United Kingdom.

England and Scotland were separate kingdoms until 1601 when the English monarch, Elizabeth I, died childless and the English Parliament invited her cousin, James VI of Scotland, to ascend the throne of England who thus became James I of England, with both Scotland and England retaining their own Parliaments.

In 1707 the governments of the two countries themselves merged by mutual agreement. Under the Act of Union, the Scottish Parliament was dissolved and, instead, the Scottish electorate (as already the Welsh) elected Members to a single British Parliament, situated in Westminster, London. The main incentive for Scots was commercial, to obtain access to English markets, including its colonies. The main initial incentive for England was security, to have a settled peaceful northern border.

By the late 20th Century a movement grew advocating the decentralisation of powers from the central government to Scotland and in 1998 the 'Scottish Devolution' Referendum was held (in Scotland alone) where a majority of participants approved the institution of a Scottish Parliament in Edinburgh, with limited powers, 'devolved', that is, granted by the UK national Parliament. Scotland continued to elect MPs to the central British Parliament in London.

In 2013 the Scottish Nationalist Party (SNP) won the elections to the Scottish Parliament and demanded a referendum on whether Scotland should remain part of the UK. The UK Parliament conceded to the demand and the date was set for September 2014.

TASK 4: *Independence or break-up?*

What precisely do we call what the SNP is campaigning for? There are a number of possible terms, all with very different connotations and evaluations. These include:

separation
secession
independence
division
self-determination
nationhood
nationalism
freedom
leaving the United Kingdom
breaking up the United Kingdom

In terms of evaluation, which is the most positive sounding and which the least? Which ones seem the most neutral?

A number of other countries observed the campaign and the outcome very closely, and sometimes nervously. Belgium is split between Flemish speakers in the north and French speakers in the south and in Brussels, and relations between the two are often fraught; many among both the Catalan and the Basque communities in Spain desire a similar referendum; in 1995, mainly French-speaking Quebec held a referendum on leaving Canada which failed narrowly, but many there would wish for another vote. At the time of writing, the Ukraine is riven by a civil war between the central government and groups who want parts of Eastern Ukraine to secede/become independent/separate/achieve self-determination (choose the term according to your political viewpoint).

10.2.2 The European Union Referendum: background

In a speech given on the 23rd January 2013, the UK Prime Minister announced that the government would make provisions for an 'in–out' referendum on the UK continuing to be a member of the European Union (EU), quickly nicknamed the 'Brexit' ('British exit') Referendum, to be held before the end of 2017.

It is, however, simplistic to analyse public views on the EU into two entirely opposing camps, For and Against. The same is true of the Scottish public on membership of the United Kingdom. In an analysis of views expressed in the English press, Partington (forthcoming) identified at least four camps or stances, as follows:

1) EU-Idealists: who are defensive of the EU, puzzled and even offended by criticism of it.
2) EU-Reformers: who acknowledge some need for reform but the solution is closer engagement and 'more Europe' (closer political union). The real problem is the UK: if only it took more responsibility it would be the solution to the EU's troubles.
3) EU-'Looseners': who wish to renegotiate institutions and treaties 'not fit for purpose' (*Guardian* 16/01/2013), the UK should engage with the EU but on an issue-by-issue basis, protecting national interests.
4) EU-Phobes: who see no good at all in the EU and cannot leave it soon enough.

However, referendums by their very nature are binary, the questions they ask compel a 'Yes' or 'No' response and, therefore, force populations into one of two camps. Nor is membership of the EU a left–right divide. Several British right-wing newspapers are constantly critical of the EU and all its works, but the following extract:

> [we are] totally committed to complete withdrawal from the European Union, or Common Market as it was originally called. That is the only way Britain can begin to regain control of its economy, sovereignty and its political powers.
>
> The European Union is a capitalist club that makes it easy for multinational companies to exploit workers throughout its member states, while the sovereignty of those states is increasingly meaningless, and we are all at the mercy of a vast, faceless bureaucracy.
>
> It is a costly business too for the people of Scotland, England and Wales; membership of the European Union means we suffer an annual net loss of at least £12 billion, simply because we are in the EU.

is not from a right-wing source, but from the Manifesto of the Socialist Labour Party, a small left-wing party for whom the EU is a 'club for capitalists' which damages workers' rights and which the UK should leave at once.

TASK 5: *The four different stances on the EU*

Each of the following extracts illustrates one of the four stances on the EU listed above: *EU-Idealist*, *EU-Reformer*, *EU-Loosener*, *EU-Phobic*.
   Match the extract to the particular stance:

A. In this new German-dominated Europe, where is Britain? Britain may never have placed itself in the very engine room of the European Union [. . .] But does Britain have to continue to sulk in a dinghy being towed along by the main vessel? (*Guardian* 2013)

B. [. . .] the modern EU has [given] a failed neoliberal model of capitalism the force of treaty, enforcing corporate power over employment rights. Claims that the single market would boost growth have proved groundless. But the EU's profoundly undemocratic and dysfunctional structures have been brutally exposed by the eurozone crisis and the devastation wreaked by Troika-imposed austerity. (*Guardian* 2013)

C. So I want to speak to you today with urgency and frankness about the European Union and how it must change – both to deliver prosperity and to retain the support of its peoples. We [British] have the character of an island nation – independent, forthright, passionate in defence of our sovereignty. For us, the European Union is a means to an end – prosperity, stability, the anchor of freedom and democracy both within Europe and beyond her shores – not an end in itself. We insistently ask: How? Why? To what end? (PM Cameron 2013)

D. This country is at risk of allowing itself to be stampeded by the Tory party and the Europhobic press into abandoning its place in Europe. Pro-Europeans should shed their anxieties. Voices that have been silent for too long need to make themselves heard. (*Guardian* 2013)

A. _____ B. _____ C. _____ D. _____

10.2.3 The wording of the question matters

The United Kingdom Electoral Commission, a non-partisan agency which oversees electoral matters, has the following official – and commonsensical – guidelines on the form of words of any referendum:

The referendum question must:

* be easy to understand
* be to the point
* be unambiguous
* avoid encouraging voters to consider one response more favourably than another
* avoid misleading voters

But the issue of how to word the question may be trickier than at first sight.

There is a body of political wisdom which argues that, whatever the issue brought to a referendum, there is an inbuilt advantage on the side of the 'Yes' over the 'No' (known as 'response bias').[1] 'Yes' sounds more positive about the future, more active and hopeful – as, for example, in Barack Obama's first campaign slogan, 'Yes, We Can'. 'No', on the other hand, can sound negative, recalcitrant, even grumpy. In 1975, when the Labour Prime Minister, Harold Wilson, ran the campaign in favour of continued membership of the EU, he framed the question so that a 'Yes' vote was an agreement to stay in, and he called his opponents 'the No men'. The leader of the SNP at the time of the Scottish Referendum agreed: 'the Yes side is important' (*BBC News* 27 May 2015). The secessionist campaign, led by the SNP, adopted the slogan 'Yes, Scotland'. Unsurprisingly, the anti-secessionist campaign, backed by all three main parties, the Conservatives, Labour and Liberal Democrats, did not adopt a slogan 'No, Scotland'. Instead, they chose the more positive message, 'Better Together'.

The wording of the Scottish Referendum

Q2

If you were a supporter of Scotland's secession, which of the following questions would you prefer the voting paper to display, and which would you prefer if you were opposed to Scotland's secession? Why?

Do you want Scotland to be an independent nation?
Do you want Scotland to leave the United Kingdom?
Do you want Scotland to remain part of the UK?

Q3

Who should be eligible to vote? Which of the following rules would you choose if you supported secession and which if you opposed it? Why?

Citizens born in and currently resident in Scotland?
Citizens currently resident in Scotland?
Citizens currently resident in Scotland and also people born in Scotland but now resident in England, Wales and Northern Ireland (approximately 600,000 people)?
All British citizens currently resident in the United Kingdom, Scots and non-Scots?

The wording of the European Union Referendum

The initial drafting of a UK parliamentary law to set up the referendum proposed the question as follows:

Should the United Kingdom remain a member of the European Union?

☐ Yes
☐ No

With this form of words, a vote for 'Yes' is a vote for continued membership, which, at the time, was the outcome favoured by the UK government. As expected, a number of EU-secessionists objected and appealed to the UK Electoral Commission. The Commission agreed that the question was not neutral and amended the ballot question to:

Should the United Kingdom remain a member of the European Union or leave the European Union?

☐ Remain a member of the European Union
☐ Leave the European Union

Another important wording issue is what the EU itself is called. We saw in Unit 7 how 'Brussels' is used by critics of the EU to deliberately conflate all the different European institutions (some of which are part of the EU, some of which are not) into one single, seemingly highly powerful entity. In another case, we see persuasive wording being chosen from those in favour of unity. Supporters of the EU often refer to it as 'Europe' and indeed the EU itself encourages the synonymy EU = Europe: its own website is entitled 'Europa'. However, the EU is not the same thing as Europe as, say, the Swiss and Albanians will testify.

Moreover, this deliberate conflation of terms can lead to dangers, even rhetorical sleight-of-hand. 'Anti-Europe' and 'anti-European' are both loaded terms and can both be used pejoratively in a way 'anti-EU' cannot. The first is also rather absurd: you might as well accuse someone of being 'anti-South America'. The second, 'anti-European', can paint critics of the EU as being automatically xenophobic, disliking all other Europeans. In this Unit, we will employ pro-EU and anti-EU as the more neutral terms.

10.2.4 The referendum campaigns: Scotland

At the beginning of the campaign in Scotland, opinion polls estimated that the 'No' (remain) vote of the anti-secessionists was ahead of the 'Yes' (leave) vote by 61% to 39% (YouGov poll, July 2014).

The pro-secessionists argued that Scotland needed to be 'free' and 'sovereign' and had to 'claw back' powers from 'Westminster'. Such arguments were encapsulated in both positive slogans such as:

Scotland's future in Scotland's hands (with a picture of a baby's hand in her mother's)

And negative ones such as:

Don't let them tell us we can't

In Unit 3.2 we discussed the difference between positive and negative campaigning and how, in the latter, a negatively evaluated 'them' is created, as here. Just who 'them' refers to does not always need to be specified.

Another positive slogan was:

We've got what it takes

which countered the argument that Scotland's population and economy were too small to be viable on their own. As we shall see, the issue of size, being big enough both to survive and constitute an autonomous sovereign nation – and not just a 'region' – was important in the EU referendum too.

The secessionist campaign was able to take control of nationalistic symbols of 'Scotland', of Scottish exceptionalness, even 'Celtic' exceptionalness, including tartans, kilts, the Scottish flag of St Andrew. These also included historical ones of a nostalgic past, when Scotland had been 'free', including patriotic songs like 'A Nation Once Again' and 'Flower of Scotland', the country's official national anthem, with openly anti-English lyrics.

The anti-secessionist 'No' vote faced a number of problems. It was essentially a vote for the status quo. It is often difficult to arouse the same emotional, hopeful appeal for things to stay as they are, as opposed for things to change, and for a rosier future. The simple theme of 'Better Together' was repeated:

Let's stick together
We are with you
Stronger together (with a picture of many hands linking)
Proud to be Scots but Better Together

The 'Better Together' camp also faced the difficult balancing act of arguing against what their opponents were calling 'independence' and 'self-determination' for Scotland, while stressing their patriotic attachment to Scotland and Scottishness. It found itself without effective emotional symbols, the Union flag coming a poor second to the Scottish flag in terms of patriotic appeal.

In terms of policies, the 'Better Together' campaign argued that Scottish sovereignty had not been 'lost' but was pooled, that is, shared with the rest of the UK, since Scottish voters send their representatives to the central Parliament at Westminster.

As all status quo camps must do, the 'Better Together' alliance exploited negative campaigning messages; that is, warnings of the dangers of change. For instance, Alistair Darling, who went on to become leader of the 'Better Together' alliance, was quoted in 2012 as saying that the Scottish people would be taking a 'massive risk' with their economic future if they voted for independence: 'the downsides are immense, the risks are amazing, the uncertainties I just don't think are worth gambling on. There are times when you should gamble and there are times when you shouldn't' (reported in the *Observer* 2012).

When the day came for voting, 18th September 2014, the turnout, that is, the percentage of eligible voters who actually cast their vote, was 84.6% – the highest for any election in Scottish history. The result was as follows:

| Yes: | 1,617,989 | 44.6% |
| No: | 2,001,926 | 55.4% |

Although the secessionists were deeply disappointed and the anti-secessionist groups greatly relieved, both sides reflected on how the pro-secessionist vote had increased by 6%–10% from the beginning of the campaign. The pro-secessionists had run a more effective rhetorical campaign. They commanded the terminology of the debate; for example, the term *independence* was adopted even by the anti-secessionists and the mainstream media, and was even the term used on the referendum ballot paper.

10.2.5 Metaphors of the UK Union

The most common metaphor in anti-secessionist rhetoric is that the United Kingdom is a *marriage*, and that, consequently, secession is a *divorce*, a painful one with dire consequences:

> Independence would not be a trial separation, it would be a painful divorce.
>
> (PM Cameron 2014)

Another metaphor is the Union is a *home*:

> For the people of Scotland to walk away now would be like painstakingly building a home – and then walking out the door and throwing away the keys.
>
> (Cameron 2014)

It is also a fabric, a cloth:

> You don't get the change you want by ripping your country apart.
> (Cameron 2014)

And a team:

> It's team GB I want to talk about today.
>
> (Cameron 2014)

And it is a family:

> [Union] really is the best of both worlds and it's the best way to get real change and secure a better future for your children and grandchildren.

> And speaking of family – that is quite simply how I feel about this. We are a family. The United Kingdom is not one nation. We are four nations in a single country [. . .]

Scotland, England, Wales and Northern Ireland different nations, with individual identities competing with each other even at times enraging each other while still being so much stronger together.

We are a family of nations.

(Cameron 2014)

which blends with the marriage/divorce metaphor:

do not break this family apart.

(Cameron 2014)

Turning the family metaphor around, the UK is a stern parent, and the SNP and Scottish secessionists, meanwhile, are 'a rebellious teenager':

The Westminster government's strategy [. . .] has been bluster and threat, typified by the recent shemozzle about whether Scotland would be able to keep the pound. The tone of voice was that of a parent confronting a rebellious teenager.

(*Financial Times* 2014)

TASK 6A: *Metaphors of the UK Union*

What metaphor is being evoked in each of the following statements?

a) The split in the Union has all the hallmarks of a vitriolic divorce [. . .] Scotland, faithful spouse of so many years, is being offered promises of a better future with another man. Cameron has pleaded for her not to break up the marriage and has promised that 'things will change'. (*Daily Telegraph* 18 September 2014, edited)
b) The United Kingdom is an intricate tapestry; millions of relationships woven tight over three centuries. (Cameron 2014)
c) In the UK, Scotland is part of a major global player. (Cameron 2014)
d) And if this family of nations broke up, something very powerful and precious would go out forever. (Cameron 2014)

TASK 6B: *Metaphors of independence*

The following are metaphors used by the pro-secession side. How is independence being represented in each of the following?

a) That is the destination of our journey: the Scotland we wish to be.
b) And we can start building. Building the Scotland we know is possible.
c) I believe that an independent Scotland will thrive.

10.2.6 The referendum campaigns: on the European Union

In a seminal study of British-based anti-EU and EU-sceptic websites, Teubert (2001) identifies a number of anxieties expressed about the EU. Partington (forthcoming) replicated this work but examining English left-leaning (the *Guardian*) and right-leaning (*Daily Mail*) articles on the EU published in 2013, the year of the referendum announcement. The first three anxieties, listed by Teubert, are familiar:

- *sovereignty*: taken away rather than pooled
- *size*: UK has become a 'province' of the EU
- *accountability*: Brussels is far away and is 'unaccountable' to the British

These anxieties are strikingly similar to those expressed by Scottish secessionists; namely, that Scottish sovereignty has been lost rather than pooled, real power needs to be reclaimed from far away Westminster and returned to a Scottish Parliament accountable to the Scottish people.

According to EU-sceptics, then, powers need to be *clawed back*, an expression meaning to retake something which is rightfully yours:

The Mail has always supported the Prime Minister in his efforts to claw back powers from Brussels before holding a referendum [. . .]
(*Daily Mail* 2013)

A more neutral term used by the *Guardian* is *repatriation* of powers; the Prime Minister himself had instead used the euphemistic metaphor of powers *flowing back* from the EU to the UK.

Both sides set up official campaigns, each with their website. The Remain campaign was called 'Britain Stronger in Europe' (website: www.strongerin.co.uk/) and the Brexit campaign was called, simply, 'Leave: EU' (website: http://leave.eu/).

One issue which grew and grew in importance was that of immigration and the claim by the 'Leave' campaign that after Brexit it would be possible to 'regain control of our borders' and limit the flow of immigrants into the UK, who, they claimed, put pressure on 'our' schools, Health Service and created competition for housing. The 'Leave' campaign was accused of xenophobia and even racism, which they vehemently denied, employing several non-white spokespersons.

Other anxieties were the perceived increasing domination of Germany over the rest of the EU, as exemplified by the headline:

Is Germany too powerful for Europe?[2]
(*Guardian* 2013)

And allied to this, many left-wing members of the 'Leave' alliance were concerned about the EU's supposed commitment to a politics of *austerity* and cuts in welfare which harm the weakest, a politics often seen as imposed by German institutions.

Being essentially the side proposing change, in common with the pro-leaving 'Yes' campaign in Scotland, the secessionist 'Leave the EU' movement used positive campaigning, the 'Yes we can' spirit, with slogans like 'Create an Earthquake' and positive reassurances such as:

> They say that the EU is the future, and that we couldn't survive outside it: but we're the world's 6th largest economy, and while the EU share of world trade is shrinking, our prospects are very good indeed.
>
> (UKIP Manifesto 2014)

which is reminiscent of the SNP's reassurance that Scotland is big enough and 'has what it takes' (see section 10.2.4). The 'Stay In' campaign, on the other hand, faced many of the same problems as the anti-secessionist 'No', 'Better Together' campaign during the Scottish Referendum. Both were proposing, essentially, a vote for the status quo and, as we said earlier, it is often difficult to arouse an emotional, hopeful appeal for things to stay as they are. Inevitably the 'Stay Together' camp employed negative campaign messages very similar to those of the 'Better Together' camp. It issued messages of *warning*, that exiting would be *mad, reckless, a historical error, catastrophic for trade* and that it would leave Britain *isolated, weakened, condemned to irrelevance on the world stage*. Along with *world stage* we find other metaphors in play: not *sliding* or *sleepwalking* (a word with negative evaluation) *towards the exit door*. The item *club* is used explicitly, in a warning by the President of the European Council, Barroso, that Britain *would pay a high price for leaving the club altogether*, presumably with a very different evaluation of the 'EU is an exclusive club' metaphor to that intended by the Socialist Labour Party noted above (see section 10.2.3). The core messages were that leaving the EU would mean 'less trade, fewer jobs, less influence both in the EU and in the outside world'. However, the Leave campaign was often at least as negative; one of the lowest points being when leading Leave campaigner Boris Johnson compared the EU to a dictatorship: 'Napoleon, Hitler, various people tried this out, and it ends tragically. The EU is an attempt to do this by different methods'.

Another difficulty the pro-EU 'Stay In' campaign shared with the pro-Union 'Better Together' alliance was in facing the difficult balancing act of arguing against what their opponents were calling 'independence' and 'self-determination' for Britain, while stressing their patriotic attachment to Britain and 'British values'. They had a similar lack of effective rallying symbols. While the 'Leave' campaign could rely on national symbols like the Union flag, nostalgic emotional appeals to history, patriotic songs and music, and national sporting successes (see Unit 3.5 on the persuasive appeal of associations), the 'Stay In' appeal to *our common European identity* felt abstract to sceptics.

TASK 7: *Remainers or Leavers?*

Do you think the following statements come from sources in favour of Remain or Leave?

a)   In recent days a string of Cabinet ministers have been wheeled out to make doom-mongering predictions about the risks of Brexit. ....

b)   What has the EU ever done for us? How about jobs, workers' rights, decades of peace, cleaner air and beaches, lower prices and dozens more reasons to vote [for us] on Thursday.........................

c)   Cameron is to blame for unleashing this reckless referendum, but above all for the anger seething underneath it. ....

d)   If we vote to leave Europe, there are no second chances and no going back. ....

e)   This is a crucial time, lots of people will be making up their minds, and I hope very much they will believe in our country, believe in what we can do. ....

f)   Former work and pensions secretary Iain Duncan Smith dismissed the warnings as a cynical scare story, saying there was no evidence Brexit would drive up inflation or spark a collapse in asset prices. ....

The eventual decision of the referendum, 52%–48% in favour of Brexit, surprised many, even a proportion of its proponents.

Further reading

Cameron, D. and Shaw, S. (2016) *Gender, Power and Political Speech: Women and Language in the 2015 UK General Election*, Basingstoke: Palgrave Macmillan.

Wilson, J. and Boxer, D. (eds.) (2016) *Discourse, Politics and Women as Global Leaders*, Amsterdam: John Benjamins.

Zappavigna, M. (2011) 'Ambient affiliation: A linguistic perspective on Twitter', *New Media & Society* 13(5): 788–806. (This work uses a post-election corpus.)

Keys and commentaries

TASK 1A:

Free response

TASK 1B: *Popular political hashtags*

1) #MakeAmericaGreatAgain #MAGA This highly successful positive hashtag was used by the Trump campaign as a central slogan.

2) #BlackLivesMatter #BLM This was not launched by any of the campaigns but was a strong political movement in the US at the time. It was triggered by the acquittal of a man for the shooting-death of an unarmed black 17-year-old and became a unifying slogan for people who wanted to draw attention to the unequal treatment of black people, particularly by law enforcement officers. In an indication of how this movement aligned politically, Clinton invited Black Lives Matters supporters to speak at her rallies. At his rallies, Trump invited police officers, who formed their own campaign 'Blue Lives Matter', to draw attention to the dangers faced by members of the police in the gun-rich US.

3) #FeelTheBern This positive slogan (a pun on Bern/burn) was used by Bernie Sanders's supporters.

4) #ImWithHer This positive slogan was popular among Clinton's supporters and was most frequent on the day she accepted the Democrat nomination.

5) #NeverTrump This negative campaign hashtag originated with Republicans in the early stages of the election campaign, when they wanted to prevent Trump being chosen as their candidate and, indeed, hit its highest peak in that period. It then spread to Democrat supporters.

6) #CrookedHillary This negative hashtag originated in a tweet by Trump in which he said 'Crooked Hillary Clinton is spending a fortune on ads against me. I am the one person she doesn't want to run against. Will be such fun!'. It was picked up by other Trump supporters and repeatedly used by Trump himself.

7) #BasketOfDeplorables This originated with a comment by Clinton that half of Trump's supporters fell into a 'basket of deplorables'. The hashtag was then used to criticise her as, for instance, in the following tweet by Trump's son: 'Look at the #BasketOfDeplorables in Pensacola Florida last night! What a horrible statement. #CrookedHillary' (illustrated with a photo of a large stadium). However, it was also used by Clinton's supporters to criticise the perceived over-reaction to her comment, as in: 'Hillary calls racists & homophobes #BasketOfDeplorables media goes nuts.

Trump insults Black, Hispanic, Gays, Muslims & Women & it's ok. Ugh'. It was also used to label Trump supporters, a popular format being to retweet a far-right tweet with just the comment #BasketOfDeplorables. To make things even more complicated, it was even 'reclaimed' (Unit 2.3) by some Trump supporters who began to wear 'Proud to be a Deplorable' and 'Deplorable Lives Matter' T-shirts, and even set up #Deplorables. This use by both sides of a polar campaign makes it quite unusual. Often a hashtag will 'belong' to one side or the other and the use of it marks out your affiliation. In this context, to use another side's hashtag in order to get their attention is referred to as 'hashtag jacking'.

8) #DeleteYourAccount This negative slogan was used by Clinton's supporters against Trump. It started with a tweet sent from Clinton's account which simply said, 'Delete your account' in response to a face-threatening tweet from Trump's account.

9) #LockHerUp This negative slogan was used against Clinton by both supporters of Sanders and Trump. It peaked on the day she accepted the Democrat nomination.

Other campaign slogans:

Clinton campaign: 'When they go low, we go high' (first coined by Michelle Obama), 'Stronger together' (note the similarity with the pro-Union slogan in the Scottish Referendum), 'Fighting for us'.

Trump campaign: 'I'm with you, the American people' (this was a reply to the Clinton campaign's 'I'm with her' slogan), 'Drain the [Washington] swamp' (referring to the 'Washington establishment' and positioning Trump as the 'outsider' candidate), 'CNN sucks' (referring to a perceived bias in the media against Trump).

TASK 2: *Political metonyms*

Fill in the gaps with *Washington*, *Wall Street*, *Main Street* or *blue collar*.

a) The arrogance of *Washington* will soon come face to face with the righteous verdict of the American voter. (Trump)

b) The Battle for *blue-collar* America: Remembering the Forgotten Men who have to live with *Washington*'s policies. (*Breitbart*)

c) We simply cannot afford four more years of an economic philosophy that works for *Wall Street* instead of *Main Street*, and ends up devastating both. (Obama)

d) *Blue-collar* voters launch hand grenade into *Washington* (*The Hill*)

e) John Kasich balances his *blue-collar* roots and his ties to *Wall Street* (*New York Times*)

REVISION TASK:

Donald Trump's victory speech: 'Binding the wounds of division'

    i. What are his main themes?

Victory; reunify Americans; serve the people; enable every American to reach his and her full potential; rebuild America and make it 'the best'; look after US veterans; build relationships with other countries.

    ii. Who does he praise?

Clinton; his own movement and voters; US veterans.

    iii. Look for pronouns, *I, you, we, us*, etc. How is each used? What overall effect does he want to achieve?

There is a very frequent use of *we* (19 occurrences), *us* (4) and *our* (22), used to congratulate his supporters and to stress the desire for unity of all Americans. *I* (9) is used in promises of future action. *You* is used just three times in one paragraph (8): 'I'm reaching out to you for your guidance and your help'.

    iv. Trump is famous for his liberal use of hyperbolic language. Can you find any examples here? Are they mostly positive or negative evaluation?

Among others we find *very, very hard-fought, major debt, an incredible and great movement, tremendous potential* (twice). As befits the moment of celebration, they are almost all positive in evaluation.

    v. Look for examples of creative repetition and contrast.

Free response.

    vi. What sort of personality (*ethos*) does he attempt to project? What logical or pseudo-logical arguments (*logos*) does he employ? And what appeals to emotion (*pathos*) does he use?

His projected ethos is one of extraordinary competence and self-confidence; he is also a visionary guide who will enable America to 'dream big'. His promises to rebuild infrastructure, and so on, are appeals to *logos*, to reason. He appeals to emotions in recalling the veterans and also in praising the American people.

    vii. Find a couple of examples of *chiasmus*.

'. . . who want and expect our government to serve the people, and serve the people it will', 'The forgotten men and women of our country will be forgotten no longer' and 'we will get along with all other nations willing to get along with us'.

    viii. 'bind the wounds of division' and this 'journey'. Neither are particularly novel. A political campaign is very frequently referred to as a 'journey' (see Task 6b) and almost every victory speech expresses the desire to bring the two previously opposing sides together.

TASK 3: *Identifying gendered evaluations*

1.

   a) Assange says Clinton has been 'eaten alive by her ambitions' (*Daily Mail* 2016)

   b) Trump's claim that Clinton lacks the 'physical stamina' to be president (*Washington Post* 2016)

   c) Hillary Clinton tries warmth as US voters go cold (*Financial Times* 2016)

   d) Hillary Clinton's charisma deficit is a common problem for female leaders (*Quartz* 2016)

   e) Hillary Should Play Up Her Feminine Side (*Newsweek* 2015)

   f) Hillary Clinton talks more like a man than she used to (*Washington Post* 2016)

   g) TRUMP: Hillary Clinton is 'trigger-happy and very unstable' (*Business Insider* 2016)

   h) Hillary Clinton's lack of empathy has her limping to the finish line (*Guardian* 2016)

   i) Hillary Clinton ripped as 'scheming, robotic liar' by Catholic bishop after WikiLeaks dump (*Washington Post* 2016)

   j) Donald Trump calls Hillary Clinton 'shrill' (*The Boston Globe* 2016)

In the majority of these, as in the discourse more generally, she is criticised on the basis of her affective face. In (a), Clinton is criticised for being overly ambitious, thus her attention to competence face is seen as damaging her affective face – apparently she can't be seen as likeable as well as highly ambitious. Similarly, in (c) and (d), it is her personal qualities which are attacked, she is not 'warm' or 'charismatic' enough to appeal to the voters (and here we can imagine the 'over-emotional' headlines that could arise if she prioritised the affective). In (e) she is criticised as not being sufficiently 'feminine', that is prioritising being a 'leader' over being a 'woman'. In (h) too, she is not empathetic enough. Likewise, in (i) she is 'scheming' and, therefore, not likeable. If we consider the meaning of 'scheming', we have a near-synonym for 'ambitious' which is differentiated by the negative evaluation which it carries. Description as an 'ambitious' candidate could flatter competence face, as we might expect a presidential candidate to possess that quality.

In (b) her competence face is threatened as she is viewed as too weak for the job (not male enough, perhaps). Also in (g) we have a criticism that primarily targets her leadership qualities – because she is 'unstable', she is positioned as not being suitable.

In (f) and (g) she is evaluated explicitly with reference to how she speaks and this was a recurring theme throughout the campaign. Gendered terms were often used to describe her, such as 'shrill', as here, but also 'yelling' (while Sanders was admired for his high-volume speeches). In speaking more like a man (f), she may be considered more leader-like (flattering competence face) but will then be seen as unfeminine which may damage her affective face.

2. Only one of the two candidates had collocates which referred to age and clothing. Which candidate and why?

   Clinton. Although the candidates were practically the same age (Clinton was a year younger), only Clinton had age references among the most significant collocates. This may have been part of the narrative that Trump's campaign aimed to tell about her being physically unfit to be President, in which illness and stereotypes of female weakness were conflated. In terms of clothing, *pantsuit* and *pantsuits* both occurred in collocates for Clinton. This suggests that her clothing was highlighted as a campaign issue in a way that Trump's was not (though presumably he too often wore trousers and matching jacket!). However, he was not immune to comments on physical appearance, and *orange-haired* occurred in his list of collocates.

3. Free response.

TASK 4: *Independence or break-up?*

Those with the most favourable evaluation include: independence, self-determination, nationhood and, of course, the 'hooray' word (Unit 2), freedom.

Those with the least favourable evaluation include: separation, division, breaking up the United Kingdom.

TASK 5: *The four different stances on the EU*

A. EU-reformer; B. EU-phobic; C. EU-loosener; D. EU-idealist.

Q2

Supporters of secession would choose the first: 'Do you want Scotland to be an independent nation?'. A 'Yes' vote would be a vote for secession, and the question also contains the positively evaluated term *independent*.

Opponents of secession would choose the third: 'Do you want Scotland to remain part of the UK?'. A 'Yes' vote would now be a vote *against* secession and the term *remain part of* suggests that Scotland *is* and *should be* a part of the United Kingdom.

In the event, the question actually adopted was the first, 'Do you want Scotland to be an independent nation?', giving the secessionists an inbuilt linguistic advantage.

Q3

Under the terms of the 2010 Draft Bill, the following people were entitled to vote in the referendum:

- British citizens who were resident in Scotland;
- citizens of other Commonwealth countries who were resident in Scotland;
- citizens of other European Union countries who were resident in Scotland;
- members of the House of Lords who were resident in Scotland;
- Service/Crown personnel serving in the UK or overseas in the British Armed Forces or with Her Majesty's Government who were registered to vote in Scotland.

These conditions were favourable to the secessionist movement, given that Scots living in the rest of the United Kingdom were excluded from voting. It is thought highly likely that most Scots living in the rest of the United Kingdom, perhaps working there, possibly with an English, Welsh or Northern Irish partner and possibly having 'British' children, would have voted against secession.

One curiosity was that the age for eligibility to vote in the Scottish Referendum was 16 rather than 18 years of age, the normal voting age in the UK.

TASK 6A: *Metaphors of the Union*

a)   a marriage
b)   a fabric
c)   a team
d)   a family

TASK 6B: *Metaphors of independence*

a)   on a *journey*
b)   *constructing* a new country
c)   Scotland as a *living entity*

TASK 7: *Remainers or Leavers?*

a)   In recent days a string of Cabinet ministers have been wheeled out to make doom-mongering predictions about the risks of Brexit (*Daily Mail* 29 March 2016). Leave.

b) What has the EU ever done for us? How about jobs, workers' rights, decades of peace, cleaner air and beaches, lower prices and dozens more reasons to vote [for us] on Thursday ('Stronger in Europe' campaign). Remain.

c) Cameron is to blame for unleashing this reckless referendum, but above all for the anger seething underneath it (*Guardian* 20 June 2016). Remain.

d) If we vote to leave Europe, there are no second chances and no going back ('Stronger in Europe' campaign). Remain.

e) This is a crucial time, lots of people will be making up their minds, and I hope very much they will believe in our country, believe in what we can do (Boris Johnson, pro-Brexit Conservative politician). Leave.

f) Former work and pensions secretary Iain Duncan Smith dismissed the warnings as a cynical scare story, saying there was no evidence Brexit would drive up inflation or spark a collapse in asset prices (*Daily Mail* 27 May 2016). Leave.

Notes

1 https://en.m.wikipedia.org/wiki/Response_bias
2 Available at: www.theguardian.com/world/2013/mar/31/is-germany-too-powerful-for-europe

Conclusion

In a modern democratic society, politics is persuasion and persuasion is conducted predominantly through language.

Throughout this book, we have studied evaluative language as employed by politicians and those around them – journalists, press agents, and so on. Evaluative language is defined as the linguistic methods of persuading us of what is *good* or *bad* – in a democracy, one presumes, good or bad for us, the people. But we have seen too that a careful study of the use of evaluative language can also tell us a great deal about the beliefs, character and strategies of the would-be persuader.

In addition, we examined a number of models and techniques of persuasion, as well as analysing various discourse types in which we can find persuasive language, principally speeches, newspaper articles and blogs, question–response discourses and satire. We observed some of the subtleties in these models, but also some of the dangers – for both author and audience – for instance, in persuasion by comparison, including in the use of metaphor and metonymy, in pseudo-logical arguments, in hidden presuppositions in questions and in the sheer seductiveness of satire.

Along the way, we noted that persuaders, in some cultures at least, do not have it all their own way. So-called 'modern techniques' of persuasion – 'spin' or 'image politics' – have their many critics. Moreover, in societies where the press is relatively free, the attempts of politicians and their hired persuaders to present to the world their picture of events and their evaluations are thoroughly scrutinised through rigorous, even hostile questioning. In a healthy society, rhetoric and spin produce their own antibodies. But only very careful attention to language and the ways it is used can help us appreciate, exploit and protect ourselves from the art of persuasion.

Glossary
(In brackets, the relevant Units)

adjacency pair (8)
a sequence in conversation where two participants each contribute one turn, such as *thank you/you're welcome*. The first part in the pair leads to an expectation of the second part occurring. For instance, a question usually leads to an expectation of there being a response.

agency (2)
See transitivity.

analogy (3, 5)
a comparison between two entities made with the intention of both explaining a certain situation and also proposing a point of view about or an evaluation of one of the entities.

assertion (8, 9)
an explicit statement or declaration that something exists, is true, has happened, and so on. (This may, of course, not be the case, in which case the speaker is either misinformed or lying.)

attribution (5)
this occurs when a speaker makes clear that the opinions and evaluations being expressed in their utterance (statement or question) belong to another party and the speaker does not take responsibility for them.

bicolon (5, 9, 10)
an expression containing two parallel phrases; for example, '. . . whether you are citizens of America or citizens of the world' (President Kennedy) or 'No creature among them went upon two legs. No creature called any other creature "Master"' (*Animal Farm*).

binomial (5, 10)
a figure consisting of two or more words or phrases usually belonging to the same grammatical category, having some semantic relationship and joined by some syntactic device such as *and* or *or*; for example, *sooner or later, death or dishonour, rules and regulations, Republicans and Democrats*.

chiasmus (5, 10)
a special form of contrasting pair where the elements of the first part are switched around in the second, such as, *he came in triumph and in defeat departs*.

connotation(s) (2, 4)
the connotations of a word or phrase are the associations it has for an individual or a group of people. The word *red*, for instance, has connotations of 'passion' and 'danger' for most westerners, while for much of Chinese culture it is associated with elegance. For many it recalls left-wing politics and for leftist sympathisers it is evaluated favourably and for rightist sympathisers it is evaluated unfavourably. For some individuals, it will have other more personal associations, perhaps with clothes, motor racing or a particular football team (see also *denotation(s)*).

contrasting pair or *antithesis* (5, 10)
a figure containing two parts which are structurally parallel but opposed in meaning; for example, 'One small step for a man, one giant leap for mankind' (Neil Armstrong) or 'In the process of gaining our rightful place we must not be guilty of wrongful deeds' (Dr Martin Luther King).

delegitimisation (1, 4, 8, 10)
In rhetoric, an attempt to discredit the right or ability of an opponent to make a certain claim or argument or to hold a certain power. Examples would include, attacking an opponent's character rather than their argument (the *ad personam*, Unit 4), questioning an opponent's abilities simply on the basis of their gender or race (Unit 10), constantly interrupting someone or even mocking their speaking style, implying that what they have to say is unimportant (Unit 8).

denotation(s) (2)
the literal meaning of a word or phrase, the definition we usually find in a dictionary (see also *connotation(s)*).

dialect (Preface)
a regionally distinctive variety of language, identified by a particular set of words and grammatical structures. One dialect may come to predominate and be considered the 'standard' form of the language, especially for writing (Crystal 1997).

dramatic irony (9)
a state of affairs in which an individual or group acts under some misapprehension of the situation he/she/they are in (is 'in the dark'), while an observer of the action (generally us, the audience or readers) is in possession of the true apprehension (is 'in the know').

dysphemism (4)
the use of language to portray some entity, event or policy in an exaggeratedly negative light; for example, Trump describing the US economy as 'carnage' in his 2017 Inauguration Speech.

ethos (1, 3, 5, 8)
the means by which a would-be persuader attempts to establish the credentials to justify why they should be listened to; for instance, by claiming to be honest, or interesting and witty.

euphemism (4, 7)
the deliberate renaming of negative, controversial or downright harmful actions in neutral terms in order to sanitise them; for example, *collateral damage*, which is used to describe civilians killed when caught between fighting forces.

evaluation (2, 3, 4, 5, 6, 7, 8, 9, 10)
very basically, the judgement of whether an entity, an event, a process, etc. is *good* or *bad* for some individual or group (usually, of course, from the point of view of the speaker or writer).

face, facework (3, 8, 9)
'face' is defined as the image we all project of ourselves to the outside world and 'facework' is the behaviour we employ to project that image. Politicians (and many other professional persuaders) have two separate kinds of face, namely *competence* face and *affective* face. One's competence face is one's image as well informed, an expert, in control and authoritative. One's affective face is one's image as likeable, good humoured, normal, 'one of us'.

ideational communication (3)
the transmission from one individual to others of facts, concepts, ideas (see also *interpersonal communication*).

institutional discourse (8)
either talk which takes place between an 'expert' or representative of an institution and members of the public, such as a medical, a police or a job interview, etc., or talk between two such representatives or groups of representatives, for example, a press conference, involving a spokesperson and journalists. It generally takes the form of a series of questions and responses.

interpersonal communication (3)
the exchange of social information; that is, the use of language to interact with others, establish relations and attempt to influence their behaviour.

irony (7, 9)
a figure of speech in which there is a mismatch, a radical difference, between the evaluation expressed in what is actually written or said (the '*dictum*') and the evaluation which is really intended (the '*implicatum*'); for example, in '[Politician X] is a genius! He's managed to upset both the trade unions *and* big businesses', the politician is clearly not being evaluated as a genius.

logos (1, 3, 5)
the attempt to present a plausible argument in a logical or at least apparently logical way.

metaphor (Preface, 1, 7, 10)
a figure of speech where a name or quality is attributed to something to which it is not literally applicable; for example, 'an icy glance', 'nerves of steel'. It is a statement of comparison between two very different entities and its main purpose is to express an evaluation.

metonymy (2, 5, 7, 10)
(including synecdoche) a type of figure of speech in which the name of one object or entity or concept is used to refer to another to which it is somehow related; for example, *the Crown* to indicate sovereignty, or *the bottle* to indicate alcoholic drink, to count *heads* meaning to count people. In a **personificational** metonym, a person stands for a structure, organisation, nation, etc. (e.g. *Bush* for the US).

In a **toponymical** metonym, a concrete place or a building stands for a larger abstract, usually political entity (e.g. *Westminster* for the British Parliament, sometimes government).

modality (2)
the degree to which speakers and writers commit themselves to a belief that something is true or is possible, or is necessary or is desirable or, indeed, the opposite of all these. In English, this belief is frequently expressed through the verbal system (with items like *should*, *can't*, *needs to*) but there are very many other ways of expressing it.

neutralism (8)
the convention that in a news interview the interviewer and interviewee both recognise and accept that the interviewer is *personally* politically 'neutral'. Even if he or she asks critical or hostile questions, these are not to be taken as expressing the interviewer's own opinions. The convention does not exist in many countries where there is no free press and where a hostile questioner may well be punished.

oxymoron (3, 4, 5)
a figure of speech in which two apparently contradictory elements are combined in a single word, phrase or epigram; for example, *living dead*, *expected surprise*, *radical conservative*, *red fascist*.

parody (9)
an imitation of a particular style of speech or writing, often with exaggeration and often with the intention of mocking those who generally use the style in question.

pathos (1, 3, 5)
the attempt to appeal to the audience's emotions.

presupposition (8)
something which is assumed or implied to exist, to be true, to have happened, and so on, but is not explicitly stated. (As with an assertion, this may, of course, not be true, in which case the speaker is either misinformed or lying.)

rhetoric (1, 2, 3, 4, 5, 6, 7, 9, 10)
the art of persuading others; that is, of influencing their thoughts, beliefs and behaviour, through the use of language.

sarcasm (9)
a particularly straightforward kind of verbal irony, with a clear 'victim'.

satire (9)
a literary form in which the vices, follies, abuses or shortcomings of powerful people (sometimes a whole group, society or the human race generally) are held up to censure by means of ridicule, derision, burlesque, irony.

simile (7)
a figure of speech involving the comparison or analogy between two entities which are deliberately very *unlike*; for example, *Encyclopaedias are like gold mines*.

Like metaphor, its main purpose is to express an evaluation (in this case, the favourable evaluation of encyclopaedias). It differs from metaphor in containing an explicit lexical indication that a comparison is being made, such as *like*, or *just as*, etc. It is often used to introduce an extended comparison between two entities.

soundbite (8)
a short extract from a speech or interview which is chosen for broadcast because of its effect.

spin (1, 3, 4)
presenting one's own or a client's case in the best possible light, usually in order to pre-empt (anticipate) eventual criticism from opponents or the press.

spin-doctor (1, 3, 5)
an agent for a politician, a business, a public service, etc., who is paid to present their client's case in the best possible light.

three-part list or *tricolon* (5, 7, 10)
a figure consisting of three parts which are the same or similar in structure; for example, *Never! Never! Never!* or 'The Good, the Bad and the Ugly'. They often build to a climax or crescendo, the third part being longer and more complex than the preceding two; for example, *the Father, the Son and the Holy Ghost* or '*Life, Liberty and the Pursuit of Happiness*'.

transitivity (2)
the grammatical system used by speakers/writers to express 'who does what to whom (and how)'. The language user can choose to place the participants and events in a particular order and this allows him or her to express evaluations of responsibility. Consider the differences between *Mary divorced John*, where the responsibility is given to Mary, and *Mary and John got a divorce*, where no responsibility is given to either participant.

References

Acemoglu, D. and Robinson, J. (2013) *Why Nations Fail*, London: Profile.

Aristotle (2012) *The Art of Rhetoric*, London: Harper Press.

Attardo, S. (2000) 'Irony as relevant inappropriateness', *Journal of Pragmatics* 32(6): 793–826.

Baker, P., Gabrielatos, C. and McEnery, A. (2013) *Discourse Analysis and Media Attitudes: The Representation of Islam in the British Press*, Cambridge: Cambridge University Press.

Beard, A. (2000) *The Language of Politics*, London: Routledge.

Bhatia, V. (1994) 'Cognitive structuring in legislative provisions', in J. Gibbons (ed.) *Language and the Law*, London: Longman, 136–155.

Bolinger, D. (1980) *Language – the Loaded Weapon: The Use and Abuse of Language Today*, London and New York: Longman.

Brown, P. and Levinson, S. (1987) *Politeness: Some Universals in Language Usage*, Cambridge: Cambridge University press.

Chang, L. (2008) *Factory Girls: From Village to City in a Changing China*, New York: Spiegel & Grau.

Charteris-Black, J. (2013) *Analysing Political Speeches: Rhetoric, Discourse and Metaphor*, Basingstoke: Palgrave Macmillan.

Chaucer, G. (2000) *The Canterbury Tales and Other Poems*. Gutenberg Project. Available at: www.gutenberg.org/ebooks/2383

Clayman, S. (1992) 'Footing in the achievement of neutrality: The case of news-interview discourse', in P. Drew and J. Heritage (eds.) *Talk at Work*, Cambridge: Cambridge University Press, 163–198.

Clayman, S. and Heritage, J. (2002) *The News Interview: Journalists and Public Figures on the Air*, Cambridge: Cambridge University Press.

Cockcroft, R. and Cockcroft, S. (1992) *Persuading People: An Introduction to Rhetoric*, London: Macmillan.

Collier, P. (2008) *The Bottom Billion. Why the Poorest Countries are Failing and What Can Be Done About It*, Oxford: Oxford University Press.

Crystal, D. (1997) *The Cambridge Encyclopedia of Language*, Cambridge: Cambridge University Press.

Darwin, C. (1874) *The Descent of Man*, London: John Murray.

Davies, M. (2012) 'A new approach to oppositions in discourse: The role of syntactic frames in the triggering of noncanonical oppositions', *Journal of English Linguistics* 40(1): 41–73.

Dodson, S. and Dodson, A. (2015) *Literary Justice*, 18 Green Bag 2d 429(2015). Available at: https://ssrn.com/abstract=2650959

Du, X. and Rendle-Short, J. (2016) 'Journalist questions: Comparing adversari-alness in Chinese political press conferences', *Discourse, Context & Media* 12: 51–58.

Duguid, A. (2007) 'Soundbiters bit. Contracted dialogistic space and the textual relations of the No. 10 team analysed through corpus assisted discourse studies', in N. Fairclough, G. Cortese and P. Ardizzone (eds.) *Discourse and Contemporary Social Change*, Bern: Peter Lang, 73–94.

Duguid, A. (2010) 'Newspaper discourse informalisation: A diachronic comparison', *Corpora* 5(2): 109–138.

Esposito, E. (2016) 'The mother's picong: A discursive approach to gender, identity and political leadership in Trinidad and Tobago', *Discourse & Society* 28(1): 24–41.

Fairclough, N. (1989) *Language and Power*, London: Longman.

Ferguson, N. (2008) *The Ascent of Money*. London: Allen Lane.

Gibbons, J. (2003) *Forensic Linguistics. An Introduction to Language in the Justice System*, Oxford: Blackwell.

Gilmour, D. (2011) *The Pursuit of Italy*, London: Penguin.

Goffman, E. (1967) *Interaction Ritual: Essays in Face to Face Behavior*, Chicago, IL: Aldine.

Goffman, E. (1981) *Forms of Talk*, Philadelphia, PA: University of Pennsylvania Press.

Hamid, S. (2011) 'The struggle for Middle East democracy', *Brookings Institution*. Available at: www.brookings.edu/articles/the-struggle-for-middle-east-democracy/

Harris, S. (1991) 'Evasive action: How politicians respond to questions in political interviews', in P. Scannell (ed.) *Broadcast Talk*, London: SAGE, 76–99.

Hart, C. (forthcoming) '"Riots Engulfed the City": An Experimental Study Investigating the Legitimating Effects of Fire Metaphors in Discourses of Disorder', *Discourse & Society*.

Heritage, J. (2002) 'The limits of questioning: Negative interrogatives and hostile question content', *Journal of Pragmatics* 34(10–11): 1427–1446.

Hirsch, E., Kett, J. and Trefil, J. (2002) *The New Dictionary of Cultural Literacy* (3rd ed.), Boston, MA: Houghton Mifflin.

Hobsbawm, E. (1994) *Age of Extremes*, London: Abacus.

Hunston, S. (2004) 'Counting the uncountable: Problems of identifying evaluation in a text and in a corpus', in A. Partington, J. Morley and L. Haarman (eds.) *Corpora and Discourse*, Bern: Peter Lang, 157–188.

Jakobson, R. (1960) 'Concluding statement: Linguistics and poetics', in T. Sebok (ed.) *Style in Language*, Cambridge, MA: MIT Press, 350–377.

Jiang, X. (2006) 'Cross-cultural pragmatic differences in US and Chinese press conferences: The case of the North Korea nuclear crisis', *Discourse & Society* 17(2): 237–257.

Johnson, S. (1755) *Dictionary of the English Language*, London: Knapton.

Jones, N. (1996) *Soundbites and Spin Doctors: How Politicians Manipulate the Media and Vice-versa*, London: Cassell.

Kampf, Z. and Daskal, E. (2013) 'Too hostile, too deferential: Processes of media answerability following political interviews', *Journalism* 14(4): 522–540.

Kurtz, H. (1998) *Spin Cycle: How the White House and the Media Manipulate the News*, New York: Touchstone.

Lakoff, G. and Johnson, J. (1980) *Metaphors We Live By*, Chicago, IL: University of Chicago.

Larsen, E. (1980) *Wit as a Weapon: The Political Joke in History*, London: Muller.

Lawton, R. (2013) 'Speak English or go home: The anti-immigrant discourse of the American "English only" movement', *Critical Approaches to Discourse Analysis across Disciplines* 7(1): 100–122.

Leith, S. (2012) *You Talkin' to Me? Rhetoric from Aristotle to Obama*, London: Profile.

Lynn, J. and Jay, A. (1989) *The Complete Minister*, London: BBC Books.

Maltese, J. (1992) *Spin Control: The White House Office of Communications and the Management of Presidential News*, Chapel Hill, NC: The University of North Carolina Press.

Mooney, A., Stilwell Peccei, J., LaBelle, S., Engøy Henriksen, B., Eppler, E., Irwin, A., ... Soden, S. (2011) *Language, Society and Power: An Introduction* (3rd ed.), Abingdon: Routledge.

Morley, J. (2004) 'The sting in the tail: Persuasion in English editorial discourse', in A. Partington, J. Morley and L. Haarman (eds.) *Corpora and Discourse*, Bern: Peter Lang, 239–255.

Obama, B. (2004) *Dreams from My Father*, New York: Random House.

Obama, B. (2006) *The Audacity of Hope*, New York: Random House.

Orwell, G. (2015 [1945]) *Animal Farm*, London: Penguin.

Orwell, G. (1946) *Politics and the English Language*, London: Horizon.

Partington, A. (2003) *The Linguistics of Political Argument: The Spin-Doctor and the Wolf-Pack at the White House*, London: Routledge.

Partington, A. (2006) *The Linguistics of Laughter: A Corpus-Assisted Study of Laughter-Talk*, London: Routledge.

Partington, A. (forthcoming) 'Europhobes and europhiles, eurospats and eurojibes: Revisiting Britain's EU debate', in A. Cermakova and M. Mahlberg (eds.) *Corpora as Discourse*, Amsterdam: John Benjamins.

Partington, A., Duguid, A. and Taylor, C. (2013) *Patterns and Meanings in Discourse*, Amsterdam: John Benjamins.

Pew Research Centre (2015) 'Women and leadership'. Available at: www.pewsocialtrends.org/2015/01/14/women-and-leadership/

Pew Research Center (2016) 'The 2016 presidential campaign – a news event that's hard to miss', *Numbers, Facts and Trends Shaping the World*. Available at: www.journalism.org/2016/02/04/the-2016-presidential-campaign-a-news-event-thats-hard-to-miss/

Proctor, K. and Su, W. (2011) 'The 1st person plural in political discourse—American politicians in interviews and in a debate', *Journal of Pragmatics* 43(13): 3251–3266.

Raskin, V. (1985) *Semantic Mechanism of Humor*, Dordrecht: Reidel.

Schäffner, C. (1997) 'Editorial: Political speeches and discourse analysis', in C. Schäffner (ed.) *Analysing Political Speeches*, Clevedon: Multilingual Matters, 1–4.

Swales, J. (1990) *Genre Analysis*, Cambridge: Cambridge University Press.

Tannen, D. (2003) 'Let them eat words: Linguistic lessons from Republican master strategist Frank Luntz', *The American Prospect* 14(8). Available at: www.prospect.org/cs/articles?article=let_them_eat_words

Taverne, D. (2005) *The March of Unreason*, Oxford: Oxford University Press.

Taylor, C. (2008) 'Metaphors of anti-Americanism in a corpus of UK, US and Italian newspapers', *ESP Across Cultures* 5: 137–152.

Taylor, C. (2016) *Mock Politeness in English and Italian: A Corpus-Assisted Metalanguage Analysis*, Amsterdam: John Benjamins.

Teubert, W. (2001) 'A province of a federal superstate, ruled by an unelected bureaucracy. Keywords of the Euro-sceptic discourse in Britain', in A. Musolff, C. Good, P. Points and R. Wittlinger (eds.) *Attitudes Towards Europe: Language in the Unification Process*, Abingdon: Ashgate, 45–88.

Thompson, G. (1996) *Introducing Functional Grammar*, London: Arnold.

Thompson, G. and Hunston, S. (2000) 'Evaluation: An introduction', in S. Hunston and G. Thompson (eds.) *Evaluation in Text*, Oxford: Oxford University Press, 1–27.

Tremain, R. (1989) *Restoration*, London: Sceptre, 160–161.

Trew, T. (1979) 'Theory and ideology at work', in R. Fowler, R. Hodge, G. Kress and T. Trew (eds.) *Language and Control*, London: Routledge, 94–116.

Vinen, R. (2000) *A History in Fragments: Europe in the Twentieth Century*, London: Little, Brown.

Whyte, J. (2003) *Bad Thoughts – A Guide to Clear Thinking*, London: Corvo Press.

Wilson, J. (2001) 'Political discourse', in D. Schiffrin, D. Tannen and H. Hamilton (eds.) *The Handbook of Discourse Analysis*, Oxford: Blackwell, 398–415. Available at: https://lg411.files.wordpress.com/2013/08/discourse-analysis-full.pdf

Zappavigna, M. (2015) 'Searchable talk: The linguistic functions of hashtags in tweets about Schapelle Corby', *Global Media Journal* 9(1): 23–37.

Index